D1712958

FRENCH WAR BRIDES IN AMERICA

FRENCH WAR BRIDES IN AMERICA

An Oral History

Hilary Kaiser

Westport, Connecticut
London

Library of Congress Cataloging-in-Publication Data

Kaiser, Hilary
[Dex amours de GI's. English]
  French war brides in America : an oral history / Hilary Kaiser.
      p. cm.
  Includes bibliographical references and index.
  ISBN 978–0–275–99398–6 (alk. paper)
1. World War, 1939–1945—Women—France—Biography. 2. World War, 1914–1918—Women—
France—Biography. 3. War brides—France—Biography. 4. World War, 1939–1945—Personal
narratives, French. 5. Women immigrants—United States—Biography. 6. French Americans—
Biography. 7. Oral history. I. Title.
D810.W7K24 2008
940.53092′244—dc22   2007030423

British Library Cataloguing in Publication Data is available.

Library of Congress Catalog Card Number: 2007030423
ISBN: 978–0–275–99398–6

First published in 2008

Praeger Publishers, 88 Post Road West, Westport, CT 06881
An imprint of Greenwood Publishing Group, Inc.
www.praeger.com

Originally published in France in 2004 by Editions Tallandier under the title *Des Amours de GI's:
Les petites fiancées du Débarquement*.

Printed in the United States of America

The paper used in this book complies with the
Permanent Paper Standard issued by the National
Information Standards Organization (Z39.48-1984).

10 9 8 7 6 5 4 3 2 1

To my three sons, who have experienced all the joys and difficulties involved in being "bi-cultural."

CONTENTS

A photo essay follows page 65.

PREFACE AND ACKNOWLEDGMENTS

As both the author of this book, which was first published in French in France by Editions Tallandier, as well as its translator into English for publication by Praeger, I have had an intimate, even a quasi-schizophrenic, association with the text appearing on these pages and have worn two hats.

Being the book's author, I have tried to make the finished text appearing here reflect as much as possible my own writing style in English. As its translator from French, and because I know the material so well, I admit that I have, at times, taken liberties which another, more objective, translator would certainly not have allowed herself to take. For example, I have sometimes included (in brackets) my own explanation of what has been translated from the original text. In a few cases, I have corrected errors that appeared in the French publication, and I have added or changed a few endnotes to make them more relevant for an English-speaking audience. Finally, in one or two of the introductions to the oral histories, I have updated some of the information or indicated the later decease of the person telling her story. Wearing my hat of author, I did this knowingly and therefore take responsibility for these various changes to the French text.

Furthermore, as I explain in the section entitled "Notes on Interviewing, Language, Transcription, and Editing for the Original French Version," I was also the interviewer and editor of the transcripts used in the writing of the first-person accounts in this book. Of the 15 accounts appearing here, only four were based on interviews done in English. These four accounts have undergone an unusual cross-translation process. After being translated into

French for publication in France, they now appear here in their original English version, with some corrections made which correspond to the editing and endnotes suggested by my French editor.

I could never have written this book without the *sacrées femmes* [amazing women] who shared their stories with me, and I thank all of them—including those I interviewed but whose stories do not appear here—from the bottom of my heart for their participation in this joint project. I would also like to thank my friend Annick Baudoin, who helped me with the original French text, as well as Maguy L. and Nathalie M. for their excellent transcriptions of many of the tapes. My thanks also go to Marie-Pierre Robert, who gave me some very practical and useful advice in finding a French publisher. My writing group, my Paris-based interculturalists' group, the board members of SIETAR France, and my colleagues at the IUT of Sceaux all encouraged me in my literary endeavors. Bernard Vincent provided many helpful editing suggestions. My heartfelt thanks also go to AAWE (Association of American Wives of Europeans) in Paris, which awarded me the AAWE Prize in 2002. The generous financial grant accompanying this award allowed me to complete the oral histories and pay for their transcription. I am grateful to Henri Bovet, Director of Editions Tallandier, who believed in my project and first published this book in French as *Des Amours de GI's* during the celebrations of the 60th Anniversary of D-Day. My thanks also go to Eric Thiebaud at Tallandier for his excellent editing and to Emmanuelle Roederer for her very professional and effective promotion of the French edition of this book. At Greenwood Publishing, I would like to thank Elizabeth Demers, Senior Editor, for her enthusiastic interest in my original French manuscript and for acquiring the English language rights, as well as Bridget Austiguy-Preschel, Senior Project Manager, and Leanne Small, Associate Managing Editor. I would also like to thank Andrew De Young, Project Manager at BeaconPMG, for his excellent copyediting.

Last but not least, I am extremely grateful to my wonderful sons Eric, Sébastien, and Marc, as well as to numerous friends and relations, for their loving support and their encouragement to complete the original edition of this book during a difficult period in my private life.

NOTE ON INTERVIEWING, LANGUAGE, TRANSCRIPTION, AND EDITING FOR THE ORIGINAL FRENCH VERSION

All of the interviews the stories in this book are based on were tape-recorded, and it is my hope that the tapes may someday be housed in an oral history archive. Although a few of them were done by telephone or in a public place, I conducted the vast majority face to face in the interviewees' homes. Using the procedures set up by the Oral History Association and the International Oral History Association as a guide, I explained my project to the interviewees and asked them to sign release forms before or after the interviews. The women and I have kept in contact over the years, and several of them have subsequently helped me fill in gaps or clarify certain details.

Although I conducted almost all the interviews in the United States, only four of them were in English. Upon learning that I lived in Paris and was married to a Frenchman, most of the women I interviewed opted to speak to me in their native tongue. The women all spoke English, but speaking French, especially when it concerned their past, appeared to be more natural for them. I also had the feeling that, owing to my experiences in France and the fact that I speak the language fluently, doing the interview in French helped create a certain bond between us. It was as if they considered me more of an "insider" than an "outsider"—as if I would understand when they spoke to me.

From a linguistic point of view, an interesting study could certainly be made from the original tapes or transcripts concerning the amount of language interference in the interviews. To illustrate, the four women who spoke to me in English often used French words and constructed their sentences in a French way. Similarly, when the women speaking to me in French did not know or had forgotten the French word or expression for something, they would use the English equivalent. Also, many of the women made mistakes in French tenses and syntax, which may have been aggravated by their knowledge of English.

Consequently, each of the French women I interviewed in the United States spoke her own particular version of *Franglais*. Sometimes these women interspersed their speech with French regional expressions or words common 50 or 60 years ago but outdated today. Other times they used Americanisms or very familiar American slang. No one made the same mistakes, and I doubt that most of the women even realized that they were borrowing from or modeling the other language. It is fortunate, then, that as the interviewer and editor of the transcripts, I knew both languages and cultures and could, when required, "decipher" what was said.

To help my readers, I have italicized words and expressions in the "other" language, often translating them (in subsequent brackets) into the language of the interview. Sometimes, even if a word or an expression is incorrect, if it is understandable, I have left it as it was said, followed by [*sic*]. At other times, I have explained words or expressions in an endnote. On a few occasions, I have changed the original words in the transcript to more appropriate ones.

One aspect of language that does not appear in the transcripts is the women's accents. Even after a half-century in the United States, most of the women still have very strong French accents when speaking English. Acquiring the proper accent in another language is a very difficult task, especially when native speakers tell you your French accent (or your American accent in *my* case!) is "cute" and that you shouldn't lose it. But having an accent can cause problems, too, as some of the women reveal in their stories. It may make you feel different or not allow you to be taken seriously. It may cause you to be stereotyped or caricatured. Finally, it may prevent *complete* assimilation into the new culture.

As far as transcription of the tapes is concerned, I transcribed the four tapes that were in English myself. Two competent French ladies, whose services I paid for, transcribed the interviews in French. When the transcripts were completed, I first checked them against the tapes for accuracy. Then I rearranged the information in mostly chronological order, eliminated my questions, corrected certain vocabulary and grammar mistakes, and deleted repetitions and verbal tics ("you know," "huh," etc.).

Using the edited transcript as a base, I then rewrote each woman's account, letting her tell her story in her own words, without any commentary or interjection on my part. My choice of the first-person narrative style was intentional. I wanted the reader to get to know each woman individually and to perceive her personality through the way in which she recounts her adventures and life experiences.

Sometimes there were memory or verbal lapses in the discourse. I have at times represented these by an ellipsis...At others, I have taken the liberty of filling in the missing words (between brackets) that I thought might correspond to the interviewee's train of thought. There were a few cases of "boasting" (e.g., "I was the youngest war bride on the ship") or misinformation (e.g., dates, names, or events). When these could be checked for veracity, I have added an endnote. I have also added other endnotes when I felt historical or cultural precision was needed.

Finally, for the sake of privacy, I have used only the first names of the women, followed by the initial of their last name.

PROLOGUE

Picture the scene: "The Top of the Mark," an elegant, revolving cocktail lounge on the top floor of the Mark Hopkins Hotel that overlooks San Francisco Bay. It is April Fool's Day 1945, and Ruth Margaret, Mary Jane, and Holly, secretaries at F.C. Phillips and Co., have come here to celebrate Mary Jane's birthday. Sitting down at their table, they can't help noticing a group of Navy officers standing at the bar. Although Germany is about to surrender, the war with Japan is still raging in the Pacific, and the officers, on leave for a week of R and R at their base on Treasure Island, have also decided to have a drink at the famous cocktail bar.

Under "normal" circumstances, these two groups of friends might possibly never meet, but this is wartime. Soldiers and sailors are living through experiences and witnessing sights that will haunt them for years to come. The women left behind are lonely; letters cannot replace the human warmth that comes from being in someone's arms.

On that evening, Ruth Margaret meets John, Mary Jane meets Sid, and Holly meets Frank. Two weeks later, at the Little Church around the Corner in New York City, Ruth Margaret and John get married. The day following the wedding, they fly back together to San Francisco. John returns to the Pacific until the end of the war, and Ruth Margaret returns to her secretarial job at F.A. Phillips. Their first child is born a year later.

Again, under "normal" circumstances, these two young people would probably not have met at all. John is a Princeton graduate, the son of a Foreign Service officer. Born in France, he has lived in various countries in

Europe and attended boarding schools in Switzerland. He speaks three foreign languages and plays tennis, squash and golf. His father's family is from
New York City, his mother's from Philadelphia. Ruth Margaret's father owns
a small coal-selling business in Milwaukee, Wisconsin. A poor student, she
left college after a few months to attend secretarial school, subsequently taking her first job in San Francisco.

Against a backdrop of war, John and Ruth Margaret meet, fall in love, and
marry, all within a time-span of two weeks. John, with his curly black hair
and grey-blue eyes, cuts a tall, dashing figure in his ink-blue uniform. By
the age of 25, he has seen half the world and has been involved in several
emotional entanglements. As for Ruth Margaret, before coming to San Francisco, she has never been out of her native Wisconsin. Her few heart-throbs in
high school were never very serious. Attractive in an all-American,
Pepsodent-smile type of way, she wears her curly, chestnut-colored hair
shoulder-length. She is a good dancer and won her school's jitterbug contest
the previous year.

Ruth Margaret becomes a "war bride"[1] at the age of 19, marrying a man
she has just met and barely knows. Perhaps she is attracted to the uniform,
the curly hair, the debonair ways. Or is it just a question of sex? John probably marries Ruth Margaret "on the rebound" after reading the letter his fiancée sent to him in Guam breaking off their engagement. Be that as it may,
they marry, and their marriage, imperfect as it turns out to be, lasts 40 years,
until the day when Ruth Margaret dies of cancer.

Another scene, another country: Paris, France, the winter of 1962. A
ground-floor concierge's *loge* of an apartment building on avenue Victor
Hugo. A 17-year-old soldier in a khaki uniform is home from his camp in
Germany for a few days visiting his mother, Marcelle. He looks around the
one-room apartment where he was raised and tells Marcelle, for the hundredth time, how he plans to find her a better place to live once he has finished his military service and found a job.

And for the hundredth time again, Marcelle looks lovingly at her son and
tells him she is fine where she is. How tall he is getting, she thinks, how much
he looks like his father. The father he has never known. The tall, grinning GI
on the tank that rolled through Paris on May 8, 1945, to celebrate the end of
the war in Europe. The one who loved her for those two short weeks and then
returned to his wife and daughter in Nebraska. The one who never left an
address or realized he had a son in France.

Why these two scenes? you might ask. Where's the connection? Different
stories, different continents, different circumstances. And yet, there *are*

threads; there *are* links. Both scenes occur because of a World War. Fighting in Europe as well as in Asia, GI's—be they officers or enlisted men, whether in the Army, Navy or Air Force—"picked up," dated, seduced, sometimes married, and often abandoned the women they encountered during the war years. Children were born in and out of wedlock. Love lasted over the years, or it didn't, as did marriages.

I, as well as other baby boomers, look back on the World War II years and try to understand how and why these romances occurred. We listen to the stories and are astonished by the naïveté of the older generation. We marvel at the romanticism of the time and the rapid decisions that were taken.

How could Ruth Margaret and John, my parents, get married after knowing each other for only two weeks? Why did Marcelle, my concierge in the 1960s, become so infatuated with an American GI? What was it about their past, their upbringing, and the period they lived in that brought all this about?

These true stories, and the questions they provoke, are the genesis of this book.

INTRODUCTION

The story of American soldiers meeting French *Mademoiselles* actually began in World War I. At that time, they were called "Doughboys" by Americans but "Sammies" (from "Uncle Sam") by the French.[1]

The war began on July 28, 1914, and lasted until November 11, 1918. Although some 3,500 "American Gentlemen Volunteers"[2]—those legendary Ivy League-bred aviators and ambulance drivers—had already come to France to help out, the United States only officially entered the war on April 2, 1917. The first U.S. soldiers arrived in St. Nazaire on June 26, 1917. But it was not until the summer of 1918—almost at the end of the war—that American soldiers, some two million of them, actually arrived *en masse* as the American Expeditionary Forces (AEF) under General Pershing. Not only did they not fight for very long in France, but the majority returned to the United States quite soon after the war was over. By the end of November 1918, 26,000 AEF soldiers had returned to the United States, and six months later, in August 1919, only 40,000 were still left in France. Total American losses amounted to between 70,000 and 100,000 men.

For Europeans, World War I was a long, drawn-out war during which some 10 million continental European and British soldiers—a whole generation of 20- to 40-year-old men—were killed. France's dead, about 1.5 million soldiers, equaled three fourths of the total American army sent to Europe, and a half a million returned permanently disabled.[3] Before the entry of the United States into the war, morale in the French army and in the public at large was at a low ebb.[4] The Doughboys thus arrived as "saviors" in war-torn

France towards the end of the war. They were numerous, young, "fresh," tall, and strong.

As military historians have often pointed out, combat and sexual activity usually go hand in hand. There was considerable concern on both sides of the Atlantic about American soldiers fraternizing with French women, particularly French prostitutes, mostly because the French and the American authorities feared the spread of venereal disease and the effect it would have on their fighting.

On the American side, the movement for "social hygiene" was in full-swing during World War I,[5] and various ordinances were issued to the troops by General Pershing. As early as July 2, 1917, for example, a general order appealed to the soldiers' sense of patriotism in preventing the spread of venereal disease. The message was: "You're expected to remain continent when you're over there." Nevertheless, the army would later provide the troops with sex education and prophylaxis, especially when it became known that the Doughboys were visiting French brothels in Nantes and St. Nazaire.[6]

In February 1918, French Premier George Celemenceau wrote to General Pershing offering to set up licensed medically-inspected houses of prostitution. General Pershing supposedly considered the proposal but first had the letter sent to Secretary of War, Newton Baker, who exclaimed: "For God's sake, [. . .] don't show this to the President or he'll stop the war."[7] Medically inspected or not, French brothels were declared strictly off-limits for American soldiers by the general order of December 18, 1917. This led French authorities in St. Nazaire and Nantes, for example, to complain that the American attitude increased *clandestine* prostitution and that the Doughboys were picking up all sorts of women in the streets. They were particularly worried that the Americans' "depravity" was spreading to "respectable" classes of women, and that "the boldness and money of the Americans toppled the resistance of some French women."[8] Indeed, because many French women—be they single, married but separated from their *poilu* husbands, or widowed—were financially destitute, they often succumbed to the Americans' offers.

In addition to the ordinances, there was a good deal of American "propaganda" that went round against fraternization with French women. Not only were the U.S. army and the government afraid of venereal disease contracted from French prostitutes, but they were also afraid of *any* French woman latching onto an American soldier. Because the Western Front was relatively stable, soldiers would come back to Paris and other leave areas, rest and recuperate, and then go back to the line. The American army and the American government feared that entanglements with French women while the Doughboys were on leave would lead to their not wanting to return to the front. Or that the women would even accompany the soldiers back to the front and distract them from fighting.

Financial concerns also prevailed. If some of these women actually *married* an American soldier, they would be entitled to an allotment from the soldier's pay, and the American army would later have to finance the brides' transportation to the United States after the war. Furthermore, should the American soldier-husband be killed in battle, a French wife would be entitled to war risk insurance benefits as the beneficiary.[9]

So the army "unofficially" made marriage very difficult. Commanding officers would restrict soldiers' leaves, or they wouldn't sign the papers giving their approval for the men under them to marry. Camp chaplains and army newspapers would campaign overtly against men getting attached to women of "dubious character" who were out to trap American soldiers for their money or insurance benefits.

Marriages were also difficult because of bureaucratic red tape. French civil law required the American soldier to produce a birth certificate and a certification of publication of wedding banns in his hometown. These requirements were later waived by French authorities, but U.S commanding officers had to sign affidavits declaring that, to the best of their knowledge, the groom was not already married.[10]

The YMCA also got involved in trying to discourage any sort of fraternization between French women and the Doughboys. Together with the army, this Christian organization set out to fill the idle time the soldiers had when away from the front and later, after the war, before returning to the United States.

To keep the boys busy, the army and the YMCA designed all sorts of activities; these included sightseeing tours throughout France and recreational and sports facilities at leave areas. Aix-les-Bains, one of these leave areas, was host to some 48,298 to 113,000 American soldiers—the first calculation being the Y's figures, the second the town's. After the Armistice, while the soldiers were waiting for ships to take them back to the United States, the AEF offered them the possibility of taking free courses ("from architecture to just plain learning to spell"[11]) at French universities in Bordeaux and Paris but also at the AEF University of Beaune, in Burgundy, where more than 40,000 American soldiers are said to have studied.

The YMCA was joined by other organizations, such as the YWCA, the American Red Cross, the Knights of Columbus, the Jewish Welfare Board, and the Salvation Army. With the approval of the U.S. government and army, some 6,000[12] American women auxiliary workers were sent to France, presumably as a diversion from French women. They worked in army canteens, which served as the social centers for the enlisted men in the camp, or in educational, library, or religious work. They also worked in "leave areas," where their duties often included playing cards, dancing, "mingling," and talking with the troops.[13]

The two American churches in Paris—the American Cathedral and the American Church—that had close ties with the American Ambulance Hospital (later to become the American Hospital of Paris), the YMCA, the Red Cross, and the YWCA also got involved. In addition to their work in war relief, they endeavored to keep the Doughboys busy and out of trouble. The idea was to provide a "wholesome" place for them to meet in the City of Lights.

The Rector of the American Cathedral, Frederick W. Beekman, for example, wrote a report in which he stated that he had been authorized by General Pershing to open the American Soldiers and Sailors' Club on the Rue Royale in Paris on October 19, 1917:

> ...The Club contained a reception room, reading and writing room and library, billiard room, canteen restaurant, offices, etc. Every Wednesday and Saturday night for fifteen months, entertainments were given. For many months, free ice cream, cigarettes and book service was established daily for (wounded) Americans in Paris hospitals. In a lesser degree, this service included many French and British soldiers. All in all, the Club distributed nine tenths of all the ice cream given the wounded in the Paris area. It established sightseeing tours for the American convalescents, which it ran during the entire period of the American fighting. Sightseeing trips to Versailles go from the Club every Tuesday and Friday...[14]

As for the American Church of Paris, during World War I, it, too, became a "home away from home" for American soldiers, so much so that it came to be called "the Khaki Church."[15] Following the announcement by General Pershing that Mother's Day 1918 should be celebrated by AEF troops, the story goes that Dr. Goodrich, the pastor of the American Church, and his wife were significant in first introducing the celebration of Mother's Day into France:

> Late in this spring of tension and anxiety, on the second Sunday of May 1918, came Mother's Day. From the founder [Ann Jarvis] of this observance a request had been sent to the wife of the Ambassador, Mrs. Sharp, that the day be made as significant as possible to American boys in France. At a conference over this matter at the Embassy, Mrs. Goodrich was appointed chairman of a

committee of women to cooperate in plans to this end. The ladies were to provide entertainment and act as hostesses at the Sunday afternoon gatherings at all the soldiers' centers throughout Paris. In order to secure cooperation by the French Catholic clergy, at whose services American soldiers might be in attendance on Mothers' Day, Mrs. Robert Woods Bliss, wife of the Counsellor of the Embassy, and Dr. Goodrich were asked to wait upon Cardinal Archbishop Amette to learn from him what could be done. His Eminence received this delegation with great courtesy and, though the idea of Mothers' Day was new to him, seemed at once to grasp its significance. He gave assurance that he would do his utmost to arrange that wherever American soldiers were likely to attend French Catholic services in any numbers, special Mothers' Day services should be appointed.[16]

During the afternoon of that Sunday in May 1918, centers for Doughboys throughout France provided food and entertainment. The soldiers in attendance were asked, "When did you write to your mother last?" A flood of letters poured into American homes as a result.[17]

The themes of "Remember your mother" and "Don't do anything she would be ashamed of" were indeed prevalent in the army and YMCA press. Various photos, drawings, and captions in the *Stars and Stripes* and the Y's *Coming Back*, which was distributed free to soldiers, stressed three things the Doughboys were supposed to remember when they were over in France. One was coming back to Mother, as in the photo of a soldier hugging his mom, with the caption: "Back to Home and Mother."[18] Another icon was "Lady Liberty," symbolized by the Statue of Liberty, for whom they were fighting. And the third was "the girl you left behind." A drawing in an April 1919 *Coming Back* showed the Statue of Liberty holding a pretty young woman with outstretched arms. The caption read: "The Torch in Liberty's Hand Is the Girl You Left Behind."[19]

Despite all of the above—the official ordinances from the army and the U.S. government, the "wholesome" activities provided by the YMCA and other organizations, and the propaganda campaigns—the Doughboys *did*, in fact, mix with local French women on a fairly large scale. The sexual relationships some Doughboys had with French women were crudely referred to in the very popular AEF song, "Mad'moiselle from Armentières." Not only was the song full of sexual innuendos—the "Hinky dinky, parlez-vous" of the refrain being just one of them—but it also created the image of the typical French woman as being loose and unfaithful. Bawdy jokes were also made about leaving *Mademoiselle* with a *"souvenir bébé."*

Not all of the Doughboys' relationships with women were "fly-by-night" affairs, however. Approximately 10,000 members of the AEF ended up marrying European women. The calculation has been that about three-fifths of them were with French women.[20] For many love-deprived French women, an American soldier husband was undoubtedly considered a fairly good "catch." Because of the heavy loss of human lives, a dearth of men existed in France following the war: there was probably only about one marriageable Frenchman for every four French women.[21]

White American soldiers met and dated "respectable," mostly working-class, girls in towns or on army bases across France. Sometimes, the soldiers were invited into French homes or became acquainted with more affluent French families at elegant leave areas. The writer of an article in a May 1918 edition of *Stars and Stripes* told his readers how "Mon Américain Makes a Great Hit with his French girlfriend's Pa and Ma."[22] After the Armistice, a May 1919 article in the same paper describes the leave area of St. Malo and says:

> As the whole vicinity is a vacation place for the people of France, and these people have a happy habit of taking their daughters along on vacation; there is no scarcity of charming dancing partners [at the "spacious casino" taken over by the YMCA] or companions on any half dozen of the interesting boat trips or overland hikes it is possible to make.[23]

As for *black* American soldiers, according to author Tyler Stovall, in *African Americans in the City of Light,* a U.S. army document entitled "Secret Information Concerning Black American Troops" was circulated among the French, whom they considered to be color-blind, warning them against intimacies between blacks and Frenchwomen. Stovall goes on to describe the stern measures that could be taken against black soldiers if they were caught fraternizing or even accepting a dinner invitation in a French home. He says that one black regiment received an order stating that black enlisted men should not "talk to or be in company with any white women, regardless of whether the women solicit their company or not." He also reports that several black soldiers were shot by military police for having consorted with Frenchwomen.[24]

But Stovall goes on to say:

> In spite of the best efforts of the American army, however, black American soldiers and the people of France did get to know one another during WWI. These contacts were not always easy, but for the most part African Americans felt that the French treated them with far more decency and respect than they had ever received from whites before. The memories of such pleasant encounters endured long after the war...[25]

Thus, despite the administrative and cultural difficulties; many romances (but fewer than originally feared) led to marriage. Some 6,000 or more Franco-American marriages were registered in town halls across France, and there were undoubtedly numerous war weddings that weren't officially counted.[26]

By marrying an American Doughboy, a foreign woman became, in fact, an American citizen and was entitled to enter the United States without a visa.[27] After the war was over, the army provided the brides with free transportation to the United States on troop ships. These transportation arrangements were intended for the wives of enlisted men with limited means; other soldiers and officers are reported to have sent their brides over on passenger ships.[28]

The brides were first transported to the ports of debarkation of Brest, Bordeaux, and St. Nazaire, where they were housed and fed in the Hostess Houses originally set up by the YWCA for female auxiliary workers. As their numbers increased, they were set up in transient "bridal camps" provided by the U.S. army.[29] YWCA and American Red Cross employees helped out in caring for and processing the brides. In addition, they often gave the women English language lessons and cultural training about what to expect in the United States.[30]

The brides paid a dollar a day for transportation to the embarkation point from wherever they lived, for room and board, for their sea voyage, and for railway fare within the United States upon arrival.[31] The greatest ports of disembarkation were New York City, Norfolk, Newport News, and Boston. Employees of the YWCA and the American Red Cross again housed, fed, and helped them with their paperwork and travel plans upon arrival. Sometimes there were problems in locating a "scared" husband, or a man was discovered already having a wife in the United States. The vast majority of the wives did not stay on the east coast. They were met at the port by their husbands or they traveled to the Middle West and the West to join them.[32]

Once they were settled in their new homes, some of these women joined local chapters of the YWCA to help in the transition of settling in a new country and to take English lessons. Others joined French groups or created local war brides associations, which oftentimes came to be called "the French ladies' group," the "Benevolent Society," and other such names. Correspondence from the French consuls in various cities mentions the existence of such groups in New York, Chicago, Detroit, New Orleans, Houston, San Francisco, and Los Angeles.[33] French women later founded a national French war brides association in 1932 when they came together in Portland, Oregon.[34]

An article in the September 2, 1919, edition of the *New York Times* states that 62 French brides returned to their old homes after obtaining divorces from their husbands because they could not adapt to the American way of life.[35] On the other hand, several months later, an article in the same paper praises the foreign brides for pitching in and helping earn "the daily bread" by working as needlewomen and cooks "when the penniless husband is scratching around for a job after his war service."[36]

In fact, it is impossible to know how many of these Franco-American marriages ended in divorce or how many French women actually returned to France. Although an incident occurred in December 1921 in which three French war brides tearfully begged French *Maréchal* Foch, who was on tour in Idaho, for his help in getting back to France, the headline of the *New York Times* article reporting the incident proudly proclaimed: "French War Brides Happy in America." And Miss Kiler of the YWCA is quoted as saying, "records show the majority of [French war brides] displaying the utmost fortitude in adapting themselves to American ways."[37]

* * * * *

War was again declared in Europe in 1939, but once again, just as during World War I, the United States did not come immediately to the aid of its European allies. It was only after the bombing of Pearl Harbor on December 7, 1941, that the United States officially entered the war. The day following what came to be called the "Day of Infamy," President Roosevelt asked Congress to recognize the state of war with Japan. Then on December 11, Hitler and Mussolini declared war on the United States. Soon afterwards, American soldiers, now no longer called "Doughboys" but rather "GI's,"[38] went off to fight in both Asia and Europe.

In the Pacific and the Far East, American troops, under Admiral Chester Nimitz, joined a coalition of allies, which included Britain, Australia, Holland, and China, in the war against Japan. An interesting "French connection" occurred in the south Pacific. Numerous GI's were stationed in New Caledonia, a French territory that had come out in support of the Free French in September 1940. As of April 1942, the local authorities allowed the U.S. Marine Corps and the other armed forces to use the island as a strategic base for their operations, particularly the Guadalcanal campaign lasting from August 1942 to February 1943.[39]

In *Tales of the South Pacific*,[40] the semi-autobiographical book written by American author James Michener, who served in the south Pacific, the narrator is asked by an officer who had fought with Patton in Africa, Sicily, and France, what war in the south Pacific was like. "Our war was waiting," he replies. "You rotted on New Caledonia waiting for Guadalcanal. Then you sweated twenty pounds away in Guadal waiting for Bougainville. There were battles, of course. But they were flaming things of the better moments..."[41]

Nevertheless, while GI's "waited" and "rotted" in New Caledonia, many of them fraternized with local women, both of Melanesian and French descent, some of whom they later married and brought back to America with them after the war was over.

The war in the Pacific would only end in August 15, 1945—three months after the end of the war in Europe—following the Americans' dropping of atomic bombs on the Japanese cities of Hiroshima (August 6) and Nagasaki (August 9).

Insofar as the European Theater of Operations (ETO) was concerned, U.S. troops began arriving in Britain in January 1942, but some 20,000 Americans were already serving in the British armed services even before Pearl Harbor. Of the 4.5 million GI's sent to Europe during the war, 3 million passed through or served in Britain.[42] GI's joined General Montgomery and the British in North Africa as of November 1942 and defeated Rommel in Tunisia in May 1943. GI's landed in Sicily and Naples with the Allies in September of 1943 and fought their way up the Italian Peninsula. On June 6, 1944, 250,000 soldiers under General Eisenhower left Britain and landed in Normandy ("Overlord"). Together with French troops, they marched on to Paris, which was liberated on August 25, 1944, and then further north and east. Other American soldiers landed in the Provence region on August 15, 1944 (Operation Dragoon). France and the Benelux countries were liberated in September 1944. Then the Allies fought their way into Germany, which finally surrendered on May 7, 1945.

* * * * *

The loss of human lives, both of soldiers and civilians, during World War II was huge. Figures vary, but one source cites the following: 20 million lives lost in the Soviet Union, probably more in China, 7 million in Germany, 5 million in Poland, 2 million in Japan, 1.3 million in Yugoslavia, 600,000 in France, 500,000 in Great Britain, 450,000 in Italy, 300,000 in the United States. There were also many losses in Canada, Australia, and numerous other countries. As opposed to World War I, "civilian populations were massively affected by illness, under-nourishment, exodus, systematic massacres and bombings."[43] In addition, millions of civilians perished in concentration camps, and about six million Jews were victims of genocide.

Mention should also be made of another violent outcome of World War II: the huge number of rapes committed by soldiers on all sides and on both fronts. Sexual violence during wartime has, alas, existed since Antiquity, and World War II was no exception. Rapes were committed by the Nazis in occupied countries, by the Red Army in Germany, by French forces in Italy and Germany, and by the Japanese Imperial Army in Korea.

A recent book, published in French and entitled *La Face Cachée des GI's: Les viols commis par des soldats américains en France, en Angleterre et en Allemagne pendant la Seconde Guerre mondiale* [The Hidden Side of the GI's: Rapes Committed by American Soldiers in France, England and Germany], underlines the fact that the GI's of World War II also committed rape. Despite the myth of their being "the greatest generation," author J. Robert Lilly says there was a "hidden side" to their behavior, and he brings out into the open this neglected chapter of American soldiers' "reprehensible acts in Britain, France and Germany."[44] In the preface to the book, French historian Fabrice Virgili reminds readers that GI's also raped Japanese women when they took over certain islands in the Pacific.

J. Robert Lilly estimates that between 1942 and 1945, some 17,000 women and children in Britain, France, and Germany were victims of rape by American GI's. Pointing out that, more often than not, it was *black* soldiers who were tried and convicted, even though white soldiers also committed these crimes, Lilly underlines the racism existing at the time in the army and American society at large and says it influenced military justice. Lilly surmises that a combination of many different factors was undoubtedly responsible for the rapes. These included: the absence of a sexual outlet (i.e., army-controlled houses of prostitution) for young, virile men who were facing death and brutality miles away from home, the abundance of alcohol, and the dehumanizing effects of racial segregation.

* * * * *

Rape is a very depressing aspect of war and military culture. But the GI's were not, by any means, all potential rapists. Many engaged in what may be called "friendly fraternization." Indeed, fraternization and marriage between American soldiers and local women occurred wherever the GI's fought or were stationed: in Europe, North Africa, and Asia. And, as was the case during World War I, the U.S. War Department, the army, the Red Cross, the YMCA, the YWCA, and other organizations all got involved.

Once again, as in World War I, GI's marrying foreign women became an issue for the U.S. War Department and the army. Starting in May 1942, various circulars and regulations appeared. Some of the points mentioned included: the requirement for a soldier contemplating marriage to obtain his commanding officer's permission; an imposed waiting period of three (later changed to two) months, and compliance with civil marriage requirements of the local country.

In 1942, military authorities asked the American Red Cross to conduct investigations into the backgrounds of potential war brides. At the time, this concerned mostly British and Australian women. But because of the bad publicity these investigations aroused among the general public, the ARC soon abandoned this practice and restricted itself to keeping up soldiers' morale and helping them with paperwork. Later, in September 1945, the ARC defined its program of assistance to alien dependents living outside the United States. Just as it had after World War I, the ARC would take part in the transportation and supervision of the war brides of American soldiers, but this time both from Europe and also from Asia.

On December 28, 1945, the U.S. Congress passed Public Law 271, the War Brides Act, which was followed six months later by Public Law 471, the Fiancées Act. Under the War Brides Act, foreign women, except for women from India and southeast Asia,[45] could enter the United States as non-quota immigrants, and visa requirements were waived for them. As for the Fiancées Act, it stipulated that racially-eligible women with proof of an intention to marry could enter the United States with visas as in-transit, non-immigrant visitors for a time-restricted period.

In January 1946, five months after the end of the war in Europe and following the passage of these two acts, the War Department announced that vessels would soon be made available for free transportation of war brides to America. This official war bride transportation operation would last 11 months and be discontinued in December 1946. However, the vast majority of GI dependents from the United Kingdom and Europe were transported to the United States by the U.S. Army between January and October 1946. Other brides journeyed to the United States by their own means, or sometimes GI's decided to immigrate to their wives' countries. The War Brides Act officially expired in December 1948, but owing to restrictive U.S. immigration legislation, some marriages were delayed or brides could not enter the United States for many years. Japanese war brides, for example, were not allowed to travel to America until 1952.[46]

During the period after the war when the shortage of ships was acute, the issue of transportation of war brides caused a good deal of controversy on both sides of the Atlantic. In Great Britain, where thousands of British women had been waiting to join their GI husbands for as long as two or three years, the situation got so tense that hundreds of war brides staged a series of demonstrations in London in October 1945. The sentiment in Washington and among soldiers and their families in the United States was: Why let war brides go first? Priority was thus given to wounded soldiers, ex-POWS, combat veterans, and men with a high number of discharge points. Thousands of other GI's also had to wait *their* turn for shipping space.

Finally, on January 26, 1946, the first group of British war brides left Southampton for the United States on the *S.S. Argentina*. Six weeks later, on March 6, 1946, some 426 European war brides and 15 babies sailed from Le Havre on the *S.S. General W. Goethals*. All told some 30 converted ships[47] would transport an approximate total of 100,000 war brides from Britain and continental Europe between January and June 1946. These figures do not include the many British women and children who had already entered America on a paying basis before the end of the war or, when the war was over, other British and European war brides who did not travel under the free transportation operation.

Exact figures for war brides entering the United States after World War II are hard to come by. Jenel Virden, in her book *Good-bye Piccadilly: British War Brides in America*, uses a 1950 Committee on the Judiciary report entitled *Immigration and Naturalization Systems of the United States* as her source to estimate the total number of World War II brides. According to her:

> The total number of all war brides in WWII was approximately 115,000. By U.S. government standards, this figure includes all people—women, men, and children—who entered the United States under the provisions of both the War Brides Act of 1945 and the Alien Fiancees and Fiances Act of 1946. However, the precise number of true war brides is difficult to determine, in part because of the variety of methods of transportation and the diverse categories of entry into the United States....[48]

Quoting many sources, Virden surmises that 70,000 probably seems a reasonable estimate of the number of British war brides that emigrated to the United States. The number of British war brides is so high because U.S. soldiers arrived very early in Britain (some as early as January 1942) and then stayed for an extended period of time. Indeed, one famous British saying about them goes: "Overpaid, oversexed, and over here." Sharing a common language with local women was undoubtedly also a factor in Americans' marrying so many British women. After British war brides, the next highest number of war brides after World War II came from Asia, with some 7,000 from Australia and New Zealand.

As for French war brides, the subject of this book, here again exact figures are hard to determine. In a memorandum concerning transportation of dependents to the United States written in August 5, 1946, by W. S. Renshaw, Chief of Military Personnel Branch, the total figure given for French brides and children shipped by the army is 5,704.[49] Ronald Creagh, author of the book *Nos Cousins d'Amérique*, speaks of 6,500 French war brides, but he does not give his source. In a letter written to the President of France, Leon Blum, on January 8, 1947, the Ambassador to the United States, Henri Bonnet, states that in addition to the more than 4,000 young French women transported to the United States by the American army, a large number of women also arrived by commercial transport. He estimates the number of French war brides in the United States to be about 6,000.[50]

It would seem, then, that about 6,000 French war brides after World War II would be a fair estimate. Coincidentally, this is approximately the same figure as after World War I. But it must be remembered that these figures are approximations, and there were undoubtedly quite a number of other French war brides who came to the United States without benefiting from the U.S. army transportation opportunity.

* * * * *

The France the brides were leaving behind was a country that had gone through six years of war and privation. Adolescents when the war began, the brides shared their countrymen's humiliation when France capitulated to the Germans in June 1940. The women's coming of age occurred in the part of the country occupied by the Germans or in the Free Zone of *Maréchal* Pétain. The atmosphere in both places was dreary and heavy and left few opportunities for personal "development" or amusement. In the Occupied Zone, the Germans had requisitioned their homes and buildings and were eating all their produce. The girls were subjected to curfews and witnessed raids, arrests, and executions. In the Free Zone, they had to live with the stifling "work, family, homeland" ethic of *Maréchal* Pétain.

Most French people, unless they produced their own food in the countryside or were able to buy on the black market, suffered from hunger during the war period. "During the Occupation, the typical Parisian subsisted on less than a third of his normal ration and lost between two and nine kilograms."[51] French people spent hours standing in lines or waiting for the electricity to come back on. There was a lack of coal for heating, a lack of fabric for sewing clothes, and a lack of leather for making shoes. An American woman, the wife of a French prisoner-of-war who lived outside Paris, in Brunoy during the Occupation with her in-laws, remembers:

With your food tickets, which you got every month at the town hall, you could buy potatoes and carrots and, in season, fruit. But sometimes everything was sold before you got to the head of the line. We never saw any chocolates or any oranges during the whole occupation. Aside from pregnant women and babies, there was no allowance for milk, so my parents-in-law bought half a cow with another family. Gasoline was reserved for people who really needed it for specific tasks. Cars could be requisitioned by the Germans if they thought they served a useful purpose. Heating was a real problem. We had a furnace, which we only used twice a week in the winter to keep the house from being too damp...[52]

Unfortunately, even after the Liberation, the penury continued, but the atmosphere in France after the arrival of the GI's would be different.

The Allies landed in Normandy on June 6, 1944, and were greeted with joy by the French population, despite the fact that thousands of civilians were caught in the crossfire and Allied aviation and artillery bombarded their towns and villages. Normans, Bretons, and all the other French people "liberated" by the Germans came out of their homes and hiding places and cheered the liberators, who were often American GI's.

Remembering the summer of 1944 in Cherbourg, two French brothers remarked how much more friendly, good-looking, and good-humored the American soldiers appeared compared to the Germans. The GI's distributed chewing gum and candy and played with the local children, and the way they drove their jeeps was "classy with a touch of wildness."[53] Normans and Americans fraternized immediately. "Hidden bottles were brought out and passed around." The soldiers were invited into Norman homes and were "unbelievably successful among French girls."[54] From the main square of Cherbourg

could be seen a multitude of Liberty ships and mountains of military supplies. ...Liberated on June 27th without much destruction, Cherbourg several months later swarmed with soldiers, airmen and sailors. The largest stores in the city had been transformed into a PX...off-limits to civilians.[55]

Some young Americans took to drinking too much Calvados and to harassing local women, and farmers in Normandy and Brittany, and later further inland on the road to Paris, began hiding their wives and daughters whenever the GI's stopped at their farms or marched through their villages. Other young men were much more inhibited. Sim Copans, an American officer who after the war would have a very popular jazz program on French radio, reminisced about one such soldier:

My driver was a boy from the U.S. south and belonged to a religious group which forbade the consumption of alcoholic beverages. [After the liberation of his town] a French high school English teacher, a widower, invited [us] for a fantastic meal. He brought out three bottles of Bordeaux wine, two white and one red, two bottles of champagne cider, a good Calvados and a bottle of Armagnac, which he opened just for us. How unhappy [he] was every time the boy refused to drink![56]

On August 25, 1944, six days after the Parisian uprising against the Germans, the French 2nd Armored Division moved into Paris through Versailles, and the American 4th Armored Division came in through the Porte d'Orléans. Although there were still pockets of Germans in the capital, the local population came out and greeted the liberators with an explosion of joy and gratitude—"a pandemonium of surely the greatest mass joy that has ever happened," according to American war correspondent, Ernie Pyle.[57]

A journalist at the *New York Herald Tribune* described the scene:

American troops found themselves the objects of more affectionate adoration than they had in any of the cities they had entered previously. . . . As the army vehicles moved down the boulevards, the yelling crowds closed in on them. Whenever the procession stopped, women and girls swarmed over tanks and jeeps, hugging and kissing the Americans with unrestrained fervor. GI faces soon became red with lipstick. Men and women swarmed up to throw flowers, fruit, bread, bottles of wine, cigarettes, and all manner of presents into jeeps and command cars. Women and girls climbed on to tanks and insisted on their riding there despite the chances of shooting starting at any minute.[58]

In the euphoria following the liberation of Paris, romance flourished, and many young French women, who before the war had only gone out in groups of friends or with a chaperone, starting "dating" GI's.

Interestingly, most combat soldiers, "the ones most deserving" of being applauded in Paris, according to Ernie Pyle, were not there that day. "Only one infantry regiment and one reconnaissance outfit of Americans actually came into Paris," he said,

and they passed on through the city quickly and went on with their war. The first ones in the city to stay were such nonfighters as the psychological-warfare and civil-affairs people, public-relations men and correspondents . . . the guys who broke the German army and opened the way for Paris to be free were still out there fighting without benefit of kisses or applause. . .[59]

Indeed, Paris was "off limits" for many combat soldiers until Germany capitulated. They would come back later, however, with dollars in their pockets, on two or three-day passes and expect the city and the population to be as welcoming as on that day in August 1944. Some of them had other expectations as well. They remembered the stories of their predecessors, the Doughboys of World War I, and planned to visit the nightclubs of Montmartre and discover the charms of Parisian prostitutes.

France was liberated in September 1944, and Germany surrendered in May 1945. But, even after the end of the war, France's economic situation remained catastrophic. Liberation had not returned the glitter to "the City of Lights." In the autumn of 1945, according to one French author:

> People were dressed inelegantly; shop shelves were empty and prices exorbitant. Passersby didn't linger in front of bare shop fronts but hurried to join an interminable queue to get, if they were lucky, a little food.... Between the Opera and the Madeleine, civilians tried to sell "souvenirs" and women, their "favors." In nearby streets, the black market, where anything could be swapped, flourished...[60]

In a talk she gave at the Red Cross Club in Paris in the spring of 1945, American writer Gertrude Stein told a number of GI's:

> Each of you should be like Boy Scouts and smile at least once a day at Frenchmen. The French...are utterly exhausted by the strain of their spiritual campaign against the Germans. Americans don't realize the depth of French fatigue. Their feeling in the Occupation was that sometime the Americans would come and then everything would be wonderful...[61]

But, a year after the Liberation, it couldn't be said that everything in France was "wonderful"; nor were the American soldiers always like "Boy Scouts." Living conditions were as bad or even worse than they were before. The country had been "looted and wrecked and it would be a long time before it would recover."[62]

As for the GI's, they had visions of "gay Paree," and it seemed "gay" for awhile, but then "it became a pretty dreary place with everything at high prices, the buildings unheated and a general lack of everything."[63] The GI's had many "gripes" about France and the French. In fact, the complaining became so bad that the U.S. army stepped in. Its "Information & Education Division" published a little booklet in Paris in 1945 entitled *112 Gripes about the French* in which it listed, according to the editors:

> the criticisms, misconceptions and ordinary "gripes" which American troops in Europe express most frequently when they talk about the French....Each comment, or question, is followed by an answer—or discussion. Some of the

answers are quite short, because the question is direct and simple. Some of the answers are quite long, because the "questions" are not questions at all, but indictments which contain complicated and sweeping preconceptions.[64]

By mid-1945, disillusionment set in on both sides.[65] The French were shocked, and the French government, exasperated, by the disgraceful conduct of certain U.S. servicemen in both Paris and the provinces. This misconduct ranged from drunkenness and rowdiness to holdups and profiteering. Unscrupulous soldiers were buying coffee, gasoline, tires, cigarettes, boots, soap, ammunition, morphine, Spam, and whiskey at the PX, and then reselling them on the black market. Despite the risk of court-martial, black marketers even got their hands on, and then sold, American arms, munitions, equipment, and war material.[66]

Many French people felt the Americans had worn out their welcome. They resented the requisitioning of their buildings, factories, and hospitals, and the financial burden of the services they provided to U.S. troops.[67] And they didn't like being treated as if they were still subjects under another occupation. A November 19, 1945, article in *Time* magazine entitled "The Wrong Ambassadors" criticized the attitude of the GI's in France and said they "swaggered about as though they were conquerors—and irresistible conquerors to boot."[68] Indeed, a French writer described a scene in which "an army of drivers with no indication of rank...threw cigarettes to onlookers as if to an African crowd."[69]

The French were tired of occupation, and many wished the GI's would go home. The truth was that the GI's themselves wanted to go home. They wanted to get back to their wives and sweethearts. But even though the war in Europe ended in May 1945, it was not until February 1946 that American soldiers started being shipped home on a regular basis. In the meantime, there was plenty of time for "fraternization."

Having been provided with condoms[70] and "social hygiene information" by the military[71] in an effort to control venereal disease, American GI's sought out prostitutes or formed relationships with French women.

Insofar as prostitution was concerned, the brothels of Paris and of other cities in France ran a thriving business. As one book on life in wartime Paris revealed, following the Liberation, men in khaki uniforms simply replaced those in green as customers in the houses of prostitution.[72] Also, as previously happened in the United States[73] and England, women and even young girls started loitering outside U.S. army camps.[74] In answer to Gripe 57 about the high number of prostitutes in France after the war, the Information and Education Division of the U.S. army explained to GI's that this was unfortunately due to the war. Having lost everything, thousands of French women, like women all over Europe, turned to prostitution as a source of income.[75]

But GI's also fraternized with other French women coming from all walks of life. There were many occasions for them to meet. In the excitement of liberation, it could be aboard a tank or jeep or while offering a glass of cider or champagne. For some French women, it was when their parents invited an American "liberator" home for a meal. Or it was during victory celebrations or at dances and socials sponsored by the American Red Cross, sometimes on an Army base. The workplace also provided an opportunity to meet. Numerous French women were employed locally by the U.S. army or in various American administrative bureaus in France. Or sometimes GI's and French women met completely by chance. Roger Lantagne remembers meeting Jeanette in the *métro* while on a three-day leave in Paris just before being shipped back to the United States. Their romance started when he offered her his seat.[76] Army doctor Arthur met his French sweetheart, Reine, when she came into a dispensary in Marseille to give blood.[77]

There were complaints in some circles that GI's "baited" women by offering them food or nylon stockings. The Information and Education Division of the army stated in its response to Gripe 57 that "the French are shocked by the rude way in which GI's talk to a woman, and by the number of unpleasant experiences decent French women have had with intoxicated and amorous American soldiers."

Indeed, unless the girls spoke English, many GI's probably had a hard time "communicating" with French women in the same way they had with British women, who at least shared the same language and cultural heritage. Moreover, owing to the stories of their predecessors, the Doughboys, they had an image of the French *mademoiselle* as being sensual and "easy." This was hardly the case with many of the women they first encountered in Normandy and Brittany, two regions which, at the time, were "essentially rural, Catholic, and conservative."[78]

Still, it must also be said that French women were not always innocent "victims" of seduction. According to some French authors, many French girls went out of their way to meet and "date" GI's. Simone de Beauvoir writes of a young woman who lived in the same hotel in Paris: "Lise's main sport since the Liberation was what she called 'hunting the American.'"[79] And in her novel, *Les Trois Quarts du Temps*, Benoîte Groult describes how, in 1945, *bourgeois* girls in the St. Germain area of Paris who'd attended fashionable religious schools quite naturally took to spending a few hours with GI's in exchange for soap, canned food, and cigarettes. Encouraged by their "innocent" mothers, the girls let themselves be seduced by Don or Steve, but because they still lived with their parents, the girls' flirting couldn't lead to a "conclusion," thus preserving their sacrosanct virginity! Groult obviously found the situation hypocritical, for she says: "The self-righteous had applauded the shaving of heads of poor girls who'd chosen the wrong uniform, but now they were encouraging these well-brought up *bourgeoises* to listen to their hearts and appetites."[80]

Not all French women, of course, went out "hunting for the American." According to Beevor and Cooper, "by the spring of 1945, American ardor was no longer appreciated by most Parisian girls, who did not like the arrogance that went with it."[81] A French girl interviewed by *Time* magazine in November of the same year complained, "I do not know why all Americans think that all French girls will make love to anybody."[82] Obviously, too, French girls came from different backgrounds and had different types of upbringing. *Parisiennes*, too, might have been more "savvy" in conducting relationships with young American soldiers.

Reports are contradictory. Nevertheless, it would appear there were various degrees of seduction and flirtation on both sides. Of course, there were also broken hearts. Although some GI's would stay on in France or later return as civilians under the Marshall Plan, most them left as of 1946, many of them never to return. As a result, numerous French girls would be left behind without any possibility of ever seeing "their" GI again or of informing them of the birth of a child. Others would be more fortunate. Their love affair would end in marriage and a new life in America.

* * * * *

As we have already mentioned, some 6,000 or more French women married GI's after the end of the war and journeyed to the United States to live, either before or after their husbands had been demobilized.

Those French women who immigrated to the United States under the War Brides or Fiancés Acts during 1946 benefited from transportation provided by the U.S. army. Indeed, all of the brides' travel expenses, "door to door," were paid by the U.S. government

Most war brides from France, who were joined by brides from Belgium and several other European countries, left by ship from Le Havre, in Normandy. Marseille was another French port used as an American staging area, and in August 1946, Bremmerhaven, Germany, would replace Le Havre as a major debarkation point.

Before going to Le Havre, many of the brides first journeyed to Paris, where they were put up at the Hotel de Paris, "converted from the Red Cross Club's Rainbow Corner to a way-point hostelry for soldiers' wives en route to the United States, from homes outside of Paris."[83] For the first group of war brides to leave Paris, a mass, attended by Jefferson Caffery, the American ambassador, was celebrated at the Church of the Madeleine on February 26, 1946.[84] The brides would then be transported by train[85] from the Gare St. Lazare or by bus to a converted U.S. army camp, or "staging area," in Gainneville, near Le Havre, called Camp Philip Morris.

Camp Philip Morris was one of the famous "cigarette camps" (named after brand-name cigarettes) set up by the U.S. army for soldiers landing in Normandy after D-Day. After the war was over, most of these camps became transit places for soldiers returning to the United States. Just before the contingents of war brides started arriving, Camp Philip Morris was used for housing nurses and members of the Women's Army Corps.[86]

The French and other Continental brides spent from three to five days at Camp Philip Morris being processed by the army and workers of the American Red Cross, who assisted with paperwork for entry into the United States and gave the brides cultural training to prepare them for everyday life in America.

The brides were shipped to the United States from Le Havre on reconverted ocean liners and troop ships, such as the S.S. *George W. Goethals*, S.S. *Zebulon Vance*, S.S. *Santa Paula*, S.S. *Cristobal*, and the S.S. *Bridgeport*. Onboard, the Red Cross and the Women's Army Corps organized recreation, ran nurseries, and provided medical facilities. According to Red Cross reports, shipboard activities included early morning church services, pastoral counseling with the chaplain, visits to the library, meetings with ARC counselors, cultural training, lunch, recreation and crafts, newsreels, dinner at 5:30 p.m., concerts, movies, and after-dinner entertainment.[87] Accommodations on board were hardly luxurious: eight or more brides, some with, some without children, shared cabins.

The majority of war brides from Europe usually disembarked in New York. Sometimes they were greeted by their husbands, who were already back in the United States, but often it was their American in-laws who greeted them and took them "home." If no one was there to greet them, the ARC or the YWCA would put them up for a few days at a hospitality center, and then ARC employees and volunteers accompanied them by train to their final destination, which could be anywhere in the country. Most brides were given an allowance for food expenses during their journey.

When the brides arrived in Alabama or Michigan, they settled into their new surroundings as best they could. Quite a few of the marriages turned out well, but many of the women had been young and "starry eyed" right after the war and had married hastily. Consequently, they hardly knew their husbands when they arrived in America. Incompatibility, lack of communication due to language differences, and cultural and socioeconomic issues often resulted. The handsome soldier in uniform would turn out to be an uneducated farm boy or an alcoholic. Or he suffered from what today would be called "posttraumatic stress disorder" and couldn't keep a job. And often, because of the acute, postwar housing shortage in the United States, couples started out their life together living with the brides' in-laws. All of these problems could, of course, lead to rocky marriages and divorce.

If the women lived in cities, meeting with other French women or joining a French Brides Club would help in adapting to their new environment. Often, French war brides of World War I would greet them and make them feel at home in the local community. The ARC and the YWCA provided English classes and other courses for French and other war brides in many communities.

Those women who ended up in isolated settings would not have such support, of course, and their transition was usually more difficult. Indeed, the reality was often not what was promised by the gorgeous GI or what appeared in American films. A telling cartoon of the time depicts a scene that obviously occurred more than once in postwar America. It shows a run-down, wooden shack with a handmade sign ("Welcum home Wally and his bride") and a returning GI (Wally) exclaiming to his wife: "But, honey, where did you get the idea that all Americans live in skyscrapers?"[88]

* * * * *

Such cartoons, as well as numerous photos and articles in the American army and civilian press of the 1940s and 1950s, and also a number of films and books, provide an interesting, and often amusing, view of how *Mademoiselle* was perceived by the GI and "folks back home" in America. For example, the popular 1949 film *I Was a Male War Bride*, a gag-filled comedy in which Cary Grant plays the role of a French army officer who marries an American WAC, made the "bride" (in this case a man) look pretty ridiculous. In addition, both the American and the French media often showed how postwar Franco-American encounters and marriages were considered on both sides of the Atlantic and the climate *Mademoiselle* had to contend with upon entering the United States.

The chronological steps by which the GI and *Mademoiselle* came into contact were illustrated in the army press. In fact, *Stars and Stripes* and *Yank* began preparing—often humorously—the GI's for going to France while they were still stationed in Britain, training and waiting for the invasion of the Continent.

For example, an article from *Warweek*, June 15, 1944, entitled "So you're going to France," declares: "It's not true that all French women are easy. Any guy who has the idea that the way to make friends and influence Frenchmen is to slip up alongside of the first good-looking gal he sees and slip her a quick pat on the fanny is going to be in for trouble." A cartoon on the same page shows a French girl and a GI "courting," followed by a whole tribe of her French relatives. The caption reads: "French cuties are well chaperoned."[89]

There were also other ways to prepare the GI's. One was teaching them how to communicate with a French girl. "Parley-Voo for Busy GI's—in One Easy Lesson, including Papa!" gives a simplified, phonetic way of saying: "*Halt!*" "*Venez ici.*" "*Je suis Américain.*" "*Où sont les Allemands?*" "*Où est Paris?*" "*Montrez-moi, s'il vous plaît*" [They're looking at a map]. *Je ne comprends pas.*" "*J'ai faim.*" Then the GI asks, "*Oui? Non?*" as he tries to kiss her. Finally, he says "*Aidez-moi, s'il vous plaît*" to a passerby after the girl's father has knocked him down and taken her away.[90]

A few days after D-Day, numerous memorable photos in the press showed French girls running up to welcome the American liberators. In a June 1944 photo in *Stars and Stripes*, for example, some paratroopers are toasting a glass of cider with a young French woman ("one version of the Mademoiselle from Armentières").[91] The caption of another photo reads: "Civilians gather around American troops in a Normandy village. One French girl offers a bottle of home-brewed wine to several of the Doughboys."[92] A cartoon from *Warweek*, September 28, 1944, shows Hubert, a funny-looking, ill-shaven GI, trying to get on with a French family living in the countryside.[93] Indeed, in the beginning of the invasion, the cartoons showed farm girls and their families, but as the army advanced and the GI's got closer to Paris, the girls get more and more chic in the photos and cartoons.

Upon reaching the outskirts of Paris, many combat soldiers on their way to eastern France or Germany were not allowed to enter the city. In a cartoon in *Yank,* poor "Sad Sack" fights his way across Normandy. The objective is to reach Paris. The signposts say, "Paris, 250 kms." Then 200, followed by 150 and 100. By the time it's 50 kilometers away, Sad Sack is dreaming about drinking with a French girl and caressing her. But when he gets to the Porte d'Orléans, he's told by an American MP: "Paris—off limits."[94]

Some soldiers of the U.S. Third Army *did* get into Paris, however, and later marched down the Champs Elysées on Liberation Day. Numerous photos appeared in the press of girls running up to the tanks or even sitting in them next to a GI. The headline on the front page of *Stars and Stripes*, August 26, 1944, exclaims: "Yanks Smash into Paris." The captions of the photos read: "Giving Lip Service to Joy of Liberation," and "The mademoiselles of Paris greeted their liberators with fervent kisses."[95]

Pictures like these appeared in all the American mainstream press, and many Americans were shocked at how free French people—especially the women—were with their kisses. Even if half the time the kisses were only on both cheeks, kissing and smooching in public were just not "the American way" in the 1940s. Another headline read: "Paris Is Free—and So Are Its Kisses."[96] In the accompanying article, the *Stars and Stripes* reporter says, "Coming in with the French Second Armored Division, I was kissed so many times it was like a multiple game of 'post office.'"[97] Further on, he admits: "After all the trouble I've had trying to convince American girls that kissing was a helluva good way to begin things, these girls in Paris were asking my permission. Boy, what a war!"

With all these photos of kisses and women, it is easy to imagine what the girls back home were thinking. A headline in the *Stars and Stripes* of September 25, 1944, ran: "Liberation Kisses Smack of Trouble Back Home." The article begins with these words: "When Johnny comes marching home again, he's going to have a lot of explaining to do about those pictures showing him kissing French girls in jeeps and atop tanks when he rolled into Liberated Paris." It goes on to quote an 18-year-old American woman in Indiana, "If the French girls kill old guys like Ernie Pyle, what are they going to do to the young ones?" The American woman obviously blames French girls for the famous war correspondent's death, whereas he actually died in an accident.[98]

All of these photos and articles in the American press illustrate the type of atmosphere that French war brides were going to face when they reached the United States. But it was not just because of the photos. It was also because of the image of French women after World War I, when they were portrayed as prostitutes and "floozies," and there was a huge campaign for the Doughboys not to get involved with them.

After VE-Day, more and more GI's were able to get to Paris, and they started feeling more welcome. However, although their salaries were high as far as French standards were concerned, they found prices—especially for items like perfume or for entertainment—very high and often complained that the French were cheating them. Although it was true that many French shopkeepers did, in fact, hike up their prices, it was also true that "the boys" from America were not always used to the savvy ways of Parisians.

In a cartoon in a December 1944 edition of *Stars and Stripes*, three young GI's stand in front of a perfume shop. One says to the other, "I wonder how you say *eau de cologne* in French?"[99] In another photo, two scruffy looking GI's are in the street, looking at chic-looking, high-heeled women with fancy hairdos and hats, rushing this way and that. Pfc[100] Hubert exclaims, "Some joker told me all you had to do was stand on a corner and beat 'em off with a club."[101]

In a long illustrated article in *Life* magazine in November 1945, numerous photos show Parisian scenes and describe the American soldiers' antics in Pigalle, which the GI's dubbed "Pig Alley." *Life* describes Pigalle as "a little sector of Montmartre devoting itself to the back-alley entertainment of foreigners. To its garish honky-tonks, penny arcades, intimate *boîtes* and amiable girls, head most pleasure-bent GI's in Paris. They are received the way their WWI fathers were received—as friendly, free-spending roisterers."[102]

One can imagine the reaction of the American public "down on the farm" when they saw these photos and read captions like: "GI kisses an *entreteneuse* [sic] after plying her with 1,000 franc champagne. *Entreteneuses* [sic] are met at bars, never in streets."[103] The words "Parisian jitterbug whirls with GI at Blue Hour. French teenagers have become quite expert at American swing dances" accompanies a photo of a French girl with a very short, swirling skirt dancing with a GI.[104] Scantily-clad women are shown dancing on stage at "night spots [where] GI's pay terrific prices for third-rate entertainment."[105]

Certain photos were really shocking "back home," especially as parts of America were segregated in the 1940s. The caption of one is self-explanatory:

> The color line in France hardly exists, especially among Montmartre artists and show people. In Frisco's, a second-story, undecorated nightclub near Place Pigalle, Negro soldiers dance with French girls, a few of whom are also Negro but most of whom are white. The girls come to Frisco's, favorite hangout for Negro GI's, because they like to do fancy jitterbugging...[106]

Many French women dated black soldiers after the war and were shocked at what they considered to be white Americans' racism, which they sometimes identified with Nazism.[107]

During the war, African-American soldiers represented about 8.7 percent of the Army but very few saw actual combat. About 78 percent of them were employed in the service branches. What happened was that after the end of the war, rather than going back to segregated America, some of these black soldiers stayed on in France after demobilization, or they returned after being disillusioned in postwar America.[108] The caption of a photo of Paul Bates from an April 1946 issue of *Life* reads:

> In officers' hotel, where he now lives, Paul Bates, 26, an ex-GI, relaxes. He was the only man from his outfit to settle in France. Before [the war] Bates earned $360 a year in Tennessee; today he works as a civilian handyman in an Army PX earning $2772 a year. He's not a bit homesick.[109]

Another subject that was touched on in the American press was how *chic* French women were. One stereotype was that most French women were very attractive, well-dressed, and had "The French look," as it was called by *Life*: "Sexier and less natural than the American look, it is the result of effort and ingenuity."[110] A caption of one photo reads: "Light, full skirts and shapely legs are the badge of French girls today. The new hairdo is down and long; five of these girls have dyed hair."[111] A 1945 *Stars and Stripes* article praised the French style of swimming togs, which they called "more and more daring."[112]

One item of clothing the Americans didn't envy, however, was French shoes. Owing to the leather shortage in France during and just after the war, women wore heavy, wooden-soled shoes that made loud, clopping noises. As a consequence, a good number of French war brides splurged on an expensive pair of leather shoes when they first arrived in New York.

Unfortunately, my sample does not include a French war bride who married an African-American. However, a file in a United States Army collection found at the National Archives[113] reveals a very moving case involving a black GI and his French fiancée. Here are some extracts from this file, the first being a letter to the Supreme Court, reprinted in its original form:

Leghorn, Italy
   Sept. 21, 1946
   Dear Sirs,
   Please inform me if, in writing to you; I am committing a breach of army regulations. I understand that as a citizen and soldier of the United States, I still am permitted to ask your decision on any perplexing problem, directly related to the administration of the Supreme Court. Since this department isn't a War Department Agency but a civilian agency, I see no breach of army regulations.

Am a regular army man, having re-enlisted for three years. Have three years and five months of honorable service in the army, of which twenty-nine months were spent overseas. Have four official battle stars, and one unofficial. During those 29 mos. My life has been in grave danger. Please forgive me for these boring details but they serve a purpose.

A French woman, with whom I have been engaged to for about sixteen months, gave birth to my child, the 16th of July 1946. In January, during her pregnancy I re-enlisted in the army at Mourmelon France for the express purpose of marrying her. Upon applying for army sanction to the marriage was denied permission by a provision of Allied Military Marriage forms that states: any member of the Armed Forces requesting permission to marry an alien must be required to conform to the marriage laws of the state in which he resides. Otherwise, if one hails from a southern state, he can't marry one of another race, even though mixed marriages are authorized in Europe and France. Does that mean that I'm still subject to discrimination, even though I'm still an American soldier. A War Department circular in 1945 stated that discrimination in any form, in the U.S. Armed Forces was unconstitutional.

As an American citizen and a member of our Armed Forces, guarding and safe-guarding the principles of the Constitution of the United States of America, and our great Democracy, I implore you to please see that justice is fulfilled and the Constitution carried out to the letter.

The Constitution states that it is unlawful to discriminate against a man because of race, color, or creed. I was denied permission to marry the mother of my child, a Melle. Paulette Hyberger, Reim, France, because I hail from W. Va. and am a Negro.

Being a soldier, and overseas at that, I am handicapped in my quest for equality and rights as outlined by the constitution. May I rest assured that the Constitution and the principles of Democracy for which we have upheld the last five years in the face of a serious menace, and for which we are pledged to defend now come to the fore and protect the minority in their uphill quest for freedom and equality?

I am begging you to represent me in my absence and render me justice on it's merits.

May I rest content that this evil shall be corrected and I be given permission to become the legal father of my kid!

Thanking you in the Interest of Democracy, I remain,

Respectively yours,

Pfc. Lawson Day

Pfc. Lawson Day, 35658773

696 Port Co.

APO 790, c/o Postmaster

New York, N.Y.

In reply to Pfc Lawson Day's letter, the Office of the Marshall of the U.S. Supreme Court answered that the Supreme Court was not authorized by law to assist, advise, or reply to affairs that were not addressed to it according to regular procedures. However, the Marshall's Office did forward Day's letter on to the Civil Affairs Division of the Pentagon. What follows is an internal memo dated October 16, 1946 from a certain Major Crook to C.P. Echols, Major General, Chief, Civil Affairs Division. This memo is included in the army file on this affair found at the National Archives in Washington:

> Memo for Record: A letter from Pfc Lawson Day, 35658773, 696 Port Co., APO 790, c/o Postmaster, New York, New York; dated 21 September 1946, addressed to the Supreme Court, complaining that he had been denied permission to marry the mother of his child because he was a negro, was referred by the Supreme Court to D/PA, and forwarded in turn to this Division for information on which to base [a reply].
>
> 1. Marriage of military personnel in the European Theater is at present governed by the previsions of Art. IV, Circular No. 128, Headquarters, USFET [United States Forces, European Theater], dated 12 September 1946. Paragraph 9 thereof; entitled, "Procedures for Handling Application for Permission to Marry", after outlining the requirements of application; specifies the action which will be taken thereon by the Commanding Officer authorized to approve it. Subparagraph 1 of paragraph 9, states, "In case of approval; the approving commander will assure himself that the applicant understands that " *** (3). The laws of a number of states do not recognize as valid any marriage contract between persons of certain different races, regardless of whether the marriage was valid where contracted."
>
> 2. From the letter of subject soldier, it would appear that the Commanding Officer to whom his application to marry was submitted for approval, misinterpreted the above quoted provision of the Circular. (If the application was prior to 12 September 1946, it would have been handled under Circular No. 51, dated 15 April 1946, which contained a similar provision).
>
> 3. It is believed that it was not the intention of USFET to discriminate against military personnel residing in states which prohibit mixed marriages, but merely to make certain that any soldier from such a state who married a person of a different race understood his position, as the soldier might be unable to return to his former residence with his wife and live with her there if the law of his state prohibited members of different races living together. The marriage; if valid where contracted, would be recognized by every jurisdiction except that of the soldier's domicile.
>
> 4. It is recommended that it be brought to the attention of subject soldier's Commanding Officer that paragraph 9 i. (3) of Circular No. 128,

Headquarters, USFET, 12 September 1946, should not be interpreted as bar-ring mixed marriages.

Because of the shortage of transport ships, many GI's faced a long wait in France before they could get back to the United States or be redeployed to the Pacific. So, as after World War I, the U.S. army set up a "university" or GI school—this time in Biarritz—where soldiers could take courses while wait-ing. The American University of Biarritz (dubbed "Sweat-it-out-U" by the students), was composed of 38 departments and offered some 241 courses, most of which they could later get credit for from colleges and universities in the United States.[114]

Some soldiers took advantage of the GI Bill[115] and stayed on in France to take courses at French institutions. A picture in *Stars and Stripes* shows two ex-GI's sculpting a naked woman: "It's art," the caption reads.

> Enthusiasm runs high at the Sorbonne in Paris, where 800 GI students are applying themselves to courses in language, science, journalism, dressmaking, hairdressing and...sculpture. The life class above shows students diligently studying sculpture. This sort of education leads to artistic careers and illus-trates what may be made of barren Army assignments.[116]

According to Tyler Stovall, thanks to the GI Bill, close to 500 African-American veterans chose Paris as the place to pursue their studies after the War. "In the late 1940s, the bill paid $75 a month, or roughly twice the aver-age wage of a French worker, for school fees and living costs."[117] Stovall believes that "the GI bill contributed indirectly to the development of the postwar black community in Paris."[118]

* * * * *

The American society of the late 1940s encountered by French war brides was quite different from that of postwar France. Food was abundant, auto-mobiles jammed the roads, and clothes and appliances filled shop windows. People lived in track homes in suburban communities and made their pur-chases in new "shopping centers." In the "return to normalcy," family values and convention became the norm.

All of this was depicted in the media. A photo in a December 3, 1945, issue of *Life* shows a GI from Indiana being welcomed home by his family. The caption reads:

> He was 26 months overseas, earned a European Theater ribbon with four bat-tle stars, as well as a presidential unit citation. Surrounded by kindly family and friends who want to know "all about it," the thing that comes out first is an account of the mud and cold of Italy.[119]

Then, in some cases, the soldier went on to announce that his European or Asian "war bride" would soon be arriving. Such news would usually be greeted with mixed emotions by the soldier's family.

Of course, besides parents and relatives, there were also all the American sweethearts and wives that were waiting for their men to come home. An advertisement of a soldier hugging his blond fiancée (who's just chosen the advertiser's silver set as a wedding gift!), with the words "Back Home For Keeps" in bold letters, appeared in the November 12, 1945, edition of *Life*.[120] An ad in the November 26, 1945, edition of the same magazine shows a "smiling bride" on the steps of the church with her GI husband. The text begins:

> And now her smile is like a brighter sun to strike all shadows always from their path—for lo! He stands beside her once again....The diamond ring that would flash one joyous fragment of this proven faith for them forever must be peerless ...[121]

There was indeed great pressure for the men to return as quickly as possible to America and to pick up their lives where they had left off before the war. Unfortunately, however, what happened was that some of these men had changed in the interim. They had been through some terrible experiences. Sometimes they couldn't re-adapt. Or they realized they'd married too quickly before leaving for the war. A December 1945 photo in *Life* shows a courtroom scene: "War marriage ends with divorce. Corporal Kenneth Dickey tells Judge Ralph Hamill how he was married in 1943 after a short courtship, went overseas, was a prisoner of war, came home to a wife who no longer loved him."[122] Or sometimes the GI had met someone else while abroad.

McKinlay Kantor's 1945 novel *Glory to Me*, later made into the award-winning film *The Best Years of Our Lives* by William Wyler, brilliantly depicted how hard it was for three GI's to adapt to their former lives upon returning to Boon City, an imaginary town in the Midwest. By way of example, Lieutenant Fred Derry's war medals don't help him find a good job, so he goes back to being a soda jerk again. And he finds his wife, whom he married just before leaving for overseas, working in a nightclub and "entertaining" other men.

The late 1940s and the 1950s were also the beginning of the "consumer age" in America. Visitors and immigrants (including war brides) were amazed at all the new goods and appliances. Raymonde Cole, a French war bride, was hired by a professional photographer to sell some of these products. In a

1952 advertisement she is seen selling a new TV set. In another, she's the mother of a family that has just bought a big station wagon. This photo could not be more typical of the 1950s: the suburban ranch house in the background, and in the foreground, the nuclear family—father, mother and two kids—standing on the front lawn and gazing at their new car.[123]

* * * * *

As for the French press after the war , it often reflected the French public's concern with the fact that French women were dating and marrying American soldiers. Pierre Lazareff, the founder and editor of *France Soir*, talked about this in a 1945 article he wrote for his paper that was later translated and reprinted in the *Stars and Stripes Magazine*:

> The misunderstanding was inevitable. On one side there were the American soldiers who were homesick and who, in their nostalgia, set up comparisons which could not [rebound] to our advantage. On the other hand, there were the French, who had just gone through four years of occupation and privations and who vaguely hoped that each American soldier would come with his rifle on his shoulder, a sack of [flour] on his back, a little coat in one hand and chocolate in the other.
>
> . . . Instead of that they saw the Americans settling down in the buildings from whence they had just evicted the Germans and requisitioning the same hotels and restaurants for their troops. To be sure, the French understood the necessities of war, but one can scarcely expect people whose feet have been much stepped upon not to have sensitive toes and to refrain from grimacing when it is a friend who treads on their corns.
>
> . . . This calls to mind my recent trip to the *Côte d'Azur*(the Riviera), which has since become USRRA. And I assure you that everybody down there is happy to see American officers, non-coms and soldiers enjoying a little of that amusement they have so well deserved. Practically all the pleasure spots have been reserved for them. They are each entitled to one guest and, naturally enough, that guest is more frequently a girl than a boy. But since some of the girls happen to be the wives and fiancées of local inhabitants, nothing in the world can prevent a husband, or a fiancé, from feeling disagreeable at having the lady of his heart whirl rhythmically in the arms of a soldier—even though that soldier is an American hero. . .[124]

Articles and photos from French women's magazines also referred to Franco-American encounters and marriages. Letters to the Editor columns abounded with requests for advice. "Should I marry a foreigner?" asks one reader in a September 1945 issue of *Marie-France*.[125] "Suffering Blondie" writes, "Two years ago, an American and I became engaged. My parents agreed. I no longer hear from him, but I know he's alive. How do I find out what happened to him?"[126] The March 26, 1946 edition of *Elle* showed photos of French war brides arriving in New York, one with the caption: "Arrived safely. Lots of kisses. The French wives."[127]

After the marriages occurred and the French brides had settled in the United States, there was concern in French official circles that some of these French women would have to be repatriated at French government expense. Copies of correspondence in the diplomatic archives at the *Ministère des Affaires Etrangères* in Paris reveal that as early as August 1946 requests for repatriation were made to the Compagnie Générale Transatlantique by French consulates in various American cities. Mention is made of the French wives' disillusionment with their husbands and their husbands' families, as well as the precarious financial situations in which they found themselves.[128]

Between August 1946 and January 1947, letters and memoranda were exchanged between French representatives in Washington at the Ministry of Public Works and Transport and the Ministry of Foreign Affaires in Paris concerning the issue of repatriation of French war brides and who would pay for it. A letter from French Ambassador Henri Bonnet to President Leon Blum on January 8, 1947, in which he requests a budget of at least $25,000, states that the various French consulates had received about 50 requests for repatriation from "disillusioned" French brides. It also says that approximately 100 more requests were expected for 1947. Although Ambassador Bonnet realizes the financial problems involved, he feels that "it is difficult for France not to assist her compatriots who are in difficulty. These women are often worthy of interest and sometimes have one or two children, who are also French."[129]

But these cases were the exception. One hundred and fifty returning war brides out of some 6,000 is not a large number. And even though there were probably some who had the funds to return on their own, we can surmise that the majority of French wives adapted and settled into the American way of life. In his letter, Ambassador Bonnet states that "most of them adapted fairly easily to their new life."[130] Comparisons, of course, were inevitable. A list in a 1946 *Elle* gives details of what French women liked in America and what they missed.[131] Among the things they liked were the convenience of everyday life, the large apartments, the launderettes, mail-order catalogues, cans and other conserved foods, the credit system, and American hospitality. What did they miss? The French way of life, *bistrots*, café terraces, dishes that cook a long time, homemade pastries, conversation, French schools, French movies, and other forms of entertainment. Photos in *Marie-Claire* in 1954 show a French war bride preparing a meal in her modern American kitchen and then in the living room with her children and husband in front of their new TV set.[132] The same issue of the magazine describes French women's perceptions of the differences between French and American women.[133]

* * * * *

The saga of French *mademoiselles* marrying American soldiers would not be complete without hearing from the women themselves. As someone who does oral history, I believe personal accounts are a valid complement to archival research. Not only do they allow the participants to share in presenting the past, but they also make history more understandable and lively for the listener or reader. Besides, everyone loves a story, and "An honest tale speeds best being plainly told." Of course, people's recollections and memories may not always be accurate insofar as certain events are concerned. Some—not all—elderly people have difficulty remembering, and a vision of "the big picture" may be missing from their testimonies. Nevertheless, to my mind, perceptions and feelings about what happened in the past also have a place in the recounting of history. Through telling their stories, women who lived through World War II and subsequently emigrated certainly provide a vision of these experiences that, until only recently, has been missing from the history books.

The first-hand accounts that appear in this book are chosen from a corpus of 25 interviews I conducted over a six-year period with French war brides who married after World War II, and with three women who are daughters of French war brides of World War I. Three of the brides of World War II originally came from Paris, three from Normandy, three from New Caledonia, two from Algeria (a former French colony), two from Marseille, two from Cannes, and one each from Nancy and towns in the Ardennes, the Vienne, the Limousin, the Dordogne, and the Meurthe and Moselle. The World War I French brides in this book came from Clermont-Ferrand, the Alpes-Maritimes, and Rochefort-sur-Mer.

Thirteen of the war brides I interviewed presently live in California, although, as with most Californians, they usually resided somewhere else first. Interestingly, in California I discovered—quite by chance—a small "colony" of French war brides from New Caledonia who all seem to know each other. Of the non-Californians, four women live in Michigan, three in Washington D.C., and one each in New Jersey, Iowa, Illinois, Kentucky, and Arkansas. Two have returned to Paris to live.

Finding the women happened in a "snow-ball" way. I told friends I was interested in interviewing French war brides of World War II, and it just so happened that the mother of one, and the sister and the neighbor of two others, fell into this category. After advertising in the *Journal Français* and with the French consulate and the *Alliance Française* in San Francisco, Los Angeles, New York, and Washington, I traveled to the United States to interview the women who responded. My contacts with the French community in Detroit helped me find those living in Michigan. The war brides I interviewed also gave me names of other women, and this led to further contacts.

I realize, of course, that a sample of 25 out of the approximate 6,000 French war brides of World War II is insignificant from a quantitative point of view. My purpose was not to do a systematic analysis. Rather, it was to interview women from different parts of France, with different backgrounds, and having different types of experience, so as to better understand what it meant to be a young French war bride after World War II and to adapt to a new life in America in the mid-1940s. Although this book includes the stories of three French war brides of World War I as they were told to me by their daughters, I regret that I was not able to gather first person testimonies. I also regret that my corpus did not include French who married soldiers of color or who were so disillusioned that they returned to France almost immediately after arrival in the United States.

About half of my interviewees later divorced, but except for two women, they nevertheless stayed on in America. Some remarried other American men; a few remained single. Several women confessed they felt they couldn't go back to France after their marriages had dissolved. More often than not, their parents and their families hadn't approved of their marrying an American and moving to the United States, but the women had done it anyway. They didn't want to go back because they didn't want to admit they'd made a huge mistake and face their family's reproaches. So they stayed on in the United States and, as one said, "got on with it."

"Getting on with it" often meant dealing with very difficult marital situations and critical in-laws, as well as the difficulties involved in adapting to a new culture, learning a new language, and taking on a new nationality. Even though most of the women I interviewed had come from modest, fairly strict backgrounds, they also often had to contend with the stereotypical American image of French women as "ooh-la-la-girls" or conniving seductresses out to catch a rich American husband.[134]

The war brides in this book aren't well-known people or heroines. They are just average women who sometimes had a tough time but who managed to survive. Deprived during the war, they married young and hastily, during a time of intense romanticism and urgency. Then they left their *milieu* and their families to start a new life in a new land. There is thus a poignant, universal quality about these women's stories that goes beyond the Franco-American dimension of their encounters and subsequent marriages with GI's.

Part I

ACCOUNTS OF WORLD WAR I WAR BRIDES

One

"St. Joseph was with us…"

Madeleine M. is a war bride of the First World War who met her "Doughboy" husband on the feast day of St. Joseph. She was still alive in 1996 and living in Philadelphia when I first contacted her daughter, Thérèse H., by telephone. Because Madeleine was 97 years old, in poor health, and thus unable to be interviewed for any length of time, Thérèse suggested I send her a written questionnaire that she could go over with Madeleine when she was feeling up to it. This I did, and Thérèse very kindly "interviewed" her mother for me and filled in the questionnaire, which was returned to me in February 1997. Sadly, Madeleine died just two months after that. Thérèse and I have recently been in contact, and she provided me with additional information, including some extracts of pieces Madeleine wrote many years ago. Like her mother before her, Thérèse is herself the proud mother of a famille nombreuse. *Here is the story I pieced together about Madeleine, told by her daughter Thérèse.*

My mother was born in August 1898 in Clermont Ferrand. Her father was a *Capitaine Commandant* in the French Cavalry. Being a military family, they were moved every two years all over France, but Mother spent most of those years in the south, in Montauban. During the Great War, they lived in Angers, and after the war they moved back to Clermont Ferrand, where her family was from. She had four brothers and three sisters, but two of her brothers died very young.

Mother attended *lycée* and two years of *beaux arts*. During the war, she tutored a young child who had pronunciation difficulties and taught catechism to five- and six-year-olds. She was quite attractive as a young girl, a lively young thing, even though timid. She met my father, Kenrick, in 1919 in Royat, a small town outside of Clermont-Ferrand. He was from an Irish family in Philadelphia and was a graduate of the University of Pennsylvania. He had been drafted into the army and was in the 312th field artillery. While he was stationed near Clermont Ferrand, he and a friend came for dinner at my grandmother's every night for about three months. My grandfather had died by then.

Mother wrote about this a long time ago, and I found what she wrote. Here's what she said:

The whole city of Clermont and the near towns, like Royat, were occupied by the American troops.

The war was still going on; everybody was talking of an armistice that finally came about on September 11, 1919. On the 19th of March, 1919, on St. Joseph's feast day, I had to go to the *rez-de-chaussée* from the *premier étage* to pay the coal man. The landlady started to talk to me about two American soldiers who wanted something, but she had no idea what they wanted. They were presented to me. They already had taken possession of a room on the first floor that they rented. The landlady thought I might be able to find out what they wanted. Ken and his friend, Joe Muldowney, with great pain, finally made me understand that they were looking for a place to take their meals regularly, preferably in a family. My knowledge of English was almost nil, especially in conversation. They tried to give me some references by showing me their rosaries.

Somehow, I felt an assurance that they were good, honest, sincere people. Then after laborious explanations I was able to tell my mother what it was all about, and she accepted to have [*sic*] them take their meals with us. Of course, St Joseph was with us in that decision. In the meantime, they went to the University of Clermont to learn French in a hurry. We were not very good cooks, neither was the maid we had at that time. But we had good moments, playing the piano, singing, reading, taking hikes in the mountains, visiting interesting places, always accompanied by a family member.

We went to visit the Taillerie de Royat with its collection of semi-precious stones, cut on the premises and mined in Auvergne. Among others, the amethyst, the lapis-lapuli, the *oeil de chat,* and very fine granite. The amethyste is a variety of quartz, purple and worn by the bishop.[1] The lapis-lapuli (an Arab word) is azure blue; the *oeil de chat* (cat's eye) is a stone of several shades of old gold and green; the granite is a rock formed by a volcanic eruption. Once Ken saw the sign, "Taillerie de Royat." This word seems to come from the word *tailleur,* so he thought, "Good, finally, I will have my suit repaired." How big was his surprise when, on entering into [*sic*] the shop, he saw cut semi-precious stones, and some in the process of being cut. To his disappointment, he knew that his suit could never be repaired at that place.

While Ken and his friend Joe Muldowney were with us, he did not seem to pay particular attention to me, therefore, was I surprised when he asked me to marry him! I was not sure I understood right; whatever language he used, English or French, I do not remember. I told him I would talk to my mother about it, because I would have never made a decision of this sort without at least letting her know, and without her advice. Evidently, she approved of it, but we were worried if it was wise. Nobody had any idea of how long the war would continue.

Ken was in good favor with the whole family. In spite of that, it was customary, necessary to look for some references about him and his family though persons who knew them well, especially having to deal with someone of another country, so far away. My mother wrote to his parish in Philadelphia, and we received an excellent report. One saintly priest in Clermont, l'abbe Germain, knew him well too. He told us that Ken was, by far, the best of the American soldiers he had ever met; he even thought he might have had a vocation to be a priest. Ken and his friend stayed with us for meals for about three months, then were sent somewhere else and later went back to the United States. We promised each other we would write, and we did. He was to come back the next year in June 1920 for our wedding in Royat. Ken was 26 years old and I was almost 22. Ken's mother came to our wedding celebrated in the church of the Sacred Heart, a plain new church close to our apartment.

Before being married at church, my parents were first married at the *mairie* of Clermont Ferrand. Then, together with my father's mother, they traveled to America on the *Rochambeau*. Since my grandmother didn't speak any French and my mother not very much [*sic*] English, my father would translate for them. Mother wrote about their trip to Paris, too:

On our way to Paris, before taking the transatlantic to the United States, the *Rochambeau*, we were invited to a very formal dinner by my uncle Charles de Chalaniat, the first cousin of my grandmother Charlotte. Ken and his mother were very much impressed to be received like royalty. We were served at the table by his valet, wearing the livery and white gloves, passing each of the numerous dishes, using a clean plate for each one.

Mother said she had a wonderful reception in America. The people were very nice to her, but she thought Philadelphia was a very ugly city. The housing was not attractive compared to France, and it wasn't a very artistic place. My parents lived with their parents-in-law in a row house in southwestern

Philadelphia for two years, and I think that was hard for her. Mother told me her mother-in-law turned out to be a very difficult person.

My parents wanted a large family, and Mother said she worried when a year and a half passed and nothing happened. But once they got started, the family grew and grew without a problem. They had nine children, but they never reached the dozen they wanted! Mother never understood why women wanted abortions. She used to say people didn't seem to realize they were forfeiting their own happiness in old age by destroying their unborn children.

My father was always a very proper gentleman, who never spoke harshly or cursed. He had a lot of control over his kids without anger or losing control of himself. He helped a lot around the house with the children, before it was in vogue for the men to help with the kids. He believed in conserving energy, so he didn't let us waste water, electricity, food, and so forth. He was a recycler long before the government encouraged it.

We were not permitted to speak English at home. My mother wanted us to learn French, knowing we would have plenty of opportunities to learn English. I remember that her ears would perk up anytime one of us wasn't speaking French. She could be up in the attic, and you in the basement speaking English, but she could hear you, and she'd call out "*Parlez-français.*" Apparently, my older siblings spoke broken English when they started school.

We lived in a three story house with an attic and a basement in West Philadelphia. I was the last of the bunch, and when I was born my oldest sister was ready to get married, and the next one was about to join the navy. Before I was too aware of what was going on around me, my next brother left for the army. So I don't ever remember all the family living together.

Mother taught me to sew when I was about 10. I love sewing and have been doing it ever since. She and my father enrolled me in ballet classes when I was eight, and I danced professionally until I became five months pregnant with my first child. Mother also taught me a love for languages, and luckily I still speak French enough that I can visit with my cousins in France and feel perfectly comfortable speaking with them. I didn't like being "different" when I had to speak in French as a child, but I sure appreciate it now.

When we children were growing up, Mother wasn't able to travel, so her family came to America for visits. She only returned to France for the first time in 1946 but then several times after that. She missed France and her family very much, but she learned to cope and made friends in the United States. I don't think Mother ever met any other war brides, but she knew a few other French people through the Alliance Française. She started teaching French right away because she didn't speak much English. She and her first students became lifelong friends. Later, she taught French in private high schools and exchanged French lessons with people for art lessons.

Mother got American citizenship in 1920 and always voted Republican. She lived to the ripe old age of 98 and died on April 7, 1997. I think she felt American because she lived here most of her life. But she felt French too, because her background was always a part of her.

TWO

AN ENTERPRISING YOUNG WOMAN

Thanks to a mutual friend, I was able to do a telephone interview of Myriam H., who is the daughter of Marie-Jeanne J., a World War I war bride. Mrs. H. also sent me many documents concerning her mother: copies of photos, newspaper articles, and letters she had written. The Sandusky County Historical Society in Fremont, Ohio, supplied me with documents about her father, a Doughboy in France and Italy in 1918. Here is the story of a remarkable woman, as told by her daughter.

My mother was born on July 14, 1898, in Fontan, near better-known Saorge, both villages in the Alpes-Maritimes near the Italian border. Her father, who was my grandfather, was originally from the Basque country, and he was working as a customs agent on the French-Italian border when he met my grandmother. They later moved to Nice. While he thought he was the lord and master of the household, my grandmother always had her way about everything. They had three daughters, who were brought up very strictly. They were never allowed to leave the house on their own. Someone always took them to school—they went to a convent school—and picked them up afterwards.

My mother's name was Marie-Jeanne. She was really super intelligent. She studied in France and Italy, and then taught French, Italian, mathematics, and psychology in Nice from 1917 to 1919. She met my father in Nice in 1919.

He came from Fremont, Ohio, where his friends called him "Shorty." His father, my American grandfather, was the owner of the Fremont hardware store. According to an article in a local newspaper of the time, my dad was a popular boy who attended Sunday school at the local Methodist church and went on to study at Oberlin College in Ohio. In 1916, he signed up as a soldier in Company K. After serving in the 6th regiment on the Texas-Mexico border, he was made an officer and, with several other young boys, enlisted in the U.S. Army Air Corps. He was first trained in the United States and then sent with 10 other pilots to Italy. This is what he wrote in a letter dated April 10, 1918, to the Fremont newspaper:

> ...It has been a good while now since I watched the Statue of Liberty fade from view—eight months to be exact...Some day when I have seen more of France, I'll give you my impression of this country... Now to the work I have been and am doing. I can't, on account of the strict censorship observed over here, tell you much about that no more than that my preliminary flying was done in Italy.... I'm just so tickled with this little plane I'm flying now that I'm glad that I came. I might as well be anyway. The thing almost had me buffaloed at first, it went so fast and was so delicate to handle and tricky. About a couple miles a minute it goes, does all sorts of acrobatics and is safe as a church, barring unforeseen accidents (joke). Looping the loop is backwoods stuff and isn't even required. One of the stunts is the spinning nose dive called *vrille* (vree) in French, which is more or less dangerous and often gotten into unintentionally so we have dubbed the camp, the "land of the *vrille* and home of the grave."[1]

While he was flying in Foggia, Italy, as a test pilot, Daddy had a crack-up. There was fog, his plane landed on top of a tree, and his leg was broken. After a stay in a hospital in Italy, he was sent to convalesce in Nice. Daddy and Maman met there at a reception given for American soldiers by Colonel and Mrs. Hayes. The Hayes family also came from Fremont, and the Hayes family home—the home of Rutherford B. Hayes, who'd been President of the United States[2]—was very near my grandparents' home.

How my mother was able to go to that reception is quite a story. As I said, my mother and my aunts never went out alone. One evening my grandfather took them to the *mardi gras* carnival in Nice. Maman found a little coin purse on the ground, with a few things inside, as well as the calling card of a certain Mrs. Hamilton with the name of her hotel in Nice. The next day my grandfather took his daughter, my mother, to this hotel to return the coin purse. Maman was very pretty, very intelligent, and she spoke fluent English. Mrs. Hamilton found her charming, so she asked my grandfather: "May your daughter come and have tea with me from time to time?"

Since Mrs. Hamilton was a very distinguished lady, he accepted the invitation, and Maman subsequently went several times to have tea with

Mrs. Hamilton. Some time later, Mrs. Hayes asked her friend, Mrs. Hamilton, if she knew of any young French girls whom she could invite to a reception she was giving for American soldiers. Mrs. Hamilton told her: "I know one, but I'd be surprised if her father will let her attend. But I can always ask." Since my grandfather respected and admired Mrs. Hamilton and since he had no way of knowing what would happen, he let Maman go to the party.

So that's how my parents met. Maman was very vivacious and lively. She had dark, green eyes, very black hair, lovely fair skin, and beautiful, even white, teeth. My father fell in love with her immediately.

So the next day he arrived at my grandparents' home with an armful of roses. My grandmother opened the door, and there was a young man with a huge bunch of flowers. This sort of thing wasn't done at the time! But he was allowed to come in. I don't know what happened afterwards. My father returned to Italy and started writing to Maman. But my grandfather always read the letters before giving them to his daughter. And then, after awhile, my grandmother took pity on my mother. She'd watch for the postman, intercept the letters, and give them to Maman. And the love story continued like that.

I don't know exactly how long all that continued, probably about a year. In the end, he asked her to marry him. I think, but I'm not sure, that he was able to come to Nice several times. But my parents were never alone until the day of their marriage. As a matter of fact, my mother was meant to marry the son of family friends who was going to become an ambassador. My grandfather had announced that his daughter would *never* marry an American soldier. But my mother insisted that her "dear American soldier" was the one she wanted. So then all my family went about trying to convince my grandfather. But before considering anything, my grandfather required letters of reference from my father's family in Fremont and from his church. Daddy came from a very devout Protestant family of Methodists.

So everything went ahead, and the wedding took place on August 4, 1919, in Nice. Maman was 21 years old, and Daddy was five years older. I have a wonderful photo where you see a very distinguished French family—the whole wedding party. Daddy is in uniform, and the other men are wearing top hats and tails.

In September they left by ship with many other couples for New York. Other soldiers were on board with their French wives. I remember a little story. Since the boys had spoken to their wives about corn on the cob, once they arrived in New York they decided to go to a restaurant to taste some. They didn't say anything; they wanted to see how their wives would go about eating it. The corn arrived, and none of the wives had ever seen corn on the cob before because it wasn't eaten like that in France then. Maman plucked up her courage and tried to spear the corncob with her fork. But it just rolled and rolled way to the other end of the table, and of course everybody burst out laughing.

My parents settled in Fremont. In the beginning, they lived with my paternal grandparents. Maman must have gotten pregnant right away, because I was born 10 months later. Her first winter at my grandparents' mustn't have been easy, but they said she never complained about anything. In fact, as well as I can remember, the only American thing she ever complained about was American gravy. She used to say it tasted like library paste!

Daddy became an airmail pilot and inaugurated the line between Chicago and Kansas City. At the time, flying a mail plane was really dangerous. In the beginning, my mother accepted this, but one night when he didn't get back on time, she made a scene. She succeeded in persuading him to give up his job, especially as she was going to have a child. At the end of the winter, they had their own house, then, in June, I was born.

Daddy was City Service Director for many years. Later, during the Second World War, he enlisted again, not as a pilot but as an administrator at McDonnell Aircraft in Memphis, Tennessee, where they built planes. Daddy was a real angel. In all his life, I never heard him be cross with anyone, and I never saw him angry. He wasn't spineless, not at all, quite the contrary. He had a lot of personality. If he let my mother have her way, it was because he admired and loved her. He also had a whimsical little sense of humor. His friends in Fremont had a favorite story about him: One day, after Maman slammed the car door shut, he said: "Wait a minute, Sweetheart. You've got my hand caught in the door!"

Three other war brides lived in Fremont, including one who had a child just three months after Maman had me. There must have been about 12 war brides in the region, because I remember their getting together from time and to time and always bringing us children. We'd play together while the mothers drank tea or had lunch. They particularly wanted to see each other to be able to speak French and to introduce France to their children. They may not have always been happy, but none was ever beaten, at least. None of the husbands in the little group I knew was anything but kind to his wife. I remember that one of the war brides was called Paulette Sparks. She was very pretty and lively. She was also a real flirt, an *allumeuse*, and she was married twice.

The three families in Fremont remained close. France, the girl who was born three months after me, became a very good friend. The poor thing!

She suffered her whole life because of her name, especially as her mother pronounced it in the French way, and kids made fun of her at school. I really liked her mother. She was very petite and cute. They weren't financially well-off, and France and her mother only got to go to France once to see their family. The boat trip to Europe was really expensive at the time.

As for me, I was privileged. Maman took me three times to France to stay with my grandparents. She was determined that I learn French. But I didn't want to speak French in the beginning. Like all kids, I didn't want to be different from the others in my class. I didn't want to speak French, or wear ribbons in my hair or short dresses like little French girls.

Maman was a teacher in a private girls' school in Toledo. She saw right away that my father wouldn't be able to send her to her parents in France every summer. So, since she was a bright, liberated woman long before we ever heard of that term, and since my father adored her and let her do whatever she wanted, she found a solution. She became a guide for a travel agency in Boston, Varsity Tours, which organized tours of Europe. And that's how she found a way to visit her parents every summer. She took me for the first time in June when I was seven. First we went to Paris, where my grandfather came up from Cannes to get me while she continued touring with her group. I didn't speak French yet, and my grandparents didn't speak English. But after three months, when Maman came to Cannes to get me, I could hardly speak English anymore! Children learn that fast. When I was nine, Maman sent me back to my grandparents' to spend nine months, and she sent me again for 15 months to go to school when I was 14.

When Maman was 29, the French department of Oberlin College in Oberlin, Ohio, decided they wanted to create a French House, and they asked Maman to set it up and to be the *directrice*. Maman stayed there for 11 years. I think it was the second French House at a U.S. university after the one at Middlebury College.

Twenty-one girls lived at the French House, and twenty-three male students came for meals. Only French was allowed to be spoken on the ground floor. The girls lived on the first and second floors, where they were allowed to speak English. Maman did a lot to encourage Franco-American exchanges. French holidays were celebrated, and they sang French Christmas carols. I remember that in the spring there was always a big tea party where everybody from the university was invited. It was when there was *muguet*, lilies of the valley, so it must have been on the first of May.[3]

Maman always found ways to make France better known. By the way, the French House was known as the dormitory where you ate the best at Oberlin!

The cook was an African-American lady, Mrs. Freeman. When Lily Pons[4] came to sing at Oberlin, the French House organized a big reception for her. It was the first time I ever wore a long dress. I was only 11. Maman influenced a lot of students, who went on to study French. As a matter of fact, in 1935 she was decorated by the French government and received *les Palmes Académiques.*[5]

Despite the fact that Maman's English was excellent and very learned, she still had an accent when she spoke. For example, she had trouble pronouncing the word "encouraging." She always put the accent on the "raging" part of the word. When I was small, my American grandfather and I would have fun trying to have her pronounce certain words.

Maman knew nothing about football and bridge when she arrived in the United States, but she became an ace at bridge, and she loved football because some of the boys on the team had their meals at the French House.

Unfortunately, it was because of a football game that she died. Despite a cold, Maman insisted on going to a game one snowy, freezing Saturday afternoon. By Tuesday, she was in the hospital with pneumonia. They were just beginning to use sulpha drugs then, but she had a reaction so they stopped giving them to her. She died 10 days later—on December 7, 1938. She was only 40.

Several hundred people attended her funeral. Maman was well-known and very popular in Oberlin. The whole town called her *Madame.* During the eulogies at First Church, one of the professors stressed that Maman could talk about almost any subject in an intelligent way. That was true. She was really very learned. She kept up to date on everything that was happening in Europe in the 1930s, for example, and asked herself a lot of questions.

As a matter of fact, she wrote some very interesting letters to a family friend, Paul Penciollelli, who was the head of Clemenceau's cabinet. In a letter dated October 13, 1938, she said:

> What a nightmare the Munich Conference was—before, during, and afterwards! I spent hours, days, glued to the radio. Of course, I immediately thought...of all of you in Paris, since you'd be the first ones hit by German bombs....The newspapers say that, from now on, France has become a second-rank nation. Hitler's Germany is now all powerful, the new star around which the little countries of central Europe will orbit. How it hurts me to hear all this! Especially as I don't know what to reply. Why did the position of Daladier,[6] which was so strong before, turn into such spineless acceptance? And why did France, for the first time in its history, let down an ally? What are people saying in France? And what do you think? And what should we think about the validity of Chamberlain's and Hitler's declaration concerning

the respective attitude of their country towards the other in case of war?[7] And of the Führer's recent speech? And of Hitler's behavior since Munich?[8]

When Maman died, I'd just turned 18 and was studying at Oberlin College. It was very hard for me, but for my father, it was horrible. He adored her, and he had always counted on her for everything. She was his "managing director."

Thanks to Maman, I learned French, and all the jobs I had after finishing college were because I spoke French. In fact, a friend once told me I was the only person he knew who'd built a career of speaking French! I was an airline hostess between the United States and Canada because I spoke French. Later on, I joined the diplomatic corps and was sent first to Saigon, then Paris, then Ivory Coast, and then Yaoundé in Cameroon, all francophone countries.

I'm proud of my mother and everything she did throughout her life. As the *Oberlin Review* wrote just after her death:

> She brought the best of French cultural tradition to America and to Oberlin. She nursed the French House, of which she was directress, from infancy eleven years ago to the outstanding place it now holds among institutions of its kind throughout the nation. . . . Madame will live just as long as men strive to reach across oceans and frontiers and bind the peoples of the world together in closer unity and understanding. . . .[9]

Three

PAULETTE RETURNS TO FRANCE

A war bride of the Great War, Paulette only spent two years in the United States with her Doughboy husband, Robert J. They came back to live in France in 1920, just one month before the birth of their daughter Liliane.[1] As it turned out, Paulette could not get used to living in America.

A mutual friend introduced me to Liliane, and we spoke at length about her mother. During our interview I learned that Paulette and Liliane had been résistantes *during World War II. Both women received the Croix de Guerre. Liliane also received the Résistance Medal, and then the Légion d'Honneur, in recognition for her work collecting documents for the National Archives.*

Mother and daughter—two strong and patriotic women. Here is Paulette's story, as it was told to me by Liliane, today, an energetic, grey-haired grandmother of 83.

Maman was born in Rochefort-sur-Mer in 1900. She had been conceived in a very pretty home which is still in the family—a kind of small manor-house situated near Marennes, where the Marennes oysters are farmed. She came from the upper *bourgeoisie*, but her family was not particularly rich, and the men were often absent. Maman's father had gone off to Senegal as a colonial administrator at the end of the century. He died there of yellow fever when Maman was 10. So my grandmother was a widow with three children: two daughters (one of whom was my mother) and a son. She had to do without a pension because her husband wasn't eligible for one, even though he only had three more months to go in the colonies before he died. So, she left her children in Rochefort with her mother, who was also a widow but of a naval officer who had "gone down with his ship" in 1870, and went up to Paris to work as a governess for some friends.

When the war started, my grandmother came back to Rochefort. Then, she and her daughters—that is, Maman and my Aunt Danièle—went to stay with some friends in Saint-Raphaël. At the time, there was a large hotel there where men from the front were sent to convalesce. My grandmother, my mother, and my aunt signed up right away to be volunteer nurses in this hospital. Maman was only 15. I have a photo where you see her in her uniform. That lasted from 1915 to 1917. Then they went back to the Charente region. During the summer of 1918, they went to see some friends in Royan who had a hotel and who'd invited them to spend several days with them.

So my grandmother, my mother, my uncle, and my aunt were having a holiday at the Hotel Richelieu in Royan, and they would go for walks along the boardwalk—the three women wearing white dresses and large sun hats. One day, my grandmother and Maman met an American sailor on the board-walk as they were walking. I'm going to read a passage that's in my book about this encounter:

> ...My father was born in the United States in 1897 of parents who had very recently immigrated from Scotland. During the Great War, he served in the American navy as radio-signalman on a ship/vessel assuring the protection of convoys landing/ending up in the Gironde region.
>
> On July 9, 1918, while he was on leave, he met a young girl who was born in Rochefort in 1900. She and her mother, who was the widow of a colonial administrator who'd died of yellow fever in St. Louis in Senegal, her sister, and her brother were all spending a holiday in Royan at the Hotel Richelieu, which was owned by their friends, Anna and Henri L.
>
> Probably to start a conversation, he asked—in English, of course, a language which was unfamiliar to her just as much as French was unfamiliar to him—for some information., which, although rather puzzled, she tried to give him once they arrived at the hotel. He wanted to know about fencing [*escrime* in French]!
>
> After some discussion, they finally discovered that it was simply a question of trying to find some ice cream!...[2]

And that's how Maman met my father.

Daddy came from Michigan. His parents, who were Scots from Kilburny, had emigrated to American right after their marriage to look for work in the automobile industry, which was really starting up at top speed at the time.

Daddy was born in 1897. He didn't go very far in his studies before signing up in the navy. But, all by himself, he built a radio set and was very proud to tell us how, when he was 18, he heard the calls of help from the *Lusitania*[3] on May 7, 1915, but that nobody believed him.

Throughout the war, Daddy kept a diary. It's in English, and it's a bit hard to read his handwriting, but here's a passage where he speaks about Maman which I'm going to translate:

> **Tuesday, July 9 [1918]**. Met Madame G. and her daughters Paulette and Danièle. Marvelous people. They live in Paris and are in Royan for the summer.
> **Wednesday, July 10**. Had dinner with Paulette, Danièle and their mother...
> **Friday, July 12**. On board the *U.S.S. Maine* today.
> **Saturday, July 13**. Had dinner with my friends.
> **Sunday, July 14**. Royan, on board all day.
> **Tuesday, July 16**. After a night of inspection, returned to Royan and got back at 8 A.M. No free time....
> **Thursday, July 18**. Spent some time with Paulette. At 5 P.M., went to the birthday party of Mademoiselle H. Her father was there. He's the Minister of Police [*sic*] in Paris....[4]

At one point in the diary, Daddy writes that he's going to ask Maman something. But I don't know what he asked her. At that time, an 18-year-old girl didn't jump into the arms of people, didn't fling their arms round people's necks; she didn't have boyfriends left and right.

My grandmother and her children probably returned to Paris at the end of August 1918. Her daughters, Maman and Danièle, who were 18 and 21, were both hired by a bank. Maman told me she remembered the day the Armistice was signed and how they were told to stop their work and to go out and celebrate with everyone in the street. As for Daddy, he remained on board his boat. I think he may have come up to Paris once or twice to see them. In his diary he talks about Plymouth. In October, he went to London, then to Brest. He was in Bordeaux in November. Then, he talks about the Armistice. On November 14, he says there was a big celebration with lots of pretty women everywhere. On November 27, he writes: "Arrived in Paris at 10 A.M. Had dinner with Paulette and her family in the evening."

My parents were married on January 11, 1919, at the town hall of Neuilly-sur-Seine. I still have the menu of their wedding meal and a photo of Maman, with her handwritten note on the back: "I'm very happy." They had a church wedding, but their marriage wasn't really a valid one because Daddy wasn't

Catholic. This was important in those days. He was Protestant, but as he used to say: "I'm Protestant but I don't protest much." Like many people at the time, my mother was Catholic, and they had to go to see the priest. My father hardly spoke French. Here's one of the family stories: Daddy went to see the good-hearted priest, who probably spoke very little English. Not really knowing what to say, and having never heard of confession or things like that, Daddy said to the priest: "Listen. I'm 21 and I'm an American sailor who's probably no better or no worse than anyone else." The priest gave him absolution, and my parents were able to get married!

Shortly after their wedding, at the end of January or the beginning of February, I think, they left for America by boat. Maman told me that on board there were some soldiers who were still mobilized and eight French war brides. Just after arriving in the United States, they went directly to my American grandparents' place. Maman told me that she wasn't very well-accepted, especially by her mother-in-law, who was a bit jealous.

I can tell a funny little anecdote about the Scottish grandmother who comes to join her daughter in America and who still speaks with a Scottish accent. Maman often told me this story. The grandmother was quite respectful of laws and religious principles, including the one forbidding working on Sundays. On Saturdays, when she knew that the whole family was coming the next day and she had to prepare the meal, bake cakes, etc., she would start to do the cooking. But when she saw that it was getting late, she would put back the clock several minutes in order to have enough time to finish baking the cakes. Like that, she could go to bed with her mind set at ease.

I don't know what my father's first job was in America, but later he worked for Sparks Withington, a horn-supplier for the automobile industry. My parents stayed less than two years in the United States. My mother was happy over there, but she didn't want to stay there for the rest of her life. So, as soon as she learned that she was expecting a baby, she absolutely wanted to return to France to be with her mother and her sister.

A few years ago, I found a bundle of letters that she sent to my grandmother while she was in America. One day, she wrote: "I want you to be the first one to know. I'm expecting a baby. My little Willy is doing well." The baby she was referring to was me! Since she wanted to return to France, my father told her: "O.K., we'll go back to France." They got back in September, and I was born in October 1920.

Daddy worked for Sparks in Paris. He was European Manager of the company. He traveled a lot and went to all the automobile shows. Later on, the company also launched the record player. You'd put on a pile of records and an arm would let a record drop one by one. There were also three or four record players around the house, and my father would play them at all hours of the day and night to check that they were working.

Daddy had a good job, and everything would have been fine. But soon, instead of going to the office, he started spending his time at the chic bars of Paris. Like many sailors, he drank quite a bit. Someone told me that the first time he'd been seen like that was the day of my birth. Everyone thought it was because he was overcome with emotion. "Robert has just had a bit too much to drink. That's all. It's nothing serious." Unfortunately, though, it continued.

For about nine years, my father earned a good living. We had a beautiful apartment, my parents entertained a lot, Maman was always very chic, and we had a maid. But then, one day, Daddy had a serious accident. It was in 1933 while he was coming back from America by ship. Daddy had been a sailor and he knew how to walk on ships. But one night, he fell backwards and hit his head so badly that he probably had a brain hemorrhage or something. He no longer knew where he was, and he could hardly talk. He was only 35 when it happened.

For several months, he stayed in our apartment in Neuilly, just sitting on a chair and not doing anything. I remember we used to play solitaire and other card games together. His situation improved little by little. But he was no longer capable of running a business. As a matter of fact, the company was obliged to let him go. Maman took care of him, but she was worried because there was no more money left. Even if he was Scottish, Daddy had never been the type to save for the future.

They had to leave the apartment they were renting. Fortunately, my Aunt Danièle, who'd also married an American who worked in Paris—a veteran of the *Escadrille Lafayette*[5] who had two sons—was willing to put us up. Maman had decided to send her husband back to his parents in America. She couldn't keep him at my aunt's in the state he was in.

So Daddy went back to America, and I only saw him once more after that. It was in 1958. My aunt and uncle were living in Connecticut then, and we went to visit them and to spend some time on Cape Cod. They'd invited my father over to see us. Daddy was better. He'd remarried, and his second wife, who was a woman he'd known as a young man, had taken him in hand and prevented him from drinking. They lived in Dayton, Ohio. After that, I wrote him for awhile at an address in Dayton, but one day the letter was returned to me with a stamp on it saying he no longer lived there. We tried to find him but never could. I don't know when and where he died; his wife never let us know. We tried to find out at the city hall of the city where he was born, but registering births and deaths is not the same in the United States as it is in France, and we didn't find anything.

After my father went back to the United States in 1935, Maman had to find work. She was 35. Like most young women at that time, she didn't know how to do much. Because of the Great War, her schooling came to an end when she was only 14. But she was pretty and intelligent, she wrote well, and she was well-mannered. Everybody knew that Paulette was looking for any sort of job. So, thanks to friends, she was able to start working as a writer at *l'Officiel de la Couture*. At the time, you didn't need any specific qualifications. Maman stayed at *l'Officiel* till the end of the last war. Then she went to Ponchon publishers, where she was editor-in-chief. She wrote articles about silk, corsets, and other subjects until she was 80 or 85 years old. I donated a lot of her articles to the archives of the Galliera Museum after her death.

Maman received the *Croix de Guerre* in 1945. Here's her Resistant's certificate, and this is what l'Officiel wrote about her:

> Our dear editor has just received the military's *Croix de Guerre* for services rendered to the French and allied forces during the last years of a merciless combat. *L'Officiel* is honored to count among its staff a zealous team which was in the front ranks of the fight against oppression.[6]

In fact, during the war, Maman and I hid allied aviators who'd been shot down over France. Our apartment was near the Porte Champerret. We risked being shot if we were discovered. I was the one who went to get them at the station and walked with them back to our place. But Maman went along completely with lodging them. That's why she also received the *Croix de Guerre*. I could never have done everything I did without her agreement.

During the beginning of the Occupation, the Germans had come to arrest Maman because she had an American passport. Her divorce hadn't been declared yet, and I had to go to different German offices to make them recognize that Maman's divorce was in process but that she still didn't have the official papers. The Germans kept her for two or three nights in the building that today is the Museum of Popular Arts. That's where they put all the American women married to Frenchmen and the French women married to Americans.

In my book, I talk about the New Year's Eve that Maman and I spent with one of these parachutists. It was at the end of 1943. Imagine the scene: a very small apartment, the bedroom where I slept with Maman, and the living room where there was a sofa for the guys we were hiding. This is what I wrote in my diary:

> Simple supper with my mother [and George, a 23-year-old fighter pilot]. . . . Danced a bit, while listening to the English radio. As much as I remember, it was neither sad nor romantic—just strange and a little oppressive. And then, without showing any more emotion, we wished each other a Happy New Year, and sensibly went to bed. 1944 had begun.[7]

Fifty-four years later, Maman died in the same apartment at the Porte de Champerret. She was 98 years old.

Part II

ACCOUNTS OF WORLD WAR II WAR BRIDES

Four

ON THE FARM

I interviewed Marcelle R. at the home of her daughter, who lives in the Paris suburbs, in 2003. Marcelle came to pick me up in her little car, which she drives like a real Parisian! She is pretty, lively, and chic. Who would have thought she began her married life in the United States on a farm in Alabama! Joanne, Marcelle's daughter, sat in on our interview and added certain details when her mother had a lapse of memory.

I was born in Mussidan, a little town next to Bergerac in the Dordogne. But when I was one year old, we came up to Paris to live in the 13th arrondissement, which was like a little village at the time. I was the eldest of five children and a little bit like a second mother for my brother and sisters. I obtained the *certificat d'études.*[1]

During the war, but before the occupation of Paris by the Germans, we returned to the Dordogne to spend a few months because of the bombings. Afterwards, we came back to Paris, and I worked in a Monoprix[2]. We didn't live far from the Panhard factory and the railway, so bombings were frequent, especially at night. We would go into the bomb shelters, such as the Place d'Italie metro station, which was very deep. But these shelters were far away, and sometimes we didn't have time to go to them. So we went down into basements of different buildings.

I remember the day Paris was liberated. I was 16. Everyone was in the streets. The American tanks arrived near the statue of Jeanne d'Arc à Paris.[3] The French militia, that is, the French police who collaborated with the

Germans, were shooting at the Americans and civilians.[4] There were bullets everywhere. We were really foolish to go out into the street like that. At one point, an American made me lie down on the ground and hide my head under his tank.

I didn't meet my husband that day, but in May or June of 1945 at a street fair at the Place d'Italie. He was with some friends, and so was I. He spoke to me, and that's how it started. He was very handsome, and very tall, too—at least two meters. My friends and I started going out with the Americans. We admired them a lot; they'd gotten us out of trouble. Moreover, the Red Cross asked us to go into the hospitals and visit wounded soldiers, so I was doing that, too.

I remember it was very hot the day I met James. He'd unbuttoned the top of his uniform. An M.P. came and asked him if he was American, because lots of Frenchmen were dressed like Americans at the time. When James answered "yes," the M.P. told him: "Soldier, dress correctly. Button up your jacket!"

James had taken part in the landings. He'd been at Omaha Beach. He was only 21. Before that, he was in England and before that at C.C. camp in Texas. The C.C. camps[5] were military training camps for young people. James was hurt in the leg during the landings and was being treated at the Salpêtrière Hospital and then at the one in Villejuif. He didn't return to the front.

A group of us would go out together to visit Paris. I spoke very little English, and he just knew a few words of French. Later, when I arrived in the United States, I learned English very quickly because I like to talk and am very chatty!

James and I went out for about seven months, and then he asked me to marry him. During this time, I lived with my parents, and he went back to the hospital every evening. He could get out during the daytime, so we'd go to the cinema or visit Paris. He took care of all the papers for the wedding. He had to ask the army, his captain [for permission], and take care of all sorts of paperwork.

I came from a very modest background, and I remember my mother telling me: "You know, Marcelle, if you're unhappy over there, don't count on us to bring you back. We can't afford it." I was only 18, and it was a really big decision. But, on the other hand, I was sick of the war, the hardships, and having to take care of my three sisters and my brother all the time. America offered another horizon.

I didn't know much about the United States, just what James had told me. Little by little, I began to understand him. He'd tell me that where he was taking me was wild, that there were snakes. He said it wasn't the garden of Eden and that it was very different from Paris.

We got married at the town hall in May 1946. A woman lent us an apartment for our wedding night. Then, James left by boat two or three weeks later. He'd write to me often. I followed him [later]. I was sad to leave my family, but I was happy to go and live in the United States. I was a little oblivious.

I left by train for Le Havre with other war brides. It felt really strange, but the atmosphere among us women was good. We stayed in the barracks for several days, and then we took the S.S. *America* to New York. James had written me to see if I wanted him to come to New York to get me. The government had contacted him and he could choose. Either he came to get me or the government put me in a train for Gordo [Alabama]. I wrote him that it was better I go by train; it wasn't worth his coming to New York.

When we were onboard the ship, they gave us shots and asked us questions. There were also meetings to tell us about life in the United States. Everything was in English, nothing in French. There weren't only French women. There were also Dutch women, etc. Most of them were going to the north of the United States or to California. Very few were going to the south, like me.

When we arrived in New York, a lot of husbands were waiting for their wives. Some of them had good jobs, others didn't. It was a gamble. Some husbands didn't show up at all, and some women had to sail back [to France]. That was awful. The Red Cross showed us around New York. It was a huge city, but I felt less out of place in New York than I did when I arrived in Alabama.

I got off the train at Gordo. There wasn't really a station there, just a hut. And when I saw my husband, I thought: "Heavens! It's like in the westerns. My husband's dressed like a cowboy!" Gordo was actually a little town, but all around was the *pampa*. It was really very, very isolated.

We lived with my parents-in-law for three or four months. They lived about 30 kilometers from Tuscaloosa and had a farm and a sawmill. James was the eldest of three brothers and a sister, just the opposite of me and my family. They all worked very hard. They'd get up at 4:30 in the morning because of the heat, and they'd go to bed early dead tired. Their whole life was centered around work and the land.

I'd get up with them. I learned how to milk the cows. I was exhausted, so they took me to the doctor. He'd fought in World War I and knew what the climate was like in France. He told them I shouldn't work so much and that the climate was too different for me. But it wasn't my parents-in-law's fault. They didn't ask me to get up so early or to milk the cows. I did it willingly because I wanted to help them out.

Then James bought his own farm. It was near a small place called Ecol, and I helped out there, too. I'd hoe the fields and pick cotton and corn, and I'd take care of the animals. There were just the two of us, and it was really hard. I remember I used to bring my little girl with me into the fields.

The women there, including those in my husband's family, were in the habit of chewing tobacco. They'd chew it all day, and then they'd spit it out. Their teeth were all black afterwards. Once, they put some in my mouth to try, but I didn't like it. My neighbors would buy flour to make biscuits. The flour came in pretty cotton sacks, which these industrious women would wash and dye and then make dresses with. My husband and his father played the fiddle. When I arrived there, they welcomed me by playing country music.

I loved my husband, but there was really too much of a cultural difference. James hadn't gone very far in his schooling, and all he wanted to do was stay on the farm. As for me, I came from Paris. He didn't want to live near a city.

When we had too much work, my father-in-law sometimes sent us some people of color from the sawmill to help us. I remember once when we'd had a good year, we'd planted cotton, and the Blacks came to help us pick it. It was like in the movies: the big bags and the Blacks singing and picking the cotton with us. I'm sorry I didn't take any pictures. It was really beautiful.

The first time I went to the sawmill, my father-in-law introduced me to the black workers, and I shook hands with them. My father-in-law told me afterwards that this wasn't done. It was in 1946. Now, things are different. The black workers used to take their pay on Friday nights and go off and celebrate. Then they'd come back with no money on Saturday night and ask for an advance on the coming week. My father-in-law didn't like that.

I always had to be careful about what I did with the Blacks. My husband was very racist. I remember there was a black woman who looked after my daughter, Joanne, and she loved her so much she would kiss her a little when no one was looking. Once I saw her doing it, and I told her: "It's okay. Just be careful never to do it in front of my husband."

Sometimes on Saturday nights my husband and I would go to Gordo. We didn't have a car yet, so we went with the horse and wagon! While James tried to sell the cotton, he would let me see friends or go shopping.

I remember once I passed in front of the drugstore and saw people eating banana splits and hut fudge sundaes. I really wanted to have one, so I went into the drugstore and I said: "I'd like a banana split with chocolate."

They didn't understand me at all. That's when I thought to myself: "That's amazing! In France, there was nothing to eat, but I could speak. Whereas here in the United States, there's lots to eat, and I can't speak!"

With all my faults, [I think] I really was rather courageous. I adapted. I didn't really mind working, but there was so much to do.

Despite all the work, we didn't earn enough. So my husband sold the farm and bought a big truck to be able to work as an independent truck driver. We went to live in Gary, Indiana, for a year. Then we moved back to Alabama and settled near Tuscaloosa. James didn't really know what he wanted. He'd go away. He became a sort of bohemian. He'd only come back every two or three months. We never knew where he was. He must have been with other women, because my daughters have a half-sister.

I found work in Tuscaloosa. I worked as a receptionist at a psychiatric hospital. Later, I bought a small car. In the beginning, James would send me a little money, but later on, nothing at all. My in-laws were nice. They'd take care of my daughters when I worked on Sundays. They didn't understand their son. Their other children weren't like that. One of my daughters thinks the reason for his behavior was that, like me, he was the eldest of five children and he'd had too much responsibility when he was young.

I made a big mistake when I married James, but when you've made a mistake, you assume responsibility for it. So, I started working a lot. My American friends were very supportive and warm-hearted. One of them rented me a big house for only $25. We really felt good there.

After five or six years, I felt like returning to France with my daughters, but I didn't have the money. I didn't talk about James anymore when I wrote my family. I didn't dare tell them, but they understood. My sister in France sent me some money to pay for our trip back, and I reimbursed her later on.

My in-laws understood why I decided to return to France. They told me that if things didn't go well, I should come back. They'd take care of the girls. They were very, very good people. I had to get a lawyer because I didn't want my husband to prevent me from leaving with the children. I got a divorce later on, but in France, where I could get legal help without having to pay for a lawyer.

After 14 years in the United States, it was difficult coming back to France. I hardly spoke French anymore. It was very hard to find accommodation because it was the time when the *Pieds-Noirs*[6] were all coming back. My sister put us up for awhile; then we were able to find our own apartment. But France lacked the modern conveniences that existed in the United States, and sometimes I regretted having come back.

I never saw James again. But my daughters [later] went to see him. He lives all alone in a big house and is still in Alabama. James's family has invited my daughters to visit several times, and I've had them here to stay in Paris. They can afford it now.

I remarried in 1983 and retired in 1986, after having worked for a long time at Galeries Lafayette department store. My life was hard, but I don't regret having lived in the United States. Quite the contrary.

Five

JACQUELINE, THE RESISTANT

Jacqueline C. S. was born in 1922 in Châteaubriant, in what is today called the Loire-Atlantique. When she was 10, her parents moved to Saint-Malo, and then later to Le Mans, where her father was an engineer with Air Liquide. At 18, she obtained the equivalent of the baccalaureate [the brevet d'études supérieures] *and began a B.A. [*une licence] *in English at the Sorbonne, which had retreated to Le Mans following the occupation of Paris. She has lived in Sacramento, California, since 1947. I was given her name by a nun who also lives in Sacramento and who knows her through a charitable organization. Jacqueline and I spoke on two occasions: the first in October 1996, and the second in October 2003.*

My father was in the Resistance. He and an Alsatian friend, who was an interpreter for the Germans, practically began being Resistants on their own. The friend was able to obtain the names of Jewish people who were going to be deported. Nobody knew exactly what their fate would be. There was talk of a camp, of extermination, but it was all very vague. I think this was in 1941 or 1942. So, since my father had this opportunity to get names on a regular basis, he began to warn a certain number of Jewish families, telling them that they were in danger and should leave the city. And Maman and I helped him, but only for a short time when he had too much to handle, because he realized that we could be caught by the Germans.

That was his beginning in the Resistance. He wasn't a member of an organization; it was just because of somebody he knew. This Alsatian friend of my father's who was an interpreter was also a very good chess player, and he played chess with people from the *Kommandantur*. Well, he was later captured and killed. They didn't send him to a concentration camp. They executed him when they realized he was talking. But, at the time, they didn't suspect my father of being in contact with him.

Papa didn't tell us everything, but he had friends who worked in the offices where identity cards were prepared. So, from early on, he was able to produce false papers for people wishing to escape the Germans for one reason or the other.

He was also very much involved in sabotage, particularly in blowing up railroad tracks just before German trains went over them. And I helped him do this. I helped him transport bombs. At the time, they were using what were called *plastiques* [sic] as explosives, and we'd hide them in a fake car battery. Papa had one made or got hold of one; I don't know where. He thought that if I was caught, the Germans would never suspect that it was hollow and contained explosives.

By that time, my father was affiliated with the OSS, the Office of Strategic Services.[1] And also with the M6,[2] with the English, and this sometimes created friction. Everything took place in Le Mans. We helped save four American pilots. We were in contact with Americans, Canadians, English people—those involved in espionage in Le Mans. Of course, they all spoke good French. I remember that one of them helped me a bit with my English homework.

I was involved in numerous activities. I'd deliver mail, hiding it in the handlebar of my bicycle. I'd remove the grip, which was made out of a kind of rubber, stuff the folded paper into the frame of my bike, and then carry the mail to the different members of the group. I also succeeded in getting the signature of the chief of police of the time. I got the mayor's, as well— he was later deported—and those of other important people. We needed these signatures for fake identity cards, which were—how should I say?— pre-dated, so that everything would coincide. I was a great forger of signatures because at school I used to forge the signatures of my friends' parents when they were supposed to sign my friends' report cards. No one suspected me because I was *numéro uno* [sic] of my class, in fact of the whole school. Really, no one suspected me at all. At the time, I could write just as well with my left hand as with my right hand because I was born left-handed. But being left-handed wasn't tolerated, so I was caned until I gave up the habit. But I could still write with both hands. You don't write at all the same with the right hand as you do with the left. I didn't know it at the time, but there's communication in the brain. That [being able to write with either hand] protected me.

Unfortunately, my father ended up being arrested by the Germans. They came to arrest him at our house and shot him at the time of his arrest. They shot at me too, but they missed me. When they saw how young and tiny I was, they said: "You almost got hit." But my father was hit in the head by two bullets and lost an eye. Then they took him away. At first they thought they'd killed him and that he was going to die. And I couldn't stop saying: "We've got to go and get a doctor." Of course, head wounds bleed a lot. My mother was hysterical. We knew a doctor who lived across the street, so I asked them to let me go ask him to come. There were about 11 men—a real contingent. They were all German, but the one who mostly talked to me was an interpreter, and he could have been French because he spoke so well. Well, they finally let me go wake up and talk to the doctor. But his wife kept saying things like "Don't get involved" to him. So the Gestapo cut off the conversation and told the doctor they didn't need him, and they took me back home.

Then I said something like: "You know Hitler wouldn't appreciate what you're doing, the way you're treating a wounded prisoner." In moments like that you say whatever comes into your mind, and that's what I did. But it surprised them. And one of them said, "We're going to show you that we're human beings," and then telephoned to have a German doctor sent for. This German doctor said he'd take care of [my father] as if he were German because he was a doctor. So they took him off to a hospital that was French but which they partially—perhaps even half—occupied. He stayed there for several days.

Maman didn't ask directly for news about his state of health, but she received some indirectly thanks to some German nurses who'd become friendly with some of the French nurses. These women contacted Maman and told her they were in contact with the nursing staff who were taking care of [Papa]. So we got news indirectly. Maman probably knew who these women were, but I didn't. But it was a clever way to at least get *some* news.

But after that, they sent my father [to prison]. When they were interrogating me, I asked them where my father was, and they answered: "You don't have the right to know where he is." In fact, they'd taken him to Angers, where there was a big prison. I found out indirectly. During a second interrogation, I asked them if we could go to Angers and see my father or at least take him a parcel of clothes and food. They said: "No, and you don't have the right to know he's there. How do you know this?" It was a little like a bush telegraph system, via the grapevine. The information [I had] wasn't completely reliable, but when I mentioned the name [of Angers], I knew that was where he was. So I asked other people who had family in that prison when visiting times were. I had to go to the police station to get permission to take the train to Angers because I was under house arrest, but I obtained authorization. Then I had to get [to the prison] by six in the morning or something like that, but once I got there, no one was in sight. Sometimes you succeeded in getting a package delivered, sometimes you didn't. At times they'd say no; they didn't want to be bothered. And the Gestapo, who were there, would interrogate me. They prodded me to give them more information.

In fact, Maman and I were also arrested and then imprisoned for several days. They interrogated and interrogated us. I had to try to keep my story straight because I was using a fabricated story as defence. Otherwise, we'd have been killed. And several people who'd helped my father would have been arrested. They never got names from my mother or me, and they probably would have if they'd tortured us. As it turns out, I was very lucky because one day the Gestapo sent for a graphologist to study my signature. But just as I was about to sign, the telephone rang, and they turned their heads. They became very agitated and wanted to go off and arrest other Resistants. Some left right away, perhaps four out of six of them. So I signed, but with the left hand rather than with the right and, because of the interruption, the expert and the others didn't notice anything. This probably saved my life. And they didn't torture me. But other people, several members of the group, were tortured. They were burnt, their nails were torn out, and all sorts of things like that.

They arrested so many people that one day they decided to put us under house arrest instead. But they continued to interrogate us twice a week. Even at the time of the Liberation we were still under house arrest. This was because they wanted to isolate us; they didn't want us to communicate with anyone. Being under house arrest meant that there were very explicit rules and regulations. They kept watch on our house. We weren't allowed to go further than the city limits. And on the two occasions when I wanted to visit my grandmothers—one lived in Paris, the other in Châteaubriant—well, I had to ask the Gestapo for permission. I had to leave alone on such and such a train and come back, alone, at such and such an hour. I had to have a very valid reason, or else.

So we were watched a lot, very closely, and two guys from the Gestapo escorted us night and day. I mean, if we went to the same place, there were two men who followed us. But if we were separated, Maman going to one place and me to another, to my work or to a class, for example, then we were followed separately. And at night, another team took over and guarded our home.

What was happening was that they wanted to capture "Uncle George." That was his name at the time. His real name was Captain Fred Floege. Uncle George was his local Resistance name. I think he also had a French name. He was a guy who was very high up in the OSS, maybe the second in command for all of France. He was a friend of my mother and father's and was in hiding. He hadn't been captured, but he was no longer in touch with London. Because the Americans suspected him of being...not corrupt, but of having committed treason through his actions. There were so many people arrested in that group. And the Germans wanted to get him. They'd captured a lot of spies but not the famous Uncle George, who wrote his memoirs[3] later on and who said one night he was so hungry—he hadn't eaten in such a long time—that he ate raw potatoes in the fields. *Bref* [in short], absolutely horrible things like that. He wanted to see Maman and me again, and he got as far as the corner of our street, but he had the feeling there was something suspicious going on and if he tried to contact us and we were being watched, then we'd all be taken. So, he didn't do it, but he wanted to, and that's just to show you how everything just hung by a thread. I might add that one of the many reasons why I dreamed about going to America was because Uncle George, who we saw again after the war, really wanted me to.

After my father's arrest, my mother had to work as a cashier in a department store. The Germans had confiscated our assets...[our way of life] changed. It took 19 years for my mother to obtain the funds that'd been confiscated at the bank by the Germans. And when they were reimbursed, it was ridiculous, because it was at the rate [of exchange] of 19 years before. This is just to say how our situation really changed. In any case, when I left France in '46, there was a recession, with shortages of everything.

It was really very interesting to be in contact with participants in the Resistance. The longer we were under the Occupation, the more we hated the Germans. But what was really very hard to accept was the attitude of the French towards Maman and me. Once my father was arrested and then sent to a camp, and while we were under house arrest, we had to go see the Gestapo twice a week for interrogations. French people no longer talked to us, either because they'd say "They were members of the Resistance" and point at us or because they were afraid and thought "If I say hello to them, the Germans will think we're sympathizers." So we went through more than a year—[perhaps] a year and a half—that was really very, very hard as far as isolation was concerned. That was another reason why I wanted to go to

America—to get away from bad memories of the Occupation and of bad French people.

In the end, Maman and I discovered that my father died in Germany while escaping from the camp of Buchenwald. No one informed us while the war was still going on. We found out more than a year afterwards that he'd died. It was a terrible shock because we'd been waiting for him [to return] for such a long time. And then we learned how much he'd suffered with the two bullets in his head that were never removed. I later learned that someone who'd also been at Buchenwald, a Polish eye surgeon, had examined him and then told him that once the war was over, he'd remove the bullets and everything would be fine.

The way we learned he'd been taken to Buchenwald was also very interesting. Someone found a small piece of paper on a railroad track. Perhaps in Angers. This paper had been pierced, pricked, by a needle. [The message wasn't written in pencil], either because my father couldn't see well enough, or because he didn't have [a pencil]. A railroad employee who was cleaning the tracks, or something like that, found the paper. How I wish we'd kept it, because it was really important! The employee sent it to us. I suppose my father had indicated our address on the paper. And the employee wrote us a little note, saying that he'd found it on the track and that he hoped... [Jacqueline does not finish her sentence here]. And on the paper my father also indicated the names of other people who were sent to Buchenwald with him.

We got news from Papa months later, [when] we received a [card] or a half-page note. The Germans had used a special liquid on it to find out if there was a secret language or secret ink. My father wrote in German that he was well. It had obviously been censored by the Germans. He said he was well, and he asked if we could send him certain things he needed. I remember these were clothes, tobacco, and several things to eat. Of course, we lacked so much, but we tried to get these things on the black market and to send them to him through the International Red Cross. And I know some of them got through to him, but not *all* the packages. I think he was only allowed one package a month, or something like that. We received two or three messages from him. I was allowed to write him, but only in German. And, you know, they opened the mail, so we had to be careful not to implicate anyone or... [Jacqueline does not finish her sentence here]. But we were lucky, because for years, a lot of my mother's friends, whose husbands were in concentration camps or other kinds of camps, never received anything at all. And the time my father spent in camp wasn't short, either. It lasted a long time for him. He was arrested in December 1943, and he probably died in May 1945. It really was a long time for him.

Afterwards, we learned he'd died. We were never sure, in fact, of the date. And we weren't able to get any sort of certificate from anyone stating that my father was dead. My mother wasn't allowed to receive financial aid because there was no proof that he was dead. We spoke to a lot of Americans, because they'd invaded that part of Germany, and we hoped to learn something [about my father] from them. I got to know a gentleman who looked like Santa Claus, with a white beard and white hair—he seemed very old to me—and who belonged to the American Red Cross. He was very nice, and he knew my father had been in a concentration camp. I told him I didn't know how we could ever obtain a certificate. We'd learned indirectly from people who'd survived the camp that my father had died, but we still weren't able to get a certificate.

[This man] said, "I see." He noted down everything. Then he said: "I'm going to take some penicillin and some pain-killers to a hospital in a village near Buchenwald. And I'll"—he didn't say "blackmail," but it was something like that—"the director of the hospital and ask him for a death certificate." And that's what he did. He came back with the certificate, with the date of death that we'd tried to estimate.

And at that time, [my father] was no longer [at] Buchenwald, but at a place near Flossenbürg.[4] Because by the time the Russians arrived in the region [of Buchenwald], the Germans had already transferred, I suppose, thousands of prisoners to Flossenbürg, which was another concentration camp. And when [the Russians] got there, the Germans had killed everyone, except for one person. And I met this person. He was an adolescent at the time. He'd been buried under a pile of bodies. I think he was wounded, and he didn't move. He was the only one who survived. I met him later in Sablé, a small town in the Sarthe where I was spending a weekend. It must have been July 4th. You know, when you meet somebody who was in a concentration camp, you ask: "Were you there? When was that? Did you meet my father?" And he'd seen my father. I think he played cards with him or something like that. Then I asked him what he'd done in the Resistance. He told me his parents were members of the communist party and that he used to distribute papers—newspapers and outlawed leaflets...I think his parents were killed in the very beginning.

It seems that during the march towards Flossenbürg, my father escaped or tried to do so. Day after day, he'd been saving pepper. He kept on doing it, all the while saying to himself: "It could be useful if ever I want to blind somebody—or an animal or something." And when they set the dogs after him, he tried to use the pepper, but he was so weak that he collapsed. He had typhus, or something else, in addition to tuberculosis. And a doctor who'd been in a camp and who survived said that when he was at Buchenwald, he suspected my father wouldn't last very long because he was so ill. Later, what Papa did in the Resistance was recognized, and he was decorated posthumously by all sorts of people.

In short, that's how Maman got the death certificate. And when I went, when we went, to Paris after the war—it must have been in '46 or almost '46—to the government office for veterans and other people who died during the war, they couldn't believe [what I gave them]. It was the first death certificate they'd seen. And what's even funnier is that when I told this story about a year ago at a party where there were several Europeans—French and Belgian people—a woman told me she'd taken care of survivors and families of survivors, that this was her job at the government office on the Place Vendôme. And I said: "I went there. I surprised them. They told me it was the first death certificate of someone who died in a concentration camp." Then I explained how I'd gotten it. And this woman replied: "I think I was working there at the time, and we were all so astonished." To think I met this same woman in Sacramento, California!

All these war memories leave a mark. When there was September 11th, I began. . . I mean, it really distressed me. I even talked to my doctor about it. That I had this problem with memories, with it all coming back. . .

In addition to helping my father in the Resistance, I also worked during the war. I worked briefly for an insurance company during the Occupation, and I also took courses. I did both. That was quite rare at the time. Since the courses I'd taken in English Studies only led to teaching, and that's not exactly what I wanted to do, I studied accounting, meteorology, different subjects. In fact, I took anything it was possible to take because most advanced-level schools, in Le Mans at any rate, had been closed by the Germans. They occupied all the buildings, so there were very few courses. As soon as a course would open up, I'd enroll in it. And since I worked for a family friend, I was able to manage my schedule.

After the Liberation, I stated to work as an interpreter. I was still a college student, but I was offered a job with the U.S. army on their base in Le Mans. I worked in an office, and it was actually quite interesting because it took place in the *mairie* [city hall]. The job involved getting in touch with owners of buildings, and sometimes of plots of land or of castles, and negotiating and arranging the location of sites that could be occupied by the U.S. army.

If there were problems, I was the interpreter, and I also translated the necessary documents. Even the *préfecture* sometimes had to deal with me, although I never really understood exactly why. Anyway, I did what had to be done. I was 21. Sometimes, I went to the Embassy because a lot of documents and interviews in French had to be translated. I also was sometimes called to be [the go-between] between people who didn't speak English very well and the personnel [of the U.S. Embassy]. While doing this job, I was able to continue my studies at the same time, and I did this until I left for America. [I took] night courses. It was very intensive.

During this time, we French girls would go out with Americans, but always in groups. Otherwise, our families wouldn't have agreed. Le Mans was a very large military base. There were tens of thousands of American soldiers. I liked to practice my English with them. We usually went to *bals*, to dances. The music was really fabulous. It was mostly swing. But from time to time, country [music], too, but this wasn't for dancing; it was for the GI's who were *nostalgiques* [homesick]. I found this music really intriguing because I'd never heard it before. The swing bands were excellent. The Andrews Sisters, for example. One of them died recently.[5] Well, I saw them in Le Mans. We had really good quality [bands].

I was a volunteer for the French Red Cross, and they often invited us to dances, where we were escorted by chaperones, who could be both men and women. I remember one of the chaperones was a French colonel who was rather strict. We went to the dances to meet Americans, but also because of the refreshments and food, which were pretty scarce at the time.

I met my husband at a Halloween party on the base at about the same time as when I heard of the death of my father. It makes quite a story. I'd just heard of my father's death and I was *en deuil* [in mourning]. In France at that time, people observed years of mourning. We dressed in black, and there was no question of going out. I said to myself: "We lived through the Occupation and couldn't do anything. I'm young and I'd like to go out with the Americans, but there's no way because people will talk, because it'd create a bad impression, and so forth."

One of my girlfriends sympathized with me and felt sorry for me. So we made up a story that on Halloween I was going to spend a quiet evening playing cards at my friend Micheline's. But, in reality, I would go to the Halloween party with some girlfriends "Since we're going to the dance in costumes, no one will recognize you," they said. So I went to the dance disguised as a Turkish woman who was wearing a little veil, because it was really important that the chaperones not recognize me. There would have been a scandal if Mademoiselle C. [the interviewee's last name] went out and had fun only a month after learning of her father's death.

That's how I met my husband, by going more or less clandestinely to the dance. So it wasn't really a *rendez-vous* or anything like that. He was an officer, a captain, and his name was Guy M. Like the other officers, he wasn't dressed in a costume. We found out that we both liked to play ping-pong, and I, of course, wanted to practice my English. In fact, I worked in the same building as he did. He worked in an office, too. So we met at lunch time to play ping-pong and sometimes to eat together. That lasted several months until when he had to leave, to go back to Butte, Montana.

We corresponded for quite awhile after that. I was transferred to Le Havre when he left. The *chef*, the commanding officer, of the base in Le Mans was transferred to Camp Philip Morris in Le Havre, and I followed him. I was his secretary from the middle of March to the end of June 1946. He'd been very nice—very *paternel*—to me when I lost my father. And I ran into this man, this colonel, one day in Santa Barbara. It was a chance meeting about 15 years ago. We were at a cocktail party. My husband heard his name and said: "It's funny. My commanding officer after the war had that name." We got his telephone number and saw him again. He was living in Carmel and had become a rather well-known artist.

When my husband left for the United States, I tried to obtain a scholarship in order to finish my studies in Pennsylvania. My husband knew about this. As for my choice of colleges, it was Uncle George's university. That was where I applied. My scholarship application was accepted; they even offered me more money than I'd asked for because they said it would take me more time than I thought. So I got a very generous scholarship. But at about the same time my husband was saying that he wanted to marry me, that we had to get married. In the end, I had to make a decision. Either go to Pennsylvania to finish my studies or go to Montana.

As it turned out, I chose Montana. If I had to do it again today, or several years ago, I might have done it differently, since my husband was a journalist and he could have found a job on the east coast. But back then, women didn't work or study, so I abandoned my project.

Then I missed the deadline for leaving on a U.S. army boat. There was a time limit [for signing up]. I was working at that time in Le Havre, and I was in contact with newlyweds, with women who were leaving. The last boat from Le Havre was in May or June of 1946, and I didn't know there were also boats leaving from Cherbourg. *Bref,* it was too late to make the sea journey for free, so my husband had to pay for a plane ticket.

I had a lot of trouble being admitted to the United States. It was rather complicated because they asked me why we didn't get married while my husband was still in France. I answered that we wanted to *réfléchir*, to think it over. I had to provide some special documents from my future parents-in-law. And in addition to everything else, I had to show them some letters of support from the American government indicating that my father had been affiliated with the OSS, the Office of Strategic Services.

We got married during the summer of 1946 in the United States—in Montana, at the place where my parents-in-law had a ranch where they stayed during the summer. The wedding took place in a chapel on an Indian *réserve* [reservation]—a very small chapel that was supposed to be the oldest church west of the Mississippi.

My father-in-law was a chemical engineer for the Anaconda Copper Company. In fact, he was [the one who signed the papers to be] my financial sponsor in the United States. In the beginning, I lived with my in-laws, and my husband worked as a journalist in Butte, but not for very long. In fact, the weather didn't agree with me at all. So my husband looked elsewhere [for a job]. He got an offer from the *Sacramento Bee*, and we moved here, to Sacramento, in 1947. He began as a journalist for the *Bee*; then he became *rédacteur* [editor] for what they called Upper California, that is, the region to the north and to the east of Sacramento. He finished as Assistant Managing Editor, but he's retired now.

I was warmly welcomed by people in Montana, but I wasn't impressed at all by the city of Butte. It was a mining town—there were abandoned copper mines—and air pollution had destroyed almost all the trees. There was very little vegetation. It had a terrible, cold climate. And it was also very isolated. *Bref*, it was pretty depressing, except for the people, who were very, very nice. I was something new for them—*la petite Française* [the little French girl]. We still go back to Montana. It's a beautiful area and is splendid in the summer. But we no longer go back to Butte, which is too depressing.

I loved the palm tress in Sacramento. We arrived in the evening, and the first thing I noticed was the palm trees. And then, the next morning, I discovered there were squirrels in the park of the Capitol [the California state capital building.] We like it here. It can get hot, of course, but the nights are cool. It's only hot in the afternoons, from half past two or three o'clock, until six o'clock. I play tennis a lot, and I'm able to play all the time, except in the afternoons.

There wasn't really a French war brides association in Sacramento, but what existed then, and what still exists today, although it's changed a bit, is a cultural club called *Les Causeries Françaises*. This club was created at the time of the First World War by women who'd been here for awhile and who were already quite old. They wanted to continue to have the opportunity to speak French. *Bref*, it was a nice club, and it was very active for a long time. We'd have speakers, and there'd be plays.

At one point we thought we wanted to be affiliated with the Alliance Française, but you had to have a library and to teach French. There weren't enough of us to do something like that. Another group that exists but has no name is a group that I think was created at the same time [as the French war brides group]. I started to go to it in '49, but it had already existed for several years before that. It was a group of French-speaking people—and they could be born in Moscow, Paris, or Sacramento—plus some Canadians and some teachers of French. This group still exists. We get together about twice a month in each other's homes, and, *ma foi*, it's a very nice group. At one point, we all became pastry-chefs because if you didn't make your own pastry, you had to go as far as San Francisco to buy good cakes. There weren't any in Sacramento.

I used to go back to France a lot, but I go less these days because my mother died. I'm both American and French—I have dual citizenship—and I feel I'm both. It's funny, because here when I want to forget I'm French, the Americans remind me I am. But when I'm in France, I realize that I've adopted American habits, the American way of doing things, an American point of view.

When I arrived here, people were really kind, and this surprised and bothered me because I was used to a much more reserved way of acting. So I had to get used to this. I liked it, but it was awkward. Over the years, several times I've met people who, for one reason or another, didn't like foreigners or people who speak with an accent. But, as my grandmother used to say, "*Vous n'êtes pas louis d'or*" [You aren't a piece of gold], which means you can't please everyone.

I've kept my French accent, because when I was studying, having an accent or not was never really important. At the time, what counted was writing and knowing the grammar. *Mon Dieu!* We managed as best we could with the pronunciation. In addition, the people here kept saying: "Your accent is so cute. You really mustn't lose it." So I wasn't going to make a big effort to!

I don't have any children, but I have a lot of French and American friends. And I've always been very active, whether doing volunteer work or working for pay. I'm a fund development person. I volunteered for a long time, but then I discovered that to be respected you had to have a profession; you had to be a professional. If you were a volunteer, they could abuse [sic] you, and that was ridiculous. Since I became good at what I was doing—I again started studying left and right, taking courses, going to seminars—I became recognized as a fund development person.

Today, I'm mostly involved in the arts. For example, for the last four years or so, I've been working with the Hmongs, with Hmong cultural art. The Hmongs are mountain people from Indochina. They fought against the communists, and since the communists won the war, they had to leave their countries[6] because their lives were in danger. A lot of Hmongs, as well as Miens and Laotians, came to our area. If you count just the Hmongs, there are 16,000 in Sacramento. They have a form of art that is very special and typical. We're trying to preserve it and to keep it going. I'm very involved in this and in getting subsidies. I'm also helping a group of professional musicians set up a little *orchestre*, a band, but only of winds [sic] and percussion instruments. All of this is very interesting.

Six

"MES CHERS PARENTS..."

Growing up, Nicole T. was no stranger to the casualties of war. Her maternal grandfather, who was a doctor in the French army, was killed in 1918, just a few weeks before the end of the First World War, and her father lost a leg and had his face disfigured on the battlefield in 1915. As a result of his injuries, Nicole's father spent four years in a hospital; then he went to work for a bank, where he met Nicole's mother. Later, after the Second World War, Nicole married a GI and discovered how difficult it was to live with a traumatized husband who had seen many of his friends killed during the Battle of the Bulge.

Nicole has lived in Louisville, Kentucky, since 1946, but I interviewed her several times in Paris while she was visiting her daughter, who is a friend of mine; we also conducted several follow-up, long-distance telephone conversations and corresponded several times. Nicole's husband died several years ago, and since then she has been making annual trips to exotic places around the world.

Nicole preferred speaking to me in English but occasionally made comments in French. What makes her story particularly poignant are not only the extracts she reads in French (or sometimes translates spontaneously into English) from the girlish letters she wrote to her parents in the 1940s—some copies of which she gave me and I translated—but also the comments she makes about them 50 years later. These letters, naïve and childish as they now appear to be, undoubtedly reflect the impressions of other wide-eyed women leaving war-torn Europe for the United States.

Born in Paris in 1921, Nicole was the second of eight children. Because her father had fought in World War I and had been decorated with the Legion of

Honor, she and her three sisters were entitled to attend the Legion of Honor's
Maison d'Education, a girls' military-like boarding school first located in St. Denis
and later in Saint Germain-en-Laye. After obtaining her baccalaureate, Nicole set
off, at 18, for England to improve her English. In 1939, the war broke out. A few
months later, she made her way back to Paris by boat and train.

All the men were gone in France at that time—they were either prisoners of war or working in camps—and the government needed school teachers. I didn't have the degree that was needed, but my father knew an inspector, so I was lucky enough to be hired. For two years I worked in a small village north of Paris, four kilometers from where my parents lived. I must say that I hated my job. I wasn't born to be a teacher; you are or you aren't. And most of my students were Polish, so they hardly spoke French! They were sons or daughters of Polish immigrant workers who worked on the farms. I did the four kilometers by bicycle in every kind of weather. It was good training for the rest of my life, and I guess after the discipline of the *Maison d'Education*, I had nothing to complain about!

When I was 21—that's when you're an adult in France—I told my parents, "I'm sick of working in the village. I'm going to find a job in Paris." And I did. First a job, then an apartment. I did different secretarial jobs. One of them was as secretary to the Aide de Camp at the French Ministry of War. It was a good job for somebody as young as I was, but I think my education had something to do with it. I worked in Paris during the whole German occupation. I remember being cold and hungry, typing with gloves. It was miserable.

I have very bad memories of this whole period. Everything was controlled by the Germans. They took all our produce and sent it away to Germany, so we suffered a lot from hunger. Fortunately, my two brothers were too young to be sent away to work camps.[1]

After the Americans landed in June 1944, I decided to leave Paris and go and be with my family in the country; they lived 30 kilometers north of the city. I wanted to hitchhike, but no French cars were on the road, just retreating German troops. They were leaving Paris via the north because the Allies were coming up from the south. So I walked the whole 30 kilometers. I was really happy to find my family again and not to have been shot down on the road!

After the Liberation of France, I met some Americans who talked a friend of mine and me into working for them near Nancy, in eastern France. I was young and nothing exciting had ever happened to me, so I went. My friend and I worked as secretaries. The American soldiers were the first men I ever went out with. That was because there were no Frenchmen in France. I asked the GIs to teach me some slang, so I knew a lot of words that weren't very nice. I didn't realize what I was saying!

Then we went to Mannheim, Germany, close to Heidelberg. The city was partly destroyed, but the scenery there was very beautiful. The GIs weren't allowed to date German girls because the war wasn't over yet, so we had our choice! When the headquarters closed, the Americans asked some of us if we wanted to go to Biarritz, France, because they were opening a university[2] there for GIs before they went home. And my friend and I said, "Why not?" She was from Paris, too, and had also gone to the Legion of Honor.

So we went to Biarritz for a few months, and that's where I met my husband, William H. Thomas. He was a master sergeant and the chief accountant for the French personnel working for the Americans in Biarritz. He took care of the payrolls and all that. I worked for him, and he was happy with my work. That's how it all started. In a way, I guess you could say I've been working for him ever since!

We started going out together on the weekends. He'd come over to the place I was sharing with my girlfriend or we'd go out for a *promenade*. I remember that one day he brought my friend and me a big box of K-rations. They weren't very good, but since we didn't have anything then, they were very much appreciated.

We got married in January '46. I was pregnant. That was because I knew we were going to get married. And he knew too. Anyway, first we got married at a very short civil ceremony at the *Mairie* in Anglet, a town outside of Biarritz. Then we had the religious wedding with a chaplain from the Army. My husband was Protestant, and I was a bad Catholic, so I thought it was better if the chaplain do it. My husband was a Methodist; he still is a Methodist, but I'm not anything. It was a very nice wedding day. Unfortunately, my family couldn't come because transportation was too bad to travel. But I had lots of friends. And the Americans made an effort for us to have a nice meal and a wedding cake at one of the big hotels in Biarritz that had been requisitioned by the Army. The cake was made from pure butter and was in the form of a pyramid. I remember having a lot of trouble cutting it in the French way.[3]

After our wedding, the Army lodged us in a lovely villa in Biarritz, and a chauffeur came to pick us up every morning in a jeep and drive us to work. I worked until March or April. My husband wanted me to go to America as fast as I could, since I was expecting our baby. I really wanted to go to the United States. For me, it was a *pays de cocagne* [land of plenty]. It was everybody's dream to go to America. And the Red Cross took care of us very nicely. They sent a lot of French war brides to the United States from Le Havre, from Camp Philip Morris. My mother saved the letters I wrote from the camp and from the United States, and I have them. Here's what I say in one of them. It's dated March 20, 1946.

Mes chers parents,

The trip went well, despite the sad good-byes. I was in a compartment with two nice young women. We ate in the train, sandwiches and fruit juice. We arrived at Le Havre at 3 p.m. and were taken to Camp Philip Morris by bus. The weather was very good. I saw cities that had been bombed, Rouen and others. The camp is situated 9 kilometers from Le Havre on a hill. It is big, and it makes me think of the Renault Camp.[4]

I am in Barracks 15, Bed Number 4. The beds are good, with sheets and *five* blankets. The organization is wonderful. Yesterday evening we had a conference with a lady from the Red Cross who told us we would stay at the camp for five days. We have a lot of papers to fill out and have to check our baggage. I have heard the boats take 9 to 10 days to cross the Atlantic. There are all sorts of girls here, but the ones in my barracks are almost all nice. Those who have never lived in a camp make faces, but I don't mind. The pregnant women and those who have babies don't eat with the others, but afterwards, with extra quantities. I think that on the boat we will also have special treatment. Here there is a nursery, a dispensary, a registration room, a reading room. Everything is well-heated, and there's a movie every night.

From time to time, we're interrupted by an announcement on the microphone. "Barracks 5 must do their baggage check." "Barracks must go to registration." I've just been for the check of the hold baggage. The French customs agent wasn't too persnickety. I was glad to check my trunk, because everything had settled on the bottom and that left an empty space, which I filled in.

I think the time will go rather quickly. I will write you again in several days and give you more details about my departure. I've already read one book, *Transparence*. The weather is marvelous.

I must go, my dear parents. Kisses to you and everyone at home.

Your big daughter,

Nicole

I can't believe I was such a good girl, writing to my parents every two days like that. All my life, every week, I wrote my parents, for 40 years! Those things are gone nowadays.

After waiting at Camp Philip Morris, we were put in a boat, the *SS Brazil*, and I talked about that boat in another letter dated Sunday, 24 March 1946:

Mes chers parents,

I'm beginning to write you today while we're still at the dock. We're leaving at one. We've been in the boat since about 2:30 yesterday. There are six of us in my cabin, which is on the middle floor, right in the middle of the boat. The *Brazil* is a very large American steamer, about the same tonnage as the *Pasteur*. It came with all its staff from America in five days. So, even at the worst, we should be over there by next Sunday, maybe even before. It is very comfortable. We have a nice bathroom for our cabin. I sleep on the bottom level and, to tell the truth, I slept well. There's a room for dancing and entertainment. Yesterday, the orchestra played, and there was a movie. We are about 500 or 600 war brides. There are also many nurses and Red Cross personnel. There's a book-store[5] and a very nicely organized nursery. The dining room is also very nice. ... Most of the waiters are *nègres*. The service is very good. Yesterday evening there was a sensational *tranche napolitaine*,[6] fruit, and so on. This morning, there was a real meal. They ask us how we'd like our eggs. We're treated like real princesses.... It's a lot different from the camp [Philip Morris], where life was rather military-like. But, of course, we had to go through that....

Your daughter,

Nicole

It's funny that I said all the waiters were *nègres*, but that's how we called them then in France. They were black civilians working for the boat, who came with the crew and the people waiting at the tables. There were three services in the mess hall, and the food was delicious, but later we were all seasick and didn't really take advantage of it. It was a real *supplice* [torture] to go down there to eat.

The boat was the only way we could go to America then. There was no other transportation for us. And before that trip, I could really imagine why people loved to travel on a ship. But after being so seasick, I wrote, "If I ever come back to France, it will be by plane. That way, if I'm sick, I'll only be sick for a few hours and not for several days!"

I remember that once we were stopped in the middle of the Atlantic for about five hours because the doctor on board had to go and perform surgery on a boat we crossed that was on its way to Europe.

All of us were French. And many of the brides didn't know what they were getting into. Half of the ones on the *SS. Brazil*[7] went back later. Many didn't speak English, and they weren't always accepted by their parents-in-law or other Americans. A lot of people then were funny about foreigners.

I wrote my parents again on the day before we arrived, April 1, 1946:

Mes chers parents,

This is the last day of our sea voyage! I assure you, we've all had enough. It's been very long because the sea was very rough several times. We should arrive in New York this evening, and the brides whose husbands are there to pick them up will be leaving the ship. The rest of us will stay onboard one or two more days at the dock while our train tickets are being reserved.

On the whole, I was really quite ill and stayed in bed half the time. Believe me, seasickness isn't any fun! It's really pretty awful. I couldn't eat anything. But you forget quickly, and today the sea is calm. We're getting close, and our morale is better...

During the crossing, there were baby contests. All the babies were very cute, and they didn't get sick...

I'll write you soon to tell you what I'm doing.

Thank you again for everything you did for me lately. I'll never forget it.

I hope you see Tommy soon. Tell him to hurry up and get over here; I really want to see him. When I think he has this crossing to do, I pity him with all my heart, and I hope he won't get seasick.

I kiss you all very affectionately. Good health, too, to everyone.

Your daughter,

Nicole

We arrived in the port of New York on April 2 at about three in the morning. We all went on deck to see the Statue of Liberty and the lights of the buildings. It was very impressive and grandiose. But it was very cold outside, too. We docked at about 7 a.m., and the women whose husbands were there got off right away. Tommy wasn't there, of course, so I had to wait. But I had a cousin living in New York who came to spend a couple of hours with me.

Then I took the train for Louisville. A Pullman train. It was something fabulous. In my compartment there was another woman going to Louisville. She was expecting, too. I'm still friends with her. She was from Tours. When her husband finished school, they moved away from Louisville. Her husband had saved a lot of money when he was in the Army, and when he finished school, he bought a hotel that became a *hôtel de passé* [a hotel used by prostitutes] without telling her. And she not speaking a word of English. They had a son. She later became a manicurist, and that was a good way for her to learn English. She raised their son, and her husband was running around. And she had a second husband who died from cancer. And a third husband, too, who was a diabetic. And now she's alone. Her son never comes to see her. She lives in Seattle.

It took us about 20 or 24 hours to arrive in Louisville. We arrived at 7:20. My husband's brother and sister-in-law were waiting for me. I recognized them because they were exactly as my husband described them. His parents were waiting for me back at home. My mother-in-law was very nice, and their house was nice, too. And what surprised me the most in America was the incredible number of cars! In France, because of the war, we didn't have so many. And all the little wooden houses! I'd never seen wooden houses before. I wrote in a letter to my parents that a friend of my mother-in-law's brought a beautiful cake with pink and green icing with the word "Welcome" on it, and we ate it with ice cream.

My sister came to see me yesterday, the sister who went to America, too, and we read the letters. We never laughed so hard. But beneath those letters was the fact that I was very much in love with my husband. And I couldn't wait for him to get back to America with me. A lot changed after that.

I'll translate what I wrote in a letter:

Time is flying. I've been here a week and I love it. And I hope that Tommy is going to come very soon. But I doubt that he's going to be here for Easter. I haven't had any news from him since I've been here.... The weather is beautiful out, but the central heating is still on! The painters are painting the house, and this afternoon my sister-in-law Luella and I are going to help. She comes back from her school around 2:30 and then we'll go out in her car. We've already taken a lot of pictures and I will send some to you. It's amazing what you can find in the States. It's exactly like in *un grand magasin* [a department store] before the war. I got a new dress with white dots, and it fits me very well. And Luella bought a beige coat. I wish you could see the quality of the material! I can't believe how many outfits Luella has. Dresses and coats. And the most interesting thing is that they all fit me! So I have *l'embarras du choix* [a fantastic choice] every morning!

Luella was very nice to me. I really appreciated it at first. She could have been mean, you know. But now I realize that she enjoyed doing everything she did for me so that she could talk about it. She was one of those talkers. She'd talk about what she was doing for me. Maybe I shouldn't say that. Anyway I am glad to say something nice about her. She just had a heart attack and she can't talk anymore. She's 83 years old.

My letter goes on [The oral comments Nicole makes as she reads are in parentheses]:

This morning I went to the hairdresser's. I really needed it. Last Saturday we went to visit the airport in Louisville, and Sunday afternoon we went to a club for American soldiers (we were close to Fort Knox)—and everybody welcomed me very nicely. (Luella talked about me so much that everybody wanted to meet me.) When Tommy gets here we're going to go for a long ride. Just to go 50 meters we take the car. It's not disagreeable. I will send you a picture of the car soon. When we go to the grocery store, I think we're in Fairyland. Bananas, pineapples, all the meat you want, fish, cakes, cheese.

Now, I think all their food is so bad, and I say to myself, "How could I write that?" I guess it was because I didn't have anything during the war. Everything is relative. We had nothing for four years.

Then I go on:

They don't realize their happiness. Only sugar is rationed. 2 1/2 kilos per person per month. They call that rationing! I'm waiting for Tommy to get here and we will prepare a big package for you. (I wish I had $5 for every package I sent my family. I sent them packages all my life. Particularly at first.) Since I've been here, I realize that the United States is a really democratic country. They don't have the least idea what social class is. Everybody's treated the same. (I've changed my mind completely about that since then.) As far as eating, we eat a lot of ice cream, of all kinds, and lots of fruit. (We didn't have any fruit in Europe during the war.) Their basement is full of canned goods. (I don't think I ever ate a fresh vegetable at my in-laws). Altogether, we eat less than in France, but what we eat is really rich. And the family food doesn't resemble army food. Thank God, for that! On Saturday, they bought a big piece of meat of about four pounds that would have made a beautiful roast. But guess what they did? They boiled it! It was very unfortunate. So when I have my home I will make some red meat, red roast. (I remember every Sunday my mother-in-law had an overcooked roast with vegetables, and she put it in the oven before she went to church. And my husband still loves it, but I don't make it anymore.) You should see the hats on display. They're very funny, but I will never, ever wear one of them.... I'm soon going to start to knit. Maman, could you send me *Modes et Travaux* [woman's magazine] every month, please? I'm going to see if I can send money to France. When you give $3 here, it corresponds to 1000 Frs., but in France 1000 Francs is $8. I don't understand. Maman, if you want something special, just tell me. I'm sure I can find it. I'm going to try to buy *socquettes* for Jean-Marie. They have them here in all sorts of colors...The lodging situation is as bad as in France, and the soldiers coming back from Europe don't know where to go.

That's why we lived at my in-laws' for six to nine months. It was against my will, but there was nothing else I could do. And I'm very grateful, but it was horrible. Not because they weren't nice. No, it was because of the heat and the noise at night. We lived in the attic, and at night it was 85 degrees up there. And down the road was the railroad switch. The climate in Louisville is terrible: hot and humid in the summer and cold and wet in the winter. I still hate the climate there, especially during the summers, because our house doesn't have air conditioning.

Afterwards, we found a housing project in southern Indiana. All the houses were one level, with a stove in the middle of the living room. It was furnished; we didn't have our own furniture. We rented another house, and then in 1954 we bought a house in Louisville, where we still are today.

The first few months I lived in America with my in-laws were very unhappy because everything was strange, and particularly because of my husband's drinking. He drank in the army when I was in Biarritz, too. I thought it was funny before. He couldn't quit. It was never one cognac. It was always a double. That's what you did in the army. You drank.

Those first years were bad years. My husband stayed in the army for awhile, but then he went back to the post office, where he worked before the war. He had a law degree from the University of Louisville, but he never practiced. He had night shifts at the post office, and he drank a lot with his buddies from the army. It lasted for many years. I cried a lot, but I never said anything to anyone. I was unhappy, but I couldn't go back to France. Not for the world. I couldn't impose myself on my parents.

My in-laws were always very nice. When we were living with them, they couldn't understand why my husband was drinking gin. They found a bottle of gin in his drawer and they, asked him, "Why are you drinking gin?" And he said, "But this is dry gin. It's gin without alcohol. It's tonic." I don't know if they believed him or not. But they made him take a teaspoon of that gin every morning before breakfast! They were such good, nice people that they didn't see evil in anything. My husband is like that, too. He's very naïve. I don't think he'd have made a good lawyer. He's too honest.

When he enlisted during the war, he told the draft board, "Put me anywhere, but not in the infantry because I have flat feet." And that's exactly where they put him!

But I have to say he was traumatized by the war. For years and years, even until now, he's talked about it. And when he starts, you can't make him stop. He fought in the Battle of the Bulge and saw his friends killed.

I cried a lot over the years. My husband was never mean. He was a nice guy, a good guy. I have a lot of faults, too. My husband was weak, and I became bossy. I'd get angry and stressed. We were happy with our daughter, who was born in August 1946, and then our son. My husband was more like a grandfather than a father to his children, and they adored him.

When I was younger, I started sewing to earn some extra money. Then I started traveling. I went to Egypt, Mexico, Canada, Haiti. My husband always let me go. "Have a good time," he'd say, rather than saying, "Let's go somewhere together." All he'd do was watch television. TV was his soul. He couldn't eat without having the TV on. I hate the TV. It makes me so upset. My husband wasn't the kind to try to improve himself. He never returned to France. France, for him, is a second rate country.

My mother later came to visit about 10 times. She had three daughters in the States because my two sisters came to live here, too. They married Americans, too—men they met while visiting me—but they're both divorced now. My mother was a remarkable woman who loved the States. She could remember the heritage from her mother. Her mother was born in Baltimore of French parents. My mother knew all the Stephen Foster songs. She spoke English with no accent, not like me. She spoke better English than I did. My father never came. He couldn't speak English.

Back in 1966 I went to live in Paris for six months. I had to get out of the house. Our son and his wife were living there, and the house was just too small for all of us. I was very depressed. I had to get away. So I got an apartment on my own in Paris and worked as a secretary to a Lebanese financier. My daughter was in France, then, too, living with a French family during her junior year abroad.

Since then, I've gone back to France every year, sometimes twice a year. I save for it. I really feel good when I'm in France. I have French friends I've had for 50 years or more. I like the old stones and the museums. People in the Midwest are very friendly, but I miss the cultural part. Where I live is not very "select." Making money is what matters. The interesting people are in the universities.

It's going to be harder for me to go back so often now. My husband has Alzheimer's. He's 86 and has lost his immediate memory. He goes for walks and gets lost, so people bring him back. He uses a cane, and last week he fell. I think he still loves me after 49 years. As for me, I don't know. I'm 73, but I don't feel 73. I still have a lot of things that I want to do, but now my husband's ill and it looks as if I'm going to have to take care of him. I sometimes read those letters I wrote to my parents in 1946 and marvel at how cheerful and enthusiastic I was back then.

Seven

NEW YORK SANDALS

Jeanne-Marie L. C. was born in Oran, Algeria, on January 12, 1920. Her father was an industrialist who owned a cigarette factory. Her mother was a housewife who had worked as a school teacher before her marriage. They had three children: Jeanne and her two brothers. When the family business was nationalized by the Algerian government in 1962, Jeanne-Marie's parents went to live in France, where they had relatives. Her father's family was from Provence. Her great-grandfather had been the Préfet *[prefect] of Marseille; and her grandfather had been elected, at the age of 28,* Député *[an elected representative of the French National Assembly] for the Hérault department before being appointed as a judge in Algeria.*

Jeanne-Marie met her husband, Tom, in Oran during the summer of 1943. He was among the American troops that arrived there just after the Allied landing in North Africa. They married in September 1944, and Jeanne-Marie immigrated to the United States in August 1945. Divorced since December 1971, she was living near Los Angeles and was teaching at a Catholic school at the time our interview took place.

At the start of the summer of 1943, my mother needed some sugar or something like that and sent me to see my aunt, who lived close by, to borrow some. That's where I met three young American soldiers my cousins had gotten to know. Since I could speak English quite well, I was able to chat with them. Over the whole summer, they continued to visit my cousins, and each time they came my aunt would invite me over. Much to my surprise, Maman, who was of Spanish origin and very strict, let me go.

That's how I became acquainted with Tom. He was a non-commissioned officer. I don't remember the number of his battalion, but it was an ordnance battalion. He was an engineer and fixed everything that had to be fixed. He'd fought on the Algerian front, and [after being in North Africa] he'd later go up the Rhone Valley and fight on the Alsace-Lorraine front and then in Germany.

Tom came from the state of Iowa. His father was a farmer and the owner of a large dairy farm in the north-eastern part of the state, about 15 kilometers south of Minnesota and 25 kilometres west of the Mississippi River.

At the end of the summer, Tom asked me if we could see each other more often. So I invited him to my house, which I hadn't ever done before. After that, he started coming once a week, then twice a week, then every day. He came so often that my family began expecting his visit. But neither Tom nor I really realized what was happening.

It wasn't until the anniversary of the Algerian landing[1] that we started realizing it. Tom asked my parents if I could accompany him to a dance taking place at a *marabout* [a shrine] on top of a mountain overhanging the bay and city of Oran. My parents gave me permission to go provided that my sister-in-law came with us! For Maman, going out alone with a young man was totally unthinkable.

So my sister-in-law came along with us. But at one point, she said she had a headache—I'm almost sure it was a "diplomatic" headache—and wanted to go home. She left me alone with Tom, and with the 250 other guests, of course, for half an hour. I don't remember how Tom asked me to marry him or if I answered favorably. All I know is that by the time we came down from the mountain we were engaged!

I was very surprised my parents didn't object to our marrying. They really liked Tom. But they told me there was one condition: I had to wait until the end of the war. So, we got officially engaged and were going to wait till the end of the war. But shortly after our engagement, someone told Tom that during the post-war period—and nobody knew how long that would last— it would be just as impossible for him to come back to Algeria to get me as it would be for me to go to the United States. So my parents agreed to our marrying rather quickly, and we started the paperwork in January 1944. However, that was when the American army began realizing that a lot of GIs had married undesirable women—sick ones and others—and that they were all going to be coming to the United States.

So the army, or perhaps Washington, decided to make it much more difficult to obtain authorizations to marry. We had to start the paperwork all over again and get affidavits from Papa's bank, from the police, etc. And I also had to be interviewed by all of my fiancé's superior officers. We wanted to get married in July and hoped the papers would arrive in time. But by the time the papers finally arrived, the landing in France had started, and Tom was put on a two-hour alert, so we had to keep waiting.

Then one day Tom arrived at my house and announced: "Guess what? We have permission! We're getting married on the 11th." It was September 5 or 6, so we had to work fast. There wasn't enough time to get the dispensations we needed to marry in a Catholic church, but we were able to publish banns at the Oran Town Hall. We were married three times on the same day, all in strict privacy, with only my parents, our two witnesses, and the chauffeur. We were first married at the Oran Town Hall, then by the Baptist chaplain of the chapel on Tom's base, and then we received benediction from the priest who'd married my parents, baptized my brothers and me, and given us First Communion.

We got married on September 11, 1944, and on September 19 Tom left for France and later Germany. I stayed on with my parents in Algeria after his departure. In August 1945, a liberty ship[2] stopped in Oran on its way back to the United States. Almost all the American soldiers had already left. The American consul asked the captain if he could take on five French women who'd married American soldiers, five war brides.

The captain accepted and we left Algeria on August 15, 1945. We were the only women onboard, and we weren't allowed to leave the upper deck. I was the only one who spoke fairly good English. After sailing along the coasts of North Africa to the strait of Gibraltar, we went down the Atlantic coasts of Africa to Dakar [Senegal] so as to cross the Atlantic from the shortest point. This was because the war was still going on with Japan, and [the Americans] were still afraid of submarines. Then we went up the Gulf of Mexico and the Atlantic coast of the United States, until we reached, first Newport News, then New York. The ship reached New York City on September 5, 1945.[3] I was 25.

Upon our arrival, we war brides were greeted by the Red Cross and then put up in a *grand hôtel* [a luxurious hotel] overlooking Central Park, the Saint Moritz. They took us to visit night clubs, museums, Saks Fifth Avenue, and other department stores. It was incredible, astounding, for us to see so many shoes, stockings, and clothes because, of course, we'd had so few of them during the war. I bought a lovely pair of shoes. As a matter of fact, this caused me some problems with my mother-in-law later on. When she saw them, she exclaimed: "What lovely sandals!" So I replied: "Yes, I bought them in

New York at a good price." "Really," she said. "How much did you pay for them?" "Ninety dollars," I answered. She almost went through the roof and let out a cry. I should add that at the time a pair of shoes usually cost about 14 dollars in Iowa!

The Red Cross accompanied us to our respective trains. Out of the five of us, three were staying on the East Coast, one was going to Cleveland, Ohio, and I was going the farthest, that is, to Chicago. I changed trains in Chicago and arrived in Postville, Iowa, at about two in the morning.

My father-in-law and my mother-in-law were the only people waiting on the platform. And I was the only person who got off the train. There was absolutely no light, either. My parents-in-law came towards me and asked: "Are you Tom's wife?" "Yes," I said. And are you Tom's parents?" "Yes," they replied. I lived with them while Tom was still in Germany. My sister-in-law, whose husband was in the army, also lived with us. Tom came back four months later; it was just before Christmas. We lived for another year and a half with his parents while our little house was being built.

My parents-in-law were good people, but we had absolutely nothing in common. And to tell the truth, it wasn't always easy in the beginning. They were of Scottish and English origin, and Tom's father's family had lived on the same farm for generations. I came from a large city, and I dressed and acted differently. It must also be said that, at the time, Iowa was a dry state and that there was Prohibition.[4] It was still very *puritain* [puritanical], very Presbyterian. There were a lot of Norwegian immigrants, especially in the northeastern part of the state, and on Sundays there was even a religious service in Norwegian.

I can tell you a little anecdote. When I left Algeria, my father gave me six bottles of champagne as a gift for Tom's family. Before leaving Algeria, I wrapped the bottles in straw and put them in the trunk where I had the linen of my *trousseau* [hope chest]. When I opened the trunk in front of my mother-in-law, she looked inside and saw the bottles. "What's that?" she asked. "It's champagne for when Tom gets back," I replied. "Champagne!" she screamed. "That'll never come into my house!" She made me store the trunk in a little shed in the farmyard. And when Tom got back, we went to look at the trunk. The champagne had frozen and all the bottles had exploded, leaving a type of frost all over my linen sheets! And when I went back into the house, my mother-in-law asked me if everything was okay. I said, "Yes, except for the champagne." "What happened?" she asked. When I told her, she said: "None of it is left?" "None at all," I replied. "Well, I'm really happy about that," she said. At that moment, I think if just one of the bottles had been left intact, I would probably have broken it on her head!

My father-in-law appreciated that I was different from them, but my mother-in-law, not at all. She would have liked Tom to marry the young woman he knew in college before the war. My mother-in-law was an educated woman—like my own mother, she'd been a school teacher before marrying—but she'd probably read that French girls were all...how can I say, all prostitutes! In fact, one day she even told me the only thing French women could do was paint their fingers and their faces and wear black underwear! But later, when disaster struck, she realized that French women weren't just the superficial Barbie dolls she thought we were. When she had massive hemiplegia in 1947, at the age of 53, I was the one who took care of her for seven years.

And she lived thirty years more! Thirty years! I think in the end she realized I was just as competent as anyone else. You know, at the time, the people of that part of Iowa were rather provincial and isolated. Some of them had never even been further than Des Moines, which was 210 miles away, for the County Fair. And on top of that, I was the first war bride to arrive in Iowa. So, of course, they made a big fuss about this. I was even interviewed by the Des Moines Register, which my mother-in-law wasn't at all happy about, since the C. name appeared in the papers.

While we're talking about war brides in Iowa, I adored the film *Bridges of Madison County*, where Meryl Streep plays the role of an Italian war bride who lives in Iowa. What I really liked in the film, and also in the book, is the fact that mature people can be [shown] falling in love without being ridiculous. My husband's aunt lived in Madison County and my mother-in-law was born there. His aunt was a member of an association that wanted to restore all those covered, wooden bridges that you see in the film.

Sometimes when I was living in Iowa, I had the feeling I was a little bit like a trained monkey. People would stare at me because my reactions were different and the words I used were different. For example, if I talked about somebody who spoke well, I'd say he was very "eloquent." But the word "eloquent" in English sounds snobbish, and the last thing you wanted to be [in that part of the country] was snobbish! And there were, of course, a lot of things I didn't know. For example, what we call a *brassière*[5] in French is not at all what they called a "brassiere." So, when I used this word for the first time, all of a sudden their eyes shot out of their sockets!

People would tell me: "You have an accent. Where do you come from?" I speak several languages. That's why my accent isn't typically French. But when I get excited or angry, my French accent gets a lot stronger. There'd inevitably be someone who'd explained to the others that I was French. And all of a sudden, you'd see the women withdrawing and the men's eyes starting to sparkle.

My husband managed his parents' property for several years. Then, in 1952, his arthritis got so bad that the doctor told us he had to leave for a drier and hotter climate. So we put all of our things into a truck and left for the West. We stopped in Phoenix, Arizona, and that's where we decided to stay. Tom got a job at Ford, where he worked before the war. He did road tests for new cars. We liked Phoenix, but in 1955 Ford transferred us to Kingman, a town 180 miles north of Phoenix and 110 miles south of Las Vegas. Kingman was once a flourishing town because of the silver mines, but in 1955, it seemed, literally speaking, like a ghost town.

I thought Kingman was at the other end of the world, and I probably cried more on the road to Kingman than I ever cried on the Atlantic! But, as it turned out, it wasn't all that bad. During the 11 years that we lived in Kingman, even if I didn't work, I was able to do what I really liked to do, that is, sing. I also gave singing lessons to a small, select group of people. As a matter of fact, before I got married, I'd begun a singing career in Algeria, starting out as a soprano at the opera house of Algiers. So when I got to Iowa and people discovered I sang, universities, churches, and associations all asked me to give recitals. They also asked me to give conferences about life in France during the war. Nobody in Iowa knew what it was like in Europe during those years. So I was very busy in Postville, and I really liked everything I did. I was able to sing in Phoenix, too.

I had to keep busy, you see, because we didn't have children. My blood type is a very rare Rh negative, and I always have to have a number on me. I got pregnant quite often, but after two and a half or three months, I'd have a miscarriage. Tom wanted children but was absolutely against adoption. Today, looking back, I guess it probably was better, after all, that we didn't have children.

In 1965, Ford appointed Tom manager of a laboratory that was being set up in Pico Rivera, California. He stayed there until Ford closed the laboratory, the assembly line, and the different facilities. While Tom was manager of the laboratory, he had to entertain a lot of engineers and other people and to take them to restaurants for "three Martini" lunches and for dinner. They went to a lot of night clubs. At the time, it wasn't really his thing, but going so often to those places, he started to drink a lot. And then one day, standing at a bar, he met another woman—a woman who soon put her clutches on him.

I went back to France to see my family in November 1969. I suspected there was something wrong, but I'd decided that whatever happened I was going to wait and wear them down, so to speak. So, I waited, waited a lot, but when I got back in August 1970 from a trip to Iowa to see his mother, Tom was gone. He'd moved out his things and left a note on the TV screen saying that if I wanted to contact him, I could call his office. But since it was the weekend, I couldn't reach him. I'm not the hysterical sort, but that day was the first and only time in my life I completely went out of my mind.

Not only was Tom gone, but he also left me without anything. He sold the house we still had in Arizona and the boat we had in the Long Beach marina. He emptied our bank accounts and piled up debts on our credit cards. And finally, he put all the Ford stock we owned under the name of his mistress.

Our divorce became official in December 1971, and they got married three months afterwards. I forgot to mention that this woman had been "kept," as we say, by several men and had also been married and divorced five times. To make a long story short, she left Tom after three months. . . . And, of course, she took everything before moving out.

After she left, Tom sank into alcoholism. They made him take early retirement. He was stopped several times by the police, and he spent several weeks in prison for drunk driving. He smoked three packs of cigarettes a day. To tell the truth, he killed himself with alcohol and cigarettes. He died on January 17, 1988.

So, as of 1970, I found myself at the age of 50 without anything. It was too late to resume a singing career. In any case, I didn't have enough money to go down that road again. That's when some friends from church suggested I start a new career in teaching. They knew that even if I'd never taught before, I was a college graduate, since I'd obtained the *agrégation*[6] in French and English at the University of Algiers. I was really lucky, because a Catholic private school recognized my degrees and offered me a job as a substitute French teacher. They hired me the following year, and I stayed there for three years.

I'll be eternally grateful to the sisters, priests, and everyone else at St. Paul High School because they took me—they gave me a chance—when I was in a terrible state. The psychological shock I had after Tom left triggered a horrible case of hives. A rash would break out first on one side of my face, then on the other. My lips and tongue were all swollen. It was awful! I looked like a monster. I never knew in the morning what I'd look like when I arrived in class. And my students didn't know either. The people at St. Paul's took me under their wing and spoiled and loved me. They were marvelous. They were my real family back then.

When my contract finished at St. Paul's in 1973, I obtained a position at Servite High School, and I've been teaching there ever since. It's a boys' high school. Most of them are Catholic, but we also have Jews, Buddhists, and Muslims. Many of our students are Asian or Hispanic. I'm head of the language department and teach both French and Spanish. I'm also the school's calligrapher. On average, I do the calligraphy for about 1,300 certificates or diplomas a year! So, of course, with all that, I spend long hours at school. I get there about six in the morning and I'm often still there at nine at night.

I intend to retire in two years. I'll go back to Iowa to live, but before I do, I want to get degrees in bookbinding and painting at Long Beach State University. Then, I'll leave. I'll be glad to leave California. I hate California now. There are too many people. And crime is everywhere. More and more, I come home and close my door. I only open it when I know who's there. I don't go to football or basketball matches anymore. For years, I used to go all the time. The place where I live, Whittier,[7] was founded by Quakers and used to be a very peaceful town, but that's no longer the case. The environment has gone downhill.

Yes, I'm going to go back to Iowa. It's a very beautiful state, and, for me, it's home. I'll live in the house where my husband was born, the same house that his father built, when he got married, on the family property. My sister-in-law and my nieces have invited me to come. I'll be near a college town that has a population of 8,500 inhabitants. Because of the college, the town is rather active intellectually, with concerts and conferences. And as I'm a qualified calligrapher, I'll be able to give courses in calligraphy in the art department of the college.

I come from a family that's always been very active. They've also all lived a long time. My mother died at 97 and was active until the end. She had an intestinal hemorrhage and was gone in a few hours. I still have family in France whom I'm very fond of. One of my brothers is dead, but the other one lives in Bordeaux.

I like living in the United States, and when I'm in France with my family, I'm happy to be there, too. But I must admit I'm rather impatient with the administrative steps you have to take in France, the paperwork, the slowness. In this respect, I've become very American. But I still cook in the French way, and when it's not during the school year, I live at a French pace.

I feel as much American as French. I have dual citizenship. I acquired American citizenship in 1948. It wasn't automatic. The only advantage we war brides had was to be able to acquire American citizenship after two years of residence instead of five. But I still had to take courses at the university on American history and American institutions and take an exam which, at that time, was very difficult. I think of myself as a Republican, but I vote for the person I think is the best one for the position. For example, I voted for Truman.

Sometimes I hear people here say that the French don't like Americans. I tell Americans that it isn't true, that it's a cliché. I explain that what the French don't like is Americans who draw attention to themselves, who wear Hawaiian shirts or walk around Notre Dame[8] or the museums of Paris in short shorts, their belly-buttons in the air, or who act like idiots. Because Americans who behave well don't attract attention; they're like everybody else.

I don't regret anything. There were war brides who went back to France. There were many whose marriages didn't last. I don't regret coming to the United States and having stayed on even after my divorce. I should say that I've always been, how should I say, a bit of a rebel. My mother was very domineering, very controlling. Marrying Tom opened up a whole world for me. When Tom left, I didn't want to go back to France and live with my parents because I really appreciate the personal freedom that I have in the United States. I'm sure I wouldn't have had that in my family. They would all have told me: "*Non, non, non!* It's out of the question that you work, that you do this or that." They would've wanted to decide for me what I should do, and where and with whom I should do it.

I never stopped loving Tom, even if he never apologized for everything he did. I always loved him, and I still love him. Not a day goes by when I don't think about him. In fact, that's the reason why I never remarried. Once he left, I decided—I was 50 at the time—that I'd never remarry. First, because I still loved him, and also because I didn't ever want to risk being fooled and hurt like that again. I'd accepted spending the rest of my life with Tom, and I couldn't conceive of—and I still can't imagine—growing old with anyone else. I know my life is lonely nowadays, but I accept it.

Even so, I think I was very lucky to have had 27 years of happiness—or rather, 26 years of happiness and one that was hellish—with Tom, and then 25 years of satisfaction afterwards. Because, after all, I've been satisfied with my lot. I'm satisfied to earn a living and to do what I want with the money I earn. I also have some long-standing friends whom I hold very dear. Yes, I must say I'm very satisfied with my life.

1917 poster depicting French women working during World War I. [Library of Congress, LC-USZC2-4067]

Poster of a book written by a woman who went to the front to marry her French soldier husband. [Library of Congress, LC-USZC2-4088]

A French poster showing the work of the American Red Cross in France during and after World War I. [U.S. Army Photo]

1918 YMCA poster. [Library of Congress, LC- USZC4-3686]

Madeleine M. ("St. Joseph Was with Us") on her wedding day, June 1920. Gift to the author by her daughter Therese H.

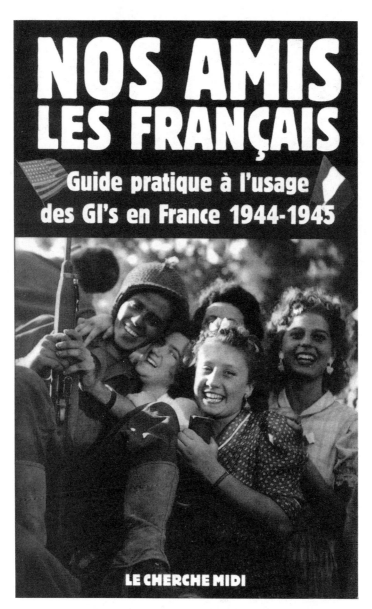

The recently translated version of 112 Gripes about the French, published by the U.S. Army in 1945. Nos Amis les Francais: Guide pratique a l'usage des GI's en France, 1944-1945. Barbino Katz, ed. Paris: Le Cherche Midi, 2003, 140 p. © Rue des Archives/ AGIP.

One of the barracks at the U.S. Army's Camp Philip Morris near Le Havre which was used in 1946 for European war brides. [U.S.Army Photo]

Jacqueline P. ("Ma Petite France") in the 1940s—gift to the author

Georgette and Glenn in New Caledonia ("From New Caledonia to Los Angeles")—gift to the author

Raymonde ("Hi Red!") as a photographer's model in the 1950s—gift to the author

Raymonde ("Hi Red!") as a photographer's model in the 1950s—gift to the author

Raymonde ("Hi Red!") as a photographer's model in the 1950s—gift to the author

Eight

MORRY AND I

Marcelle S. was born and raised in Oran, Algeria. Her mother, who was of Spanish descent, was born in Grenada. Her father's parents were French, but he was born in Spanish Morocco. The two families had immigrated to Algeria, and Marcelle's parents met in Oran. They married and then had five children in five years. Following the death of Marcelle's mother from heart disease at the age of 32, Marcelle and her brothers and sisters went to live with their maternal grandmother and their aunt, uncle, and cousins, all of whom lived together in Oran. In 1962, when the French had to leave Algeria after its independence, Marcelle's family went to live in France. By that time, Marcelle was already well-established in Chicago.

When I went to interview Marcelle at her apartment in north Chicago, a gentleman in a wheelchair opened the door for me. Maurice ("Morry"), Marcelle's husband, had had a stroke five years previously and was partially paralyzed. But his memory and his sense of humor and repartee were sharp as a whip. Indeed, before leaving us to go and take a nap, he helped Marcelle out with certain details and dates during the first part of our conversation.

Marcelle and I spoke in English, the language she feels most comfortable in at this point of her life. I have tried to retain all of the liveliness of our original conversation in the following edited version of our interview.

Morry was the most gorgeous officer! I took one look at him and said, "I don't believe this!" It was one of those things. I fell head over heels. By and large, I don't believe this can happen, but it happened to me!

That was back in July 1944. We got married five months later and have been together ever since!

The funny thing is that I never should have met him. I was already engaged to a Frenchman who was fighting at Tripoli. It was really a ridiculous circumstance. This friend of mine called and invited me to a party with a lot of British and American soldiers. Remember, we were in Algeria, not France, so it was a different kind of war that we had there. We had parties and picnics. My friends were desperate because they needed one more woman. They didn't usually invite me to their parties because I was engaged. This friend of mine really kept insisting, but I told her I couldn't afford to be seen at a party like that. Finally, she said, "You know, the Americans are coming and they're bringing chicken." Well, that did it ! So, for chicken, I went to that party and met Morry! I fell—I went *gaga* [crazy]—and that was it. But, afterwards, this created a lot of problems for me.

I started feeling very guilty, so I decided I wouldn't see Morry again. Then, a few weeks later, there was this outing at a beach, Lourmel, I think it's called. Lourmel is lovely—it has beautiful dunes—and my friends told me that the Americans were going to bring the food. We didn't have all that much food during the war. My family was rather lucky because we could get some stuff from my grandmother's farm, but still. Anyway, I decided to go to the picnic, and that did it ! Then I really had to send a letter to my fiancé. It was very hard, very traumatic, for me to write to him, to cut off ties. We had a lot of friends in common. We were in the same *bande d'amis*, the same gang, for years and then got engaged. My grandmother hadn't let us marry right away, though. And now his family was seeing me going out with an American.

Believe it or not, my grandmother and my aunt and uncle accepted Morry right away. They were absolutely ecstatic that I wouldn't be involved anymore with my fiancé. My family didn't want me to marry into his family because they were rather nouveaux riches. You know, French people in those days, maybe even still, were quite strange with regard to mixing with people, and it was not considered a good tie if I married him. They really didn't even mind that I wanted to marry an American and would probably leave for the United States They were just worried that we wouldn't have enough money after we got married. Morry couldn't speak French—he still can't—so they all started learning English to be able to speak with him.

As for me, I was so crazy about Morry, I don't think I worried at all about leaving the country, having enough money, or not speaking the language. I felt we would make it. But we had to wait several months because there was a 90-day "cooling off" period before I could get my papers. The Army didn't want people getting married easily. They interviewed me, but they were very nice. My husband's captain—Morry and he were friends—told me, "You're going to find it difficult." But, at that point, nothing was going to change my mind. Morry was sent to Italy, but his captain encouraged him to come back to Oran to see me. He'd say, "When are you going to see your queen?" Morry came back four times. What's really interesting, too, is that he was able to get a jeep from the Army for our honeymoon. We went to Tlimcen, in the Algerian mountains, to the same place where Paulette, the friend I met on the boat to America, went with her husband a month before. In fact, the Army gave us the jeep, the flowers, and all sorts of things. That was nice.

Morry was very kind, very human. He represented a sort of anchor for me after my funny childhood—being raised without parents and so on. My mother was sick from the time I was born. She was always in bed. I don't ever remember seeing her up. She had some sort of dramatic heart disease, but in those days no one knew much about it. After my mother died, my father became totally dissolute. Or maybe he'd always been that way and we didn't realize it. We lived in a big place and didn't really know what our mother and father were doing. In those days, maids and a governess always took care of us children, and we lived in a different part of the house. My father came from a family of bankers; he had money and didn't have to work. Maybe he owned property, I don't know. After my mother's death, my maternal grandmother became our legal guardian. My grandmother also had a big house and money; she was a very intelligent woman, and we never really lacked anything. We hardly ever saw our father again after our mother's death, though. I didn't invite him to my wedding, but I saw him in town from a distance several times.

I was one of the first war brides to leave Oran. There were five of us. Just after the war was finished with Japan, like a week later, somebody knocked on the door—this is the truth—and said, "Can you be ready to leave here in two or three hours?" I was staying with my grandmother again because Morry was in Italy. My family and I were all in a panic to get ready; I didn't want to miss the opportunity to leave. But if I had known that Morry was going to stay in Italy another four months, I wouldn't have left then. I would have waited.

The five of us [war brides] left Oran on a merchant marine ship. It was a very slow boat and we spent nine days on board. There was me; Jeanne, whom you met;[1] Paulette, who's about my vintage but a year younger—you know, a real youngster; a girl going to Michigan who was pregnant; and a very sick lady who died about two months after we got to the States. Paulette lives in Cleveland, and she and I have remained friends over all these years. I lost contact with Jeanne. What a coincidence that you found her in Los Angeles! When I met her, she had married an American and was on her way to Iowa, a place called Strawberry Hill or some name like that. She had a little shipboard romance with the captain. He was nuts about her. Gosh, he was terrible! Jeanne was a good-looking girl then and very outgoing. We had to keep a watch on her.

I arrived in Chicago on Labor Day 1945. Morry wasn't back from Europe yet, so I stayed with his brother and sister-in-law for four months. They had children, and he thought it would be easier for me to get along and be with them than with his parents. Being here four months without my husband was kind of weird. I thought I spoke English, but I didn't really speak it well at all. They were very kind, very lovely people, family oriented, so that part was nice. But they didn't have my kind of education. My sister-in-law, for example, had only gone to high school, and that's it. This was a common thing in those days, for the little *bourgeois*.

My husband's family was from eastern Europe. His father was from Russia, and his mother from Latvia. He went two years to a liberal arts college and then took voice lessons. He sang in a nightclub or something like that before enlisting in the Army. That wasn't much of a profession. But he got an enormous education in the Army. He did well; I mean, he went up and up. First he was a sergeant, then a lieutenant, and then a captain by the time he came home. He is a baritone and had this booming voice, so they used him as a training officer. He even sang at our wedding—"Through the Years," I think it was.

I married into a family that didn't have my type of education or background, if you will. I came from a rich family. But since we've been married, with everything we've done, he's grown to my stage. I mean, he's just as well informed about politics and the arts. We're great opera lovers, and we go out all the time, even now. I take him everywhere, to the opera, to the theater, to concerts.

Morry was raised Jewish, and I was brought up Catholic. When I came to Chicago, I met mostly Jewish people, which was quite interesting. His family, though, has intermarried a lot, and there are probably now just as many Christians as Jews. Morry jokes and says that I'm now more Jewish than he is!

When my husband got out of the army, he decided he had to make some real money for us to live on, so he went to work for a company that made washable uniforms. He stayed with them for 15 years and then moved to

Marshall Field's, which is our big department store here. He sold office furniture, things like that, for 20 years and then retired at 65. We lived in different places in the beginning, in Minneapolis, Pittsburgh, and then back to Chicago. We're city people and never moved to the suburbs; that wasn't our style. We always lived in apartments in the city or in Evanston, which is a university town, not really the suburbs.

I didn't work during those first 15 years. I was a lady of leisure and had a wonderful time. I discovered golf. I learned how to play bridge. I went to all kinds of lectures and improved my mind. I really had no problem filling my time. I traveled a lot with my husband when he went out on the road. He taught me how to drive right away when we went to North Dakota. There were these huge highways with nobody on the road but me.

Unfortunately, we couldn't have children, and I didn't want to adopt. So, when Morry started at Marshall Field's, I decided I wanted to teach. I had a *licence* [B.A.] in chemistry from the University of Alger and had taught some classes in math and chemistry before getting married, but I couldn't do much with my degree here. Everything in the sciences was different, and I'd have had to take a lot of classes even to get an American bachelor's degree. But I was able to get a master's degree quite easily in the humanities because I'd done a lot of philosophy and literature in Algeria. And, thanks to a sister from Loyola University whom I met at one of my night classes, I got invited by Loyola to a party given for the new French consul for all the chairmen of French departments at universities in the city and the state. That's where I met the chairman of the French department at the University of Illinois, who gave me a job. I taught French at their Chicago campus for about nine years—all levels—but I never seemed to escape doing 101 [classes]!

When I look back, I'm extremely grateful to my grandmother. She had extraordinary intelligence. She was a very, very modern woman. She knew that because my sisters and I didn't have any parents, we would have to have resources; we would have to get jobs. And not jobs sewing or embroidering. So we went to university, and it was rather traumatic because we had to leave home and go and live in Alger. There weren't many girls who did that at the time. As a girl, it really was a privilege to go to school. As it was, we mostly had our own classes, even at university, separated from the boys.

At *lycée* [in high school], I was lucky enough to have Albert Camus[2] as a teacher. His wife was very involved in the school; she was like a—I don't know how you would call her here—like a *surveillante* [supervisor of students]. Camus was absolutely astounding. He was very, very charismatic, very nice, a very human type of person. He was young then—we all were!—probably about eight years older than me.

Where were we? Oh, yes, getting back to my life in America, my Americanization was pretty much total. I took American citizenship and gave up my French. I'm a Democrat and was very active politically in the 50s during the McCarthy era. The milieu I moved in was not conformist, and I was never a conformist myself. I was involved with university people.

I like it here. I like the ease with which we do everything, the fact that we don't worry if somebody doesn't like what we are doing because "the Joneses" are doing it. I've seen my sisters and my brother in France, the way they operate. They say, "What are people going to say? What are they going to do?" After 50 years, I don't care what people say or do when I do something. I'm a free agent, but they are not. Before Morry had his stroke, we used to go to Europe every year and stay with my sister. She lives in a little town near Geneva. It's lovely, and she has a lot of friends, but they are always saying, "You cannot do that. Madame So and So is coming." I don't live like that at all.

My life in America has been wonderful, really, and my family was always happy that I adapted so well. My husband is a wonderful man and we have had a very interesting life. First of all, because everything in Chicago is the best! Our symphony is the best, our opera is superb. And the Art Institute is magnificent. And then, Morry and I did a lot of traveling. We went to Australia, New Zealand, Fiji, Hong Kong, China, and Japan. When he was with Marshall Field's, he had a lot of vacation time, so we would go away for weeks. When we went to Australia and New Zealand, we used the money my aunt left us when she died in Paris. And she told all the nephews and nieces, "I don't want you to buy a chair or table or a piece of cloth. I want you to use it for fun." So we blew it on our trip and were gone for 42 days!

Maybe one of the reasons I adapted so well here is because of my temperament. I make friends easily. They may not be intimate friends, but I have a lot of people around me that I can call on if I need something or if I want to go for lunch. I don't mind being the head of a group, either. I don't mind working for an association. I was chairman of the French group of the International Women's Association here for 10 years. It used to be part of the International Visitors Center. I also go into the schools and teach children how to appreciate opera. That type of thing.

I feel very American and feel more comfortable speaking English now than French. I'm sometimes surprised when people here ask me, "Where are you from?" So, I turn and say, "Why are you asking?" I'm a very assertive person, quite outspoken, actually. They don't believe it when I ask them that, they get embarrassed. But they say, "Well, you have an accent." I don't resent that. To tell you the truth, I don't care. You have to have the attitude, "OK, I'm different." And, actually, most people like French accents. And nowadays, you know, a lot of people are of Spanish origin, this type of thing.

I think my great pleasure is that I can be a little bit of everything here. I can buy a book and read it in English, French, or Spanish. I can use my languages —I speak Spanish, French, and a little Arabic—with the people who are newly arrived in Chicago. I really don't miss anything.

Regrets? I have very few. I regret that Medicare won't pay for physical therapists for my husband anymore and that we have to spend all our savings on medical bills. I also regret that ever since Morry's stroke we can't get back to France to see my sisters and my brother. It's been five years. And, of course, the situation today in Algeria makes me very, very sad. It is such a beautiful country. The last time we went back there was in 1953. The terrorists are ruining it. It seems beyond repair at the moment. And very few foreigners live there these days. My brother, who is a teacher near Paris, used to go back every year and spend his summer vacations. But about five years ago, his friends told him not to come back anymore because they could no longer insure his safety. And that crushed my brother because he really is an Algerian at heart.

Nine

FATHER KNOWS BEST

Energetic and outspoken, Denise Berthier lives in Fullerton, California, with her third husband, Predrag, who is of Croatian descent and a teacher of English and Spanish. She was more than eager for me to interview her at her home, even more so when she learned that I was an American married to a Frenchman, spoke fluent French, and lived, at the time of our interview, in the same town in the Parisian suburbs as a cousin of hers. After our interview, Denise sent me an article about her that appeared in Aller-Simple, *a now-defunct French language publication in Los Angeles, which I have used to fill in some of Denise's biographical information. Denise and I also had follow-up telephone conversations both a year and then five years after our interview.*

Denise began and ended her interview with me in French, but the central part was in English. Denise preferred it this way. When speaking French, she has a Parisian accent and uses many Americanisms. Her English is colloquial, almost Californian slangish, tinged with a heavy French accent. Enthusiastic about telling her story, she often went off in many different directions, and I have had to "piece together" the events, anecdotes, and impressions, all the while leaving most of her original words. Her style is frank and open, especially where her relations with men are concerned.

Denise was born in Paris in April 1926. Her parents first owned and ran a large café, Le Café des Oiseaux, which still exists at Anvers metro stop. Later they sold the café and bought a bureau de tabac *[cafe selling cigarettes and tobacco] in the Buttes-Chaumont district. The family lived in the nineteenth arrondisement. Denise was an only child, and, because her parents were so busy, she was mostly raised by a* nourrice *or nanny. At the age of five, Denise came down with an illness and was sent off to a convent in Arcachon to recover. Returning to live in the Paris area, she was then sent to a girls' boarding school in Colombes. Unhappy living away from her parents (she was only able to go home once a month), Denise convinced them when she was 12 to let her live at home and attend the local school and then the Lycée of Vincennes. When Denise's father went off to the front, Denise, her mother ,and a waitress ran the* bureau de tabac. *Her father was later captured by the Germans, but fortunately he managed to escape and return to Paris before the end of the war.*

When asked about her diplomas, Denise insisted that she possessed a B.A. in philosophy from this lycée and spoke at length about the problem of equivalences between French and American diplomas. Indeed, she felt that this issue had been very damaging to her in America, insofar as prestige and advancement at work were concerned. Until her retirement, Denise worked at a variety of jobs, including that of computer programmer at North American Rockwell.

My first husband's name was Eddie Muschwitz. We met in Paris in August 1944. I was 18 years old, and he was 20. The Americans had arrived in Paris and we were all gung-ho to thank them and invite them home. My father was very pro-American, so when some neighbors were having an American for dinner, he asked them if they could see if he knew of another officer who would like to come to our place. So the American said, "OK, I will find them a very nice guy." And he did. He sent us a very attractive man, well-bred, good family, from South Pasadena, and not just any Pasadena, but San Marino, actually. The Muschwitzes were originally from Pittsburgh, and his father, who was dead, had been a CEO in an iron works factory. His mother was from Cleveland. So, there was really nothing wrong. Except for one mistake: he wasn't an officer, he was a sergeant. He was stationed at Eisenhower's headquarters near the Champs-Elysées. He could do drafting, so he worked in an office. I don't think he was ever a combat soldier. He was drafted when he was twenty, and was in the war for seven years; first in Alaska, then London, then the European area.

Anyway, one day Father sends me to the Arc de Triomphe to pick Eddie up and bring him back to our place for dinner. I waited for him there. When he came, I said to myself—just like a kid—"Well, at least he's good looking." There was really no depth to my mind or my personality then. I had to do all the talking during dinner because I was the only one in the family who could speak English. After that first time, we invited him over on Sundays for lunch. He and I would go for a walk together afterwards, so I guess we saw each other every Sunday from one to five. I was still going to school during the week. I was doing my last year of the B.A.

It was kind of glamorous in a way. I had this very attractive boyfriend who was 26 or 27. But I was not attracted physically because I was not that type of person. He was more sexual than me. He had lots of experience. Then one day Eddie gets on his knees and says, "I would like to marry you." I was really shocked. I was completely naïve. I was not emotionally or sexually ready for marriage.

When I got home, I said to my parents, "Guess what? The American asked me to marry him!" The biggest silence followed, and my heart went in my feet and I thought, "My God, they take it seriously." I'd been in boarding school for a long time. I was never with my parents, except for maybe five years, that's all. I didn't know my parents. I didn't know how to approach them. I didn't dare. With their business, they were working all the time. I didn't know the communication system. But never in a million years did I think that my father would say yes, because all the other parents were against those marriages. And I would have loved it for my father to say, "Wait six months, and if you still feel that way, we'll see." My father had to give permission and everything because I wasn't 18; so he gave all his consent to everybody because he was really the one who wanted to go to America. He wanted to immigrate to America when he was about 20, and then he met my mother and his plans didn't work out, but they never left his mind.

Eddie and I got married about 13 months after we met. I wasn't really in love, but when you're 19 you're always a little in love; it just wasn't very profound. I had this idea of a big wedding in my head, so I said to myself, "It doesn't matter. I will divorce if it doesn't work out." That meant the marriage was condemned from the start. Because I've learned since that if you want to stay married you have to want it. I didn't realize the consequences, and my father didn't either.

We first got married at the *Mairie* [City Hall] of the nineteenth *arrondissement*. Then I was married in the church of St. Georges. I cried and I cried because suddenly it hit me what I had done. I just didn't have the courage to go against my parents. I was brought up to obey. I was an only child; I didn't dare say anything. My father was a very strong man. France is a patriarchal country. I even got my B.A. with honors. When I got the telegram with the exam results, I went to tell my father. He was with a customer, and he said, "What good is that for a girl?"

When the time came that I could have said something to my father, it would have taken more courage than I had. But one day my mother suddenly . . . she must have seen that I had a long face because she said, "You know, you don't have to do it if you don't want to." She must have seen in my face that

I was a reluctant fiancée. But I knew what a mess we were in, so I said, "Oh, no, it's okay, Mother," and I just went and did it. I guess it was my destiny; we all have our destiny.

So, I got married on September 12, 1945, and I was 19 years old. That is awfully young. I think I was the youngest war bride, by the way.[1] My father gave $2,000 to Eddie as a dowry. He thought Eddie could set up a business in America. My father being intelligent, he never thought that other people were less intelligent than he was.

Anyway, Eddie and I went on a three-week honeymoon to Nice [on the French Riviera] to the Negresco Hotel. I think it still exists on the Promenade des Anglais, the big white hotel. We stayed three weeks. Everything was paid for by the American army. It was *formidable* [wonderful] for a girl who had lived through five years of war. But the wedding night left me cold. I don't think I was really ready for things like that at all. It didn't improve anything. I didn't really love him, and I probably hurt him.

Eddie was discharged in November '45 but I don't remember where. He went back to California, to Long Beach, to be with his mother. She had a big villa on the bayshore. I came six months later. I wasn't even 20 years old. I wasn't thrilled to leave France. But I went through with it, probably because I'm a naturally curious and happy person.

I came over on a war ship. I'm not sure of the name because it was my parents who booked it. We left from Le Havre. I was not seasick at all. I was like a little kid jumping over other people sitting on the floor watching movies when the sea was rough. We landed in New York. I don't know if we did the Ellis Island thing but we must have because there were lots of people. I remember a person, an American woman, a volunteer [probably from the American Red Cross], who was in charge of taking the women going on to Los Angeles by train. She was very nice. She didn't want to lose us. We stopped in St. Louis in the afternoon on the way, and she took us to see a movie.

When I arrived in March, Eddie was living in a big house with his mother on the beach, and it was perfect. We used to cross the bay in a canoe. It was fun. I made myself a bathing suit right away. At that time in France we already had the mini skirt; we already had the open-leg, one-piece suit. So here I come, and I see all these ugly bathing suits, with skirts and all that. So the first thing I did was I made myself a two-piece bathing suit up to the navel. I didn't show my navel because I wanted to be respected, respectful. But I had the round leg, not the normal leg, and in those days you only saw things like that in Palm Springs, so people were really looking at me.

We lived with my mother-in-law for about two or three months. But then —I was so stupid—I said, "We're supposed to be living in our own place." So we moved out. We got a place, something really poor on seventh street, which I decorated. I had never decorated in my life, but I had to do something. I'd never lived in such a poor place before. I lived well with my parents in Paris.

Eddie wasn't working when I arrived at his mother's. He was spending all his time building a car. And that caused our first fight. I was French. French women are very strict. I mean they like to have leisure *after* they're done with their work. So I arrive here and I am 19 years old and I see a guy that doesn't work. I say, "What's the matter?" That was my first sensible question, but I was probably too straight. I had no sense of humor, obviously.

Eddie went back to the place where he used to work, where his father was a CEO, and they gave him a job drafting. But the man was 27 years old; he was not 18. He felt insecure. He felt bad inside. He felt he was not at that level. He was probably more mature than they were, after seven years of seeing war. He couldn't readapt. Back then, people didn't talk about the difficulties GIs had readjusting to normal life.[2] It was just like for the soldiers coming back from Vietnam. People just didn't realize.

Eddie didn't stay with that company. It was like a slap in the face asking him to do the same work he did at 18 before going off to the war. He felt humiliated. But he couldn't find any other work, he wasn't qualified, and he didn't want to go back to school. So, without asking me, he used the $2,000 my father gave him to buy a cleaning business. We had a cleaning shop in Long Beach, and I learned to press. We had a woman who was doing the repairing. But the business didn't do very well. I wanted to have trucks and things, but Eddie didn't want to; he was very stubborn, very set. We couldn't talk; there was no communication. The business really started dwindling after I got mad at the Mafia. We had this counter selling uniforms to bus drivers at a discount. And one day these two strong men came up to me—I was only 20—and ordered me to do something. I said, "No, I won't." And they said, "If you don't, you'll never be able to sell those uniforms again." I said, "I don't care if you take those uniforms." Then the guy told me, "You're wrong. You don't know how wrong you are." He was right. I didn't know they were the Mafia. They took away the uniforms and the business we had with the bus drivers.

After the cleaning business failed, we had another business. My mother-in-law and her second husband helped us start a picture framing business. I learned to frame pictures, and my husband worked very hard, long hours, trying to get contracts. My husband was a dreamer; he didn't share with me. There wasn't enough money to live on, and he had to start working in a shipyard. I got pregnant and then had a son, a lovely boy born in March 1948. He's still a lovely boy, by the way.

About three months after the baby came, Eddie came home one night from work and said we had no money for the rent. The rent was only $33, so that was a real shock. It really made me angry. I felt I had to make a decision. But my feeling that way probably spoiled everything between us, because you know things have a way of working out. I didn't have to jump in like that. But I did. I got a job as a waitress. I found a French restaurant and got a babysitter. I had never worked in my life except for helping Eddie out. I didn't like being a waitress, and it made Eddie very upset. He was always afraid of losing me. And sure enough, I became more independent after that, and I later found a smarter, a more intelligent man.

There was nothing wrong with my husband, and I don't think there was anything wrong with me. It was just the circumstances. Somehow he was not able to be manly enough with me, I guess. I don't know. He was bewildered. I think he always felt I put him down, in a way, because he was not educated like me. We couldn't communicate. We had nothing in common at all. I think I also realized I shouldn't have chosen him in the first place. My whole life got screwed up back then because I didn't marry a man I loved. At least when you love somebody, you have the courage to endure a lot more.

Our marriage wasn't going well; it was just a matter of time. I had a kind of affair. Then in 1953, when my son was five, I went back to France for a long vacation. I wanted to stay there, but my parents wouldn't help me. There was no satisfaction with them at all. It was a mistake going back there because when I got back home with Eddie it was worse. I got very depressed, very sad. There wasn't all this self-help stuff then—even TV now teaches you a lot of things. I had these resolutions to tell Eddie, but the minute I would see his face at the door, I couldn't say anything. Finally, I just left. Left all the furniture and everything. The marriage only lasted about eight years.

I went back to Paris again in 1956 and stayed six months. I wanted to stay that time, too, but again my parents said no. And again I obeyed them because, well, if they didn't want me to stay in France to be with them, I had no real advantages to stay there. By then I was established in America. I had a car and could move around better. So, my choice was to remain in America, but I would have done it for them. It is hard working in a cafe, and we could have bought a bigger place, and I could have helped out a lot. It's funny, they pushed me away, and yet they were crying. But, as it turned out, it was Father's plan to go to America.

In fact, my parents came twice to this country. They first came in 1946 to see how it was and stayed six months. They rented their own place, and Father took a look at what he could do. This was America. He was a businessman and he saw right away what he could do, which was build apartment houses. But he couldn't do this then because DeGaulle at that time would not let French money go overseas. My parents finally came over in 1960. They sold the café in Paris and Father bought a building on Ocean Boulevard in Long Beach, right there, the best. He really knew what to do. They immigrated here and even became American citizens. By that time, I had remarried a Swiss doctor—partly because I needed his signature to buy a house so that my parents could stay with me. Then they moved into their apartment building. Unfortunately, though, my father got arteriosclerosis, a hardening of the arteries, and died in January of 1967. My mother, who had worked all her life with my father, she says, "You know, I would really like to sell this apartment house and just have an apartment and live from my income." Business-wise, it was not a good idea on my part to say yes, but I did. My mother died in 1974 of breast cancer.

If I had to do it all over again, I probably wouldn't have married Eddie and come to America. I would have said *non* to Papa. I would have been more courageous. I was a person brought up to obey men. Mother was doing all these little tricks where Father was always right. I never confronted my parents. What good would it have done? What's done is done. Besides, I might have married another GI or an alcoholic or something a year or two later because I could speak English and was at the age where you are beginning... [Denise does not finish her sentence]. I don't regret anything. Because you might regret your life. There is nothing you should regret, nothing. Because you don't know what the other side might have been.

I met some other war brides in Los Angeles at a war brides association for French women. It was started by French women of the First World War, and I belonged to it for a few years. But I stopped going because it was in Baldwin Hill and was too hard to get to from Long Beach. And those women from the First War were really boring and *pédants* [pedantic]. But I met some other women my age. They had problems here, too. Many of their American husbands were alcoholics but they didn't dare say anything. We had all married men who were maladjusted, just like those of the war of Vietnam. Nobody knew this then. There were marriages with just anyone. We believed them. And it was sad because we couldn't go back to our families in France. We were ashamed. The French women I knew were good women, too. They weren't "consumers" of American men, as some people called us. Many didn't have any money. They had children and had to work at little jobs. They didn't have any security, any retirement. Many didn't have an education or an independent spirit like me.

For many of us, too, there was the big problem of diplomas. In the '40s in France we got the *brevet* at 16 and the "bachelor's" at 19. That's where all the confusion begins. We finished high school at 16. Then we went to *lycée*. We had our B.A. at 19. It was like an elite thing, only two percent or less got it. We did philosophy, letters, science. It wasn't just a high school diploma. Then we went to university to do a *licence*, a *maîtrise*, and a *doctorat*. We had very few universities. Here you have a university every block!

I could probably have done one year at university here and gotten my American B.A. But Eddie said, "If you do that, you won't love me anymore. You will find someone else of your level." I was stupid not to go back to school. In America, you're not treated well if you don't have a degree.

Back in the '40s, I felt really demeaned when I had to go out and be a waitress—having an accent and the people joking about it. It really embarrassed me and still does today when I say the word "chocolate." People would say, "Honey, why don't you say it again?" And I would start crying from the pressure of the words. In those days, the men were much more aggressive and familiar with the waitresses than they are now. It is laughable today when they talk about sexual abuses. Harassment? My God, it was so prevalent here!

Later, in the '50s, I became a computer programmer at North American Rockwell. I fought terribly because they wanted to keep me in data-processing. They were really prejudiced against women then. I love computer programming and thought I deserved the job. So I felt I had a right, I had broken the barriers. I love American women, but I found the women there very meek. They accepted things. I would try pushing them to unite, to ask for raises. At Rockwell once when I asked for a raise—I was divorced again by then—I asked the boss, "How come I didn't get my raise?" And he said, "Denise, we only give raises to men with children, with families." That still happens today. No matter how educated a woman is, you cannot do a thing without a man here. Your "second half" [better half] has to be a man with ambition and *savoir-faire*. It's a lonely struggle.

When I was 45, Rockwell laid me and 30,000 other people off. I never got back to what I was. I took it very badly and started to drink. Then I went to A.A.. I met Predrag, my third husband, and things got much better. I bought a café and called it "Denise's Café," but I sold it after two and a half years because it was hard getting personnel, and Predrag wanted me to come with him to Zagreb for awhile every year. I later worked in a bank and retired in 1990.

I became American in 1953. I was working at Rockwell and needed a security clearance, so I had to give up my French citizenship. I think now I have the right to take back my French citizenship. I'll do that in Paris. It might be easier for my husband when we travel in Europe. He's Croatian and American.

There are a lot of things I criticize about American society, but I love America and American people. There's no truth to the idea that French people don't like Americans. It's just that we criticize and have a mind of our own. And there *are* certain things that I don't like. I don't like the way America feels superior. I don't like the way Anglo-Saxons are hypocritical and never say what's really happening. I don't like the complications, the fears, like losing your job. Free enterprise here means an authorization to abuse people. A good employee can just remain sweeping the floor. In the United States the schools are very poor. Ignorant people teaching the ignorant. My husband had trouble in the school system. He was almost fired at 60. He's a French teacher, but he had to teach English and Spanish. Unlike in France, here the students are always right, the customer is always right. I don't like American men as much as American women. American men don't like women. They bury themselves in the TV. I don't know what they do in their marriage bed! Marriage is just a framework. They go to church together, that's all. When I got divorced in 1953, I was like the plague. Many husbands of my girlfriends said, "Don't do anything with Denise. She might give you wrong ideas." I married two foreigners because I couldn't find any warmth in American men. I also wanted to go to the theater, to do things like that. I couldn't communicate with them.

In the beginning, when I came here in the '40s, I couldn't breathe; it was so dull. I came from very intellectual surroundings, and here all I found was women who drank coffee, didn't work, and had stupid husbands who had stupid jobs that they would keep for 30 years. It was very depressing. But now things have changed. I love American women. They are very easy to talk to. They are courageous and very nice. My French friends say, "American women don't do anything. They don't care about what they cook." But I think French women who speak like that are jealous. I tell them I've mostly seen American women making a lot of effort to get everything together.

When I was young in Paris, I never thought about America at all. In school, I learned about America like I learned about Canada or any other country. Under the Germans, we didn't see any movies, but we did read *Gone with the Wind* and pass it around to each other. Oh, yes, we read something about a co-ed at college, and I remember thinking how free American girls were. And we weren't free at all. We were all Catholic and virgins and living in a patriarchal society.

After my retirement, I started to feel that I wanted to go back to my roots. I have American friends, but the conversation always seems to stop somewhere. I always feel different, as if I've come from the Moon, or Mars. I realize now I get on best with people from my native country. I really believe it's where you went to school that marks you for the rest of your life, and I went to school in France. I'm now more pro-French than I was before. I am distressed about Quebec not being able to secede. I read *Paris Match*. I've been back to France many times and I keep up with everybody. I took my grandson to Paris when he was 14, and I'm going to take my granddaughter when she's ready. I belong to the Alliance Française. I am a shareholder in a French magazine, *Aller Simple*. I give a French party once a year and invite many French people. We get together, speak French, laugh a lot, and don't have to be on our guard.

Before, I used to feel discriminated against. I'd be really hurt when people said, "When are you going to get rid of your accent?" or "Where are you from?" Now, I don't care. I am an American citizen, but I am also French. I'll always be French, and this is to be treasured. Before, I never had time to know who I really was. But now I do. Yesterday was Halloween, and I opened the door and there was this adorable little kid about four years old with his mother. And she said, "You have an accent." And I said, "Yes, I am French." And she said, "Oh, I went to Paris last year and bought a book for the children but I cannot translate it." So, I gave her my card and said, "Come on over anytime. I won't charge anything and I'd have pleasure doing it." That's what I do now. I teach French to anybody who wants to learn.

Ten

"HI, RED!"

Raymonde D. is a pretty woman who does not look her age. An only child, she was born in Mons, Belgium, in 1927. When she was five years old, her parents moved to Valenciennes, where they stayed more than 76 years, all the while retaining their Belgian citizenship. As for Raymonde, she considers herself to be Valenciennoise *[an inhabitant of Valenciennes] and remains very attached to the north of France.*

I interviewed Raymonde twice at her home in a residential suburb of Detroit where she lives with her second husband. The mother of two children by her first husband, the G.I. she met in Valenciennes, she has three grandchildren.

Easy to talk to and an extrovert, Raymonde put me in touch with other war brides in the Detroit area and showed and lent me photos. Her original account in French was charmingly "sprinkled" with American words and English expressions. In the following translation, I have used italicized French expressions to render this use of "franglais."

I was very young, about 12, when the war began. It was as if I grew up during the whole time it lasted. Papa was a coal merchant, and Maman helped him by taking orders. In a way, during the war, I was lucky my father had his own business, because we were able to do a bit of trade—what they called *marché noir* [black market trade]—which helped us to survive.

The Germans would come knock on our door, often at night, whenever they wanted something, and we had to give it to them. My father had a hangar where he kept his coal and his truck, and they'd come at night, even at four in the morning, and say, "We need 100 kilos of coals, or we need..." So my father had to run around and give them whatever they wanted. And they'd often ask my father if he had any children. When my father answered he had a daughter, they'd say, "*Ach, gut,*" and then give us some bread. The bread was as hard as wood, so they told us to wet it and to roll it in a towel and then we could cut it. We were often happy to have at least that.

I remember once a friend and I went to a potato field that was guarded by Germans, that is, a German guard kept watch over the field by walking back and forth. And when he was on one side, my friend kept watch while I dug into the earth with my hands and pulled up some potatoes, and then afterwards it was my turn to keep watch while she dug. Maman was furious with me afterwards and told me I could have been killed. But I was happy and said, "But at least we have some potatoes to eat!"

At one point, the Germans requisitioned my father's hangar. This was because they wanted to bring horses from the front, from the battlefield, there. When horses were wounded, they were sent up to our part of the North, since there were German veterinarians near my father's hangar. The veterinarians treated the horses, bandaged them, did everything they had to. And if the horses survived, they'd send them back to the front in trains going through our part of the country. If some of the horses couldn't be fixed up, they'd kill them, and we were the ones who ate them, because the Germans would sell the meat to the butcher, and he sold the meat to civilians. This was in 1942, 1943, and 1944, and we were happy to be able to get horsemeat.

During the summer, there were horrible invasions of flies! That's because there were all the horses and their open wounds. We used a lot of things to combat the flies, and they'd fall everywhere. So if you were in a café or at home, you'd have to cover your glass all the time because of the flies. You had to be careful. And when the horses died, the Germans buried them in the fields. A lot of people got sick. We didn't know from what exactly; it came from everything.

It was very dangerous in the North where I lived because German airplanes flew over us on their way to London. So we heard them all the time. We also heard the bombs during the night, and we often had to go down into the basement to protect ourselves. Everything was requisitioned. We didn't have anything to eat. It was really hard.

The Germans requisitioned my aunt's house, but fortunately they didn't requisition our house or my school. I could go to school, and I got my *certificat* [after finishing primary school] during the war. The Germans were around all the time. Afterwards, in 1945, when there were battles with the Americans, the Germans left Valenciennes. Then the Americans came and settled in our region. The war wasn't even over yet.

I met my husband in March 1945. He'd just arrived. The Americans had set up camp in a silk *fabrique* [factory] where the Germans were before them. I'd often see the soldiers passing by our house on their way to the factory, where there was a mess hall. When my friends and I were outside, the Americans would say, "Hello." I saw this one man pass by two or three times a day, and I thought he was cute. I had red hair at the time, and he used to call out "Hi, Red!" I didn't understand what he was saying. "Red?" I asked myself. "Why does he call me Red?" After seeing him several times, he stopped one day with a friend who could speak French and could translate. The friend said, *"Bonjour Mademoiselle. Comment allez-vous?"* Then he asked what my name was and if my girlfriend and I could come and meet them sometime. After that, we'd go out for walks, and I'd show them the town and so on. Then one day my parents invited him over and gave him something to drink. He came over more and more after that, and *voila*!

He was charming, but at the time he didn't speak French, and I didn't speak much English, just a few words. In the beginning, his friend from New York would translate, but later on I taught him to speak French.

The Americans had a Rec Hall [*sic*] where we danced on Friday, Saturday, and Sunday. I'd never danced before. I was only 18, and, of course, during the war we didn't go out. I went with him to the Rec Hall, but Maman would take us and be our chaperone. My girlfriend came, too. We learned how to dance there; it was really nice. We'd never seen anything like it because we'd grown up during the war and never had anything like that. We learned how to dance the jitterbug. I really liked music and could play a little piano.

That's how it happened. And it happened fast because I met him in March and come July, I was married.

My husband was a sergeant in the Signal Corps. He took care of all the wedding papers. He asked for permission from the army in May, and it took two months to have the papers. The army didn't like those marriages, and it took a long time. They tried to dissuade the soldiers and would say, "Wait till the war is over. Come back [to France] later." Maybe they had doubts that the marriages would last. I don't know. There were a lot of marriages in my city, though—about a dozen. My neighbor married a month after me, and I have another friend who married two months afterwards. There were a lot of marriages, but a lot of divorces, too. As for me, I actually stayed married for 20 years.

Our wedding took place in Valenciennes on July 16, 1945. We had to publish the banns for two weeks before that. We were married by the town mayor. We didn't get married [afterwards] in a church because my husband was Jewish. His parents were Russian Jews who had immigrated to the United States. I'm a non-practicing Catholic.

My husband went back to America when we'd only been married for four months, so we were separated for several months. I only came to America in March 1946. He wrote me and I wrote him, too, as best I could, since my English wasn't very good. As for his French, he could speak it, but writing it was quite difficult. And we couldn't call each other at the time. In 1946, it wasn't like it is today.

I was really in love with my husband when I married him. Later on in life, a psychologist told me that I probably also wanted to get away. That's possible. Valenciennes was a small city. I'd spent the war there; everything was destroyed. We didn't have anything. We'd been occupied by the Germans. We couldn't do anything during the war. Everything was closed at nine at night. We couldn't turn on the lights; we had to use candles. If the Germans saw a little bit of light, they tapped on the windows. With all that, four, almost five, bad years of our youth went by.

In addition, my parents were very strict, very old-fashioned, French people. Maman was particularly strict with me, and since she helped Papa and they ran their business from our home, I could never invite friends over to the house. And I wasn't allowed to go out. They were protective because I was their only child. But I always had, more or less, a sense of adventure. So maybe underneath, when I met my husband, what with my personality.... And since my husband was good-looking and I was attracted to him, or rather, let's say I was attracted to him at the time, perhaps I seized upon the opportunity....

It was very hard when I left my parents to go to the United States. For me, but especially for my mother. I'll never forget the moment when we said goodbye at the station. Poor Maman! It was the beginning of March, and the weather was still bad. My train left Valenciennes at six in the morning. I was with a girlfriend who'd come up from Paris so that we could travel together. That's because I'd never been anywhere. I'd never traveled by myself before. I was an only child and my parents really watched over me. Maman protected me all the time.

Since I was a war bride, people were waiting for me in Paris. The American army organized everything. They told me where to be, what day, what time, what hotel I had a reservation at. Arlette helped me a lot. She accompanied me to the hotel. I don't remember the name [of the hotel]. Arlette had also known an American, but, unfortunately, he didn't marry her, and Arlette was always sad because of this.

Two or three days later, we were sent to a camp for war brides. They took us in buses, big buses, and it was good [for me] because it was according to the alphabet. My married name began with an "A," and the "A's" were the first, followed by the "B's," the "C's," etc. I never was really badly off, because I was in the *premières lettres*, the first letters.

They sent us to Le Havre, to Camp Philip Morris, where I stayed two or three days. The weather was bad; it was March. [In fact], we probably stayed four days. It was cold, and I think it was because of the bad weather that we stayed a little longer than planned. We were in large rooms lined with beds; we must have been at least 20 girls, if not more, to a room. And the room was heated by a large *poêle à charbon* [a coal stove] in the middle of the room. It had a long pipe, and German prisoners came during the night, even while we were sleeping, to put coal in the stove. Since it was so cold, the stove had to be kept on. The German prisoners also cleaned the camp and made our food, since all those women had to be fed. The camp and the kitchen weren't very clean, because American soldiers were there before the war brides; they lived in the camp before leaving for America. The W.C. [toilets] and bathrooms weren't very private. There were often 20 or so of us washing ourselves in the same room.

During the day, they called us by groups to explain what was going to happen. There was a large room where we ate, and in the evening they'd show American films, often those with music. There was also ping-pong, since the soldiers had been there before.

I remember there were some old, bearded men smoking pipes standing on the dock the day the ship left. They shouted: "We'll be seeing you again. You'll come back. You'll see." And I said to myself, "Whatever happens, I won't come back here."

Onboard the ship there were Italian, German, French, and Belgian women. All sorts of nationalities. We mixed, but there were language differences. I made the acquaintance of a young woman whose husband was waiting for her, as mine was, when we arrived in New York, and [the husbands] introduced themselves. I wrote to her two or three times, but over the years, [our friendship] came to an end.

Our ship was the S.S. *George W. Goethals*. It was the first war bride ship to leave Le Havre. We were about 600 women. I was in a nice cabin with four bunk beds for eight women and a bathroom. We chatted a lot. There was an Italian woman in the bunk above mine, and she spoke a little French, so that was fine. But she was continually seasick and kept to her bed. She was really very sick. The journey took six days because of the bad weather. It was March and the weather was really awful. There were American films, but I don't remember having English lessons or hearing conferences on board about American culture. We were the first war brides to embark from France, so perhaps afterwards they did that.

When we arrived, we saw the Big Lady, the big statue. And then, when the ship arrived at the dock, it was really something. We saw all the taxis, all the cars. *Mon Dieu!*

What commotion! They'd call out on the *haut-parleur* [loudspeaker] the names of the women whose husbands were there, and you had to come down. My husband came from Detroit by train, and he was waiting for me. But how to recognize him! He was no longer dressed in uniform but in civilian clothes. I didn't recognize him at first. He was different. But he came and took me in his arms and lifted me. But I was surprised at first because, as the saying goes, a soldier's uniform makes a man look better.

He was good-looking, but it was still a change. He had wavy black hair and black eyes. He was about five feet ten inches tall. He was, he must have been, 23. After getting back to America, he'd re-enlisted, but by the time he came to get me in New York, he'd just been *congedié*, discharged.

In fact, my husband had been *appelé* [drafted] at 19. Then he got promoted several times until he became sergeant. I guess it was *juste après avoir reçu son diplôme* [right after graduation] from Cleveland High School. He was originally from Cleveland, Ohio, but his parents moved to Detroit during the war. So after being discharged, he went to Detroit to live with his parents. He could have signed up again, but his father wanted him to come to Detroit to help him with the business.

The day I arrived in New York was St. Patrick's Day. This was a surprise for me because in France we didn't know about St. Patrick's Day. There was music and a *défilé* [parade] on Fifth Avenue. My husband and I stayed two days in New York because he had some family, two aunts, whom we went to visit. He took me to Radio City Music Hall. I'd never seen people tap-dance before. There was a movie after the show.

Then we went to Detroit by train. My parents-in-law were waiting for us at the Detroit station. They lived on Seven Mile Road and Livernois, near Palmer Park. It was a pretty nice neighborhood 50 years ago. Seven Mile Road was called "the avenue of fashion" then.

We stayed at their place for three months. I had a large trunk and several suitcases that I never unpacked. I didn't like living like that. I also felt that

they didn't like me very much. I couldn't communicate with them. I spoke
French with my husband, and my mother-in-law didn't like that. She was
an old-fashioned woman who'd come from Russia when she was 18. Her
husband had also come from Russia. She couldn't stand that I spoke French
with my husband. "You're in America," she said. "You must speak American
[English]." Later, she was afraid our children would have an accent. *She* had
an accent and she didn't like that. She thought it was horrible to have
an accent.

She also thought French women were *légères* [frivolous, easy]. It was a
mother-in-law thing. As a matter of fact, many American men and women
still imagine that French women are sexier. When my husband wrote to his
parents that he was marrying a French girl, his father wrote back that he'd
better be careful because French women were *coquettes* and *frivôles.*

My mother-in-law also thought that France was *la brousse*, the back country—that we didn't have anything. She thought we didn't have any movie theaters, any indoor plumbing or comfortable housing, anything worth seeing.
She made me work a lot. Back then, there were no *lave-vaisselle* [dishwashers]
or things like that. I did the dishes, I scraped the vegetables, set the table,
cleaned the house. My sister-in-law, who was a shorthand typist, also lived
with them, but she wasn't very hardworking. My mother-in-law did the cooking and the washing, and I did the ironing.

After three months, I'd had enough. I told my husband we had to go away,
that we had to do something. I kept pushing him. But my husband wasn't
making much money then. He worked for his father, who only paid him
$25 a week. His father was very *radin* [tight], not very generous. He was in
non-ferrous metals. He bought old metals and then resold them wholesale
to companies. My husband always worked in the family business. His
brother, who's 12 years younger, is now taking care of it.

So, my husband worked in the business and his father paid him a salary.
And when my husband asked him for a raise to be able to buy a home, his
father didn't want to give it to him. That's why the only house we had later
on was a little "GI home," which cost at the time about $9,500.

I kept saying, "I want to get away from here." But in 1946, you couldn't
find any accommodation. You had to rent a tiny apartment and buy the
furniture that was already inside it. It was really difficult to find something.
We finally found a room to rent in the home of a widow who lived on Dexter
Street. She needed some money. She had a son who was a little *retardé*
[retarded] and another in the army in Korea because during that time the
Korean War was going on.[1]

So we rented this room, which also had kitchen privileges. The lady let me have a shelf in the refrigerator. We had hours when we could eat in the kitchen. She had her hours, and I had mine. We lived there for awhile, and I really liked this woman because she was like a mother for me. She taught me English and showed me the shops and what to do.

Back then, I had a very strong French accent. In fact, I still have it. I remember once I said to a *laitier*, a milkman, "A bottle of milk, please." And that evening, when I served the milk at the table, my husband drank it and then exclaimed, "But this is butter milk!" The milkman had understood "butter" and not "bottle." We laughed a lot about that.

I'd go to English courses for war brides in downtown Detroit. I'd take the Woodward Avenue streetcar. I remember that my husband showed me how to put the money in the box and where to get off. There were German, Italian, French, and Belgian women in class. I made friends with several of them, but we couldn't see one another very often. We didn't have much money because all the husbands had just come back from the war. And we didn't have any transportation; we didn't drive. So we wrote one another letters and notes. Later on, when we had a telephone, we'd call.

The women at the war brides school pointed out on the map the different parts of the city, and they'd show us around. It was very well-organized, and they were very nice to us war brides.

Detroit was a really great place 50 years ago. You could walk everywhere There were a lot of shops and *grands magasins* [department stores]. The city was clean. There weren't all those broken windows boarded up the way there are now. But back then, the whites got on at the front of the bus, and the blacks at the back. And public toilets were separate.

Several months after moving to Dexter Street, we had to decide about another place to live. I was seven months pregnant and we couldn't stay at the woman's. We had to find something bigger. So my husband bought a GI home. We moved and I cried because I didn't want to go away or leave the widow. She was really like a mother to me.

I found myself all alone in the GI house. My husband would go off to work early every morning and come back late at night, and I was stuck at home. At that time, we didn't have a television or a car, and it was really, really hard, especially the last two months when I was expecting the baby. We lived in the suburbs, in Park Michigan, which is really crummy now. The house was a little brick bungalow. All I had was a radio. I liked music and listening to songs. I tried to understand a little English by listening to them, but I didn't understand much when people sang or talked.

We really didn't have much money. My husband's father increased his salary to $50 a week after the birth of the baby, but we had to pay for our house, for food and everything else with just that. I couldn't work because I couldn't leave the baby. I didn't have any help. As a matter of fact, I'd never worked [in France] because my parents thought I was too young and didn't want me to. So, I didn't have a profession.

We didn't have many electrical appliances back then. For example, I didn't have a washing machine for a long time, so I washed clothes by hand. I had something that resembled a big pot, and I'd boil water in it and put the clothes inside. My mother-in-law gave me a sort of wringer where you'd put the clothes and then turn a handle. But we did get a TV set back in 1950, I think. It was a Muntz TV.[2] Their ad used to say, "Up in the sky with Muntz TV."

It was still much better, much more comfortable, than what we had in Europe. During the period between 1940 and 1945, we had to heat with coal or wood. We didn't have hot running water all the time the way they had here. And we didn't have central heating, either. I liked the amenities in the United States right away.

My husband and I liked to go to the movies and went once a week. We had to walk because we didn't have a car. We bought our first car when my son was about two. It was a Plymouth, *d'occasion* [second-hand]. Later, I learned how to drive.

Once we got a telephone, I was able to speak with my French friends. We invited one another, along with our husbands, on weekends. I knew French women by then because I belonged to a French war brides club. It was on Grand Boulevard, and I'd take the streetcar to get there. The club was an association created by the first war brides, those of 1918. They died off one by one, and it became the club for the war brides of World War II. It was called the French Women's Benevolent Club, and it still exists. But it changed names about three years ago. It's now called the French Women's Club.

[Raymonde shows me some photographs.] This lady is 94 years old. She is from World War I. Here's the current president of the club.

This one was from Rouen. In fact, they're all French women married to GIs. This one is vice-president. Her parents were Italian, but she was born in France. This one is a French teacher. She's American and she teaches French. She really likes our group and comes often. Otherwise, all the others are French. *Mais non*, this one was born in Belgium like me. She speaks very good French, but she remained Belgian. I was brought up in France, but she wasn't.

We have a lunch every month. Last May four French people came to visit us, because there's going to be a celebration for Cadillac, for Lamothe Cadillac.[3] He was from a small village in France, whose name I can't remember.[4] These people are from the village, and they were invited to come to America to see the place where the party to celebrate Cadillac de la Motte [*sic*] will be held. So, we had a little buffet for them.

After eight years in our GI home, we moved to Oak Park. Our little street there was very nice. We were all young couples, and our children played together. The neighbors were charming, and we'd entertain one another once a month in different homes. We'd have a "pot luck" every month. I liked that because you got to know everybody. We also had little Christmas celebrations. And we women would go out together to the movies. We'd see good films with actresses like Mirna Loy. They're playing those old movies again. I really like American *cinéma*.

When my son was four and a half, I learned how to drive. I also wanted to work, but what could I do? I'd never worked. As it turned out, I began by doing modeling, that is, picture work, photographic modeling. Since I wasn't very tall, I couldn't do *la mode*, fashion modeling, so I did interiors and cars. I worked freelance.

I did lots of different things. I had agents. There were several agencies here in Detroit. I was with three different agencies. When the automobile show was on, I went to *castings* [auditions], and if I was chosen, I could work for at least a week and make quite a lot of money. That was good. But after 10 years, things slowed down. So then I taught modeling to little girls at the American Beauty School of Modeling. But I didn't do that very long, perhaps for two years or so. I didn't like it very much.

My husband didn't really like me to work. He was a little jealous. And then, once I started working, I started to evolve, but he didn't. So I found him *ennuyeux* [dull]. We didn't have anything in common. The only thing we had in common was that he lived in France during the war, that he visited it afterwards with me as a tourist, and that he knew my parents. So we could talk about France and my parents, but otherwise.... There was also the difference in religion and the problem with family, with his family.

They were Jewish but non-practicing. But we still had to eat with them *every* Friday night. I think my father-in-law liked me, but my mother-in-law was really hard with me. For example, she kept telling me she wasn't a babysitter and that she didn't want to take care of our children. I remember when my son was a year and a half, I had a cyst taken from my breast. We were afraid; we didn't know. I had to ask my mother-in-law to take care of the baby because I didn't have anyone else. She did it, but she brought him back the next day. Couldn't she have kept him a day or two longer?

Unfortunately, my husband always took her side. He didn't defend me. I remember the first time my parents came to America. At the end of their visit, my husband, my son, and I drove them down to New York so they could take the boat. I cried a lot in the car on the way back, but instead of taking me home, my husband took me back to his parents'. When I asked him why we couldn't go back to our house, he said his mother wanted us to eat at their place. I was very tired from the trip and I'd just left my parents. I would have preferred to go home, but we had to go [to his parents']. While we were at the table, all of a sudden I started to cry. And my mother-in-law said to me, "Why are you crying? Come on. Stop it, already. You should have known better. You didn't have to marry my son." I was crying for Maman and everything. [My mother-in-law] really had no heart. She was a very hard woman.

When my husband was 40, he had a *dépression* [a nervous breakdown]. I had to take him to the hospital downtown. He stayed there for a month, and they gave him *traitements par électrochocs* [shock treatments]. He was never the same again. He didn't have any *cran* [backbone] afterwards. I was the one who ran everything after that. The disease must have been in the family, because his youngest sister also had a breakdown two years before. The same psychiatrist who took care of her also took care of my husband. I saw him every month, and once he told me, "Your husband's mother is the one who should be here speaking to me."

When my son was almost 20 and my daughter 14, things weren't going at all well between us, and we got divorced. I got four years of *pension alimentaire* [alimony] for my daughter until she went to college, and afterwards he helped a bit for her studies. My son left for California. I had to work more, so I learned hairdressing and *esthétique* [esthetic work]. I did *soins de visage* [facials] and *maquillage* [make-up] in good salons. And when my daughter went off to college and I found myself alone, I bought a little house in Royal Oak. I was *célibataire* [single] for 11 years. Then I remarried. I've been with my second husband for 18 years. My ex-husband remarried twice. After me, he married a woman 12 years younger, and now he's with one who's 20 years younger! I saw him last year at *la remise des diplômes de ma petite-fille* [my granddaughter's graduation].

My parents were a little disappointed I got divorced, because in Europe divorcees are looked down upon. My parents came to America three times to see me, and I used to go back often to France when they were still alive. My mother died at 84 and my father at 90.

I remember the first time I went back to France. People in my small city used to point at me and say, "There's the American. She's come back to the home-country." And when I was a little girl at school, I was called *sale belge* [dirty Belgian]. I was like a *paria* [an outcast]. That was why I was glad to come to America 50 years ago. I could be myself. People liked me for who I was. And when I used to say I was born in Belgium, they were really interested.

But, on the other hand, we war brides were too young to come to America. We weren't very *cultivées* [cultured]. We hadn't gone to college. I have French friends in the United States who've never liked living here. They're 70, 72, and they still say, "Oh, France is this, France is that." They miss their families. As for me, I like France. I like going there to visit, but I'm more American now. I also don't have anybody left in France. I became an American citizen two years after my arrival in America. My children are also American, and I raised them in the American way.

After all these years, I've become more modern, more *ouvert d'esprit* [open-minded]. I had to learn a lot of things, like how to defend myself. I think a woman should be independent. I always say that if you get divorced, if you have to work to bring up a family, to buy a house or a car, you need to be independent. I've gotten used to America. I like the people. They're kind and warm. I had two or three bad years in the beginning, but I still have had a good life here, and I'm grateful.

Eleven

FROM ANTOINETTE TO TONY

It took a certain amount of perseverance on my part to be able to conduct an interview with Tony K. Two of her former colleagues—both professors at the University of California, Berkeley—had told me parts of her story, saying she would be a wonderful person to interview for my project. As Tony was coming to France in the spring of 2000, we agreed, by letter, on a date for an interview. And upon her arrival in Paris, we reconfirmed our appointment. However, when I rang the bell of her friend's flat on the given day and at the given time, I was told that Tony had had a small stroke that morning and had been rushed to the American Hospital in Neuilly. There'd been no time to warn me. Fortunately, Tony recovered and was later able to return to California. But our interview had to be put off.

In October 2000, I was in California for a week and once again arranged for an interview with Tony—this time at her home in Orinda (north of San Francisco). But when I arrived at her home, Tony told me she'd been expecting me the day before, not that day! Despite this misunderstanding, she agreed to speak with me, and we subsequently spent two delightful hours together. Tony showed me her notebooks and lent me photos of her and her husband, as well as articles she'd written for Le Courrier Francais des Etats-Unis. *Two weeks later, we met again on the Berkeley campus so that I could return these documents and ask her several additional questions.*

Two years passed and the letters I wrote to Tony remained unanswered. Later on, the friends who'd introduced us told me that Tony was living in a retirement home and that her lovely home had been sold. I tried to arrange a visit to see her when I was again in San Francisco in October 2002, but I was told that Tony didn't remember who I was and refused to meet with a stranger! Tony succumbed to the ravages of Alzheimer's for several years and later died in 2005.

My maiden name is T. It's a name from the Limousin, which is a region in the center of France. My first name is Antoinette. But in the United States, Americans find this too long to pronounce, so they call me Tony. I was born in 1917. I'm 83, but I'm very energetic. I'm like an old peasant-woman from the Limousin who works the land until she's 100. Many people think I'm younger [than I am].

I was born in Paris. I was conceived in December 1916. Papa told me one day: "You were conceived during the Christmas holidays of 1916." Papa fought in World War I. He was sent home from the front and...*voilà*. I was born in September 1917. He was the driver of a colonel or a captain who always wanted to take leave. That's why Papa could come back to Paris.

My father's profession was as a little bit of everything. In the beginning, he was a taxi driver. Then he worked for a big trucking company. He was a *compagnard* [a man from the country], and the character of men from the country is not the same as that of men brought up in Paris. One of my uncles, my grandmother's eldest son, helped Papa come up to Paris, and that's where he met Maman.

My parents ended up by buying a little notions shop, a *bonneterie*. They had four children, but only two survived: my older sister and me. Maman often lamented over this.

I lived at my grandmother's in the Limousin until the age of six or seven because I was the fourth child. Maman wanted to be spoiled. She was tired, so she left me in the country. In a way, they made a *compagnarde* [a country woman] of me. I really enjoyed being with my grandmother. It was lovely. She'd had 12 children, and Papa was the youngest. I think of Grandmother all the time, and on Mother's Day, she's the one I pray for. I wrote a little book, a book from the heart, in which I tell everything about her. Later, I had to leave my poor grandmother and return to Paris to go to school. But she remained my mother—the loved one of my childhood.

I spoke *Limousin* [the language of the Limousin region] when I was little. As a matter of fact, that's why I felt so good in the medievalist group [at Berkeley]. During the Middle Ages, *Limousin* was the favorite language of the troubadours. Nowadays, we say *Limousin*, but before it was called *Limongeaud*. I didn't speak French—I mean *Parisien* [the French of Paris]—until I was seven years old. *Parisien* became the national language because Paris is the capital [of France]. It's a bit like the French of the north.

So, I arrived in Paris at the age of seven and went to school. My first year wasn't a great success, but afterwards—I don't mean to boast—I was often the most intelligent [pupil]. I had a dual experience: that of the country with my grandmother and [that of the city] with my mother and father. I was quick-spirited. I wanted to know everything. Things went much better my second year at school. Every week I'd get what was called "the honor card" [for best student]. I'd go home with my honor card. But one day, I went home and Maman asked: "So, where's your honor card?" "I don't have one this week, Maman." She slapped me, so I told her: "Maman, it was just a joke."

When I was 13, I took some business courses. All the children in the upper grades had to take a test. The answer was 1608.83 or something like that. I was one of 10 winners in all of Paris.

Papa wasn't getting on with my mother anymore, so he left us when I was 10. He disappeared from our existence, and we didn't see him anymore. I began to replace my family life with my school life. That's why I was less affected by the family situation than my sister. She was five years older than me, and she stayed at home most of the time. I was really hurt when my father left, but not as much as my sister. She almost died. She was weak, ill. But I continued to be okay.

Afterwards, we'd go to see Papa once a month. Each time we went, I wanted to have a new dress from the shop and would say to Maman, "I'd like a new dress for Papa. He has to see this one." Papa, my sister, and I would have a meal in a restaurant. The waitress would ask us what kind of wine we wanted, and I'd answer, "Some Vouvray, as usual."

Maman got fed up running the *bonneterie* by herself. She couldn't have fun; she couldn't have a boyfriend; she had to stay home all the time. I also think she was afraid. I was turning into a young woman of 15 or 16. I was flirtatious, and boys would look at me. My sister wasn't at all flirtatious. She was more *pôt-au-feu* [of a house-body].

One day, Maman told us, "It's over. I'm leaving the shop. It's slavery. I can't manage on my own. I'm sending you back to your father." So she sold the house, and my mother and father shared the money. But, surprise! The woman my father was living with, and with whom he'd had a child, turned out to be a friend of my mother's. We didn't know this before. This woman was ugly! And my mother was so pretty!

I didn't get on with my stepmother at all. I have a very strong personality. And when I'm happy, I'm happy. But when I'm unhappy.... So, I told my father, "Papa, it's really easy. Just leave this woman and live with us." He didn't leave her, and later things went badly. In the meantime, I caused a whole lot of misery to that woman. She deserved it, since she'd been a friend of Maman's.

As it turned out, my sister married Pierre, who was that woman's son. He first wanted to marry me, but I didn't want him. He had pimples on his face, and I didn't want a man with pimples. When I got to that woman's house, her son told me: "When I'm 25, I'm going to ask Papa for your hand." And I said to him: "You could ask *me* as well!" So, in the end, he asked my sister to marry him. He wanted to be Papa's son—*le fils à Papa.* I think that was why. He missed not having a father. He called my father "Papa," and by marrying my sister, he became Papa's son, and so he was happy.

Maman lived in Paris, and we lived in the northern suburbs. When I went to see her, she told me how my sister had announced she was marrying Pierre, that she was letting Pierre marry her. "You see, we're walking calmly down an avenue where there are some benches. Your sister says she has something to tell me, that she's going to get married. I answer: '*Bon, très bien.* Who with?' 'Pierre,' she says. Fortunately, there was a bench because otherwise I would have fallen to the ground. Imagine, marrying that woman's son!"

We lived with Papa in Saint-Denis, which is the former royal city of France. But as soon as I could, as soon as I came of age, I left Papa's house and returned to Paris, where I felt "big" [grown up]. I worked in business. I liked that, and I liked working. And also after the war, I managed all right. I was a bit of a flirt, I dressed well, I had boyfriends, I had nice legs. I still have nice legs!

During the Occupation, I helped people cross over [the Line of Demarcation]. I'd go to my family's place in the Limousin, which was still the Free Zone. I liked doing that. There were a lot of people who crossed over. It was as if you were getting out of prison. Our village was called "Saint Angel." There was a boy in the village that I liked a lot. He was a *beau garcon.* Saint Angel is very pretty. I went back there several years ago.

I crossed the line between the Occupied Zone and the Free Zone about eight times. I must say that once I was very courageous. I crossed over with an old couple, some Jewish friends. When they found out that I'd already crossed the line, they asked my father if I could help them cross over. Then my father asked me one evening, "Some friends want to cross over. You know the way. Could you help them?" I accepted. All of us young people were crazy. We wanted to do so many extraordinary things.

So, those people and I took the train and arrived in Angoulême. And in the train, the gentleman, Monsieur Abelson, explained to me the philosophy of I-don't-remember-who. Then we got to Angoulême. And when the woman at a farm where I'd already crossed over from saw the Jewish couple, she didn't want to take care of them. She said, "I've never done that." I replied, "But, Madame, you've already helped me pass over. You're not going to let these people be killed." She said, "All right. But go into the pen with the sheep."

When the shepherds returned, we left, crossing the fields at nightfall. We weren't supposed to make any noise. There was a big white road that shone in the night. And that was the road the Germans who were patrolling also used. And one of the two guides our Jewish friends had paid [to come with us] told us to cross over one by one. Monsieur Abelson had heart trouble, and he was afraid. We crossed over one by one without making any noise. But at night we couldn't see if there were twigs or not. In short, we all got across. Then the young guides said: "We're in the Free Zone." We kissed each other and were very happy. I'd imagined myself dead, because if I'd been captured with them, everything would've been all over.

We walked several more kilometers, and I thought that Monsieur Abelson was going to drop dead during the trip. Then we got to a little café where we were told that [because it was two in the morning and we were supposed to arrive at midnight] our friends had waited for us but then left for Limoges. So we had to continue walking to Limoges. We got to a hotel. Monsieur and Madame slept in one bed, and I slept in another small one in the same room as them. During the night, I had to go to the toilet and got out of bed. Monsieur Abelson woke up and said, "What's that? A rat?" "It's nothing Monsieur Abelson," I said. "It's just me!" We separated the next day. They stayed for months in the Limousin, near Limoges, until the end of the war. I was happy. Nothing happened to us. I knew others who died crossing over the line.

I can tell another story about something that happened when I was crossing over. I was sitting next to a young man in a bus, and I said to him, "*Enfin!* Thank heavens we're now in the Free Zone!" He replied, "*Non.* For you, perhaps, but not for me. I'm Jewish."

The bus stopped, and they asked for our papers. I had my student [identification] paper. The young man gave his papers, and the gendarme told him to get off the bus and to go with them. The young man looked at me, as if to say: "You see. I was right. They're not letting me through." So you see, it was the French in the south who turned over that young Jew to the Germans.

Another time I was coming back to Paris and was crossing over at Vierzon. The weather was good, but there was a lot of mud near the river. I was wearing a little hat in *velours* [velvet] and looked quite elegant, but my feet were covered with mud. I arrived at the station and continued walking. Ahead of me was a German, who was looking at me from head to toe. Despite everything, he saw right away I wasn't Jewish. But he kept looking at my feet and making fun of me. "So, you too crossed over the line?" I told myself it was over; I'd been caught. I didn't say anything. I just looked at him and smiled. I didn't risk being killed, but I did risk being arrested. I reached the train, and the conductor said to me: "Hurry up, Mademoiselle. Have you just crossed over?" I said, "Yes, but the German has just seen me." But the German went on and entered an office. I was waiting for him to call me, but nothing happened. He let the train leave, and he left me alone.

Another time, we got to a farm with a boy who'd just escaped from prison or something like that. He really wanted to sleep with me. I said, "Listen, Monsieur. I have no desire to sleep with you. Leave me alone or I'll call the farmers." He answered, "Come into my bed." I said, "*Non.*" Suddenly, he got into my bed, but the bed broke, and so forth. That really made me laugh, and he didn't bother me anymore. He was a thief or something like that. He would have liked to take advantage of the young woman who was crossing over.

I crossed over so many times for different reasons. I had family in the Free Zone and was sick of Paris. I wanted to go somewhere to relax and have a vacation. You couldn't relax in the Occupied Zone. And once I started, I took a liking to doing it. I helped the Abelsons one way, and then I had to get back. Another time, I went to spend the holidays with my family, and I had to come back. Young people wanted adventure. After the war, I met a young woman when I was working for the Americans who told me she, too, had crossed over eight times. We were happy to talk about our experiences. It was Adventure with a capital A. When you weren't Jewish, that is. Because I had my Paris student identity paper. And my last name, T, was everything except [anything but] Jewish. It's a local name that's associated with the land.

During the war, when we lived with Papa, no one could go out at night. We closed the shutters and put up navy-blue curtains to prevent light from going through. We girls never went out at night. We stayed at home. Papa locked us in. We were supposed to go down into the basement, but we didn't do this.

I remember one day I was walking down the Avenue de l'Opera and a German said to me, "Show me your legs." I never went out with Germans during the war. There were girls who didn't care. As for us, we hated them. Well, it wasn't hatred, but we didn't like them. They were foreigners. After the war, the girls who'd slept with the Germans lost their hair.[1] We knew right away [what had happened to them] when we saw girls wearing woolen caps.

My sister's husband—my stepmother's son—was in the FFI [the French Forces of the Interior, or the French Resistance]. He was almost killed. He was married and had a baby. One day, a German came to my sister's place. "Where's your husband?" he asked. "I don't know," she said. He was in the FFL [the Free French army] and was a spy. Fortunately, the German left.

Then the war was over. I was living in Saint-Denis, but later I moved to Paris and lived near Maman. We laughed a lot the day the Americans arrived. Everyone was happy. My mother never remarried. She was a flirt, but one husband—that was enough [for her].

Since I'd done a business course, I was able to work for a company as a shorthand typist and bookkeeper. I worked for a long time for the Abelsons. They were the Jewish couple I'd helped cross over to the Free Zone. Madame Abelson really liked me. She taught me English and spoke to me in English all the time. She knew German, English, and French. She was very beautiful. Her husband wasn't handsome, but he was nice. He was a good man. After getting into the Free Zone, they stayed in the Limousin. But in 1944, the Germans left, so they wanted to go back [to Paris]. They finally returned to Paris and to their apartment, which was once again free, but the Germans had taken everything inside it. Samuel's face was horrible when they got back. His beard scratched us when we kissed him. And Madame Abelson, who'd been the prettiest and best-dressed woman in all of Saint-Petersburg, was dressed like a concierge, like a poor woman.

The Americans settled in Paris. A friend told me I should work for them. "You'll be well-paid," she said. So I began working for the Americans. And *voilà*! My Jim arrived in Paris. He'd been a regular soldier. He landed in Normandy, crossed France, and then went into Germany. He drove in a convoy and continued as far as Berchtesgaden. I have some photos.

He came to Paris and worked in my office. He was my boss and was very nice. We were all friends, both the men and the women. Then one day, Jim asked me, "What would you like me to bring you back from Switzerland?" I answered: some stockings. At that time, we painted our legs with colors because we didn't have stockings. When Jim came back, he brought me a bracelet, but no stockings.

Jim returned to America. When he left, there was no question at all of our marrying. We were good friends. We wrote for about a year. We liked each other, and he liked to read and write in French, so he was happy. We'd tell each other a whole lot of things, and we got to know each other very well. I learned that he was an intellectual, that he wanted to teach. One day, he wrote me, "Come to America." I answered, "No, it's too far, and so on."

He courted me for a year by letter. I'd say *oui*, then I'd say *non*. I couldn't decide. I thought he was a little crazy, that I couldn't depend on him. He was nice, but he wasn't a father, a mother or an uncle. "But Tony, don't you understand?" he asked. He explained that he wanted to marry me. I finally came to a decision. One day when he asked me whether it was *oui* or *non,* I answered *oui.* Later, Jim used to say, "You drove me crazy that year with your *oui/non, oui/non.* That was in 1947. I was 29.

It was easy to have a visa, because I was a war fiancée. I left for America by plane in 1947. At that time, people who'd fled from France during the war—Jewish people and others—were coming back to Paris, and they needed apartments. I had a very small apartment that wasn't worth much at all—it was just a room with a kitchen and a bathroom—but a Jewish family said to me, "If you let us have it, we'll pay your way to America."

So, I arrived in America. Jim, who was originally from Seattle, was waiting for me in San Francisco. We were married almost immediately by a judge at San Francisco City Hall. One of my husband's friends was our witness. Later on, were married at the French church of San Francisco. The priest wrote to my priest in Paris. We spent our honeymoon in Carmel. I was happy to be called Mrs. K.

I liked Americans' cheerfulness. The country I was coming from was *triste* [sad]. We'd lost family members, friends, Jewish people. The Germans.... We wanted to forget all that, all those memories. And here [in the United States] people had a lot of money. My husband had a small veteran's pension,[2] and we lived very well. We ate well. We were gay and joyful. After four years with no laughter or pleasure, with a lot of danger, all of a sudden we could go out at night. In France, we couldn't do that during the war. I never went out at night during all my youth in France. That was *triste* for a young woman.

Everyone was very nice with me—except for my in-laws. We went to see them in Seattle. Jim's mother had a new husband, and he drank too much. My brother-in-law, the husband of Jim's sister, was the brother-in-law of a captain in the American navy who'd been killed by a Frenchman. So, of course, [he had to talk about] the bad reputation of French women. "Marrying a French woman, are you?" He said to his wife, "Your brother is half-crazy. That doesn't surprise me." They housed us, but they were cold. They were rather *bourgeois,* so even if there hadn't been the war or if they weren't Americans.... Jim and I were a bit Bohemian.

Jim drank a bit much to my mind. We French drink, but that's all. When we visited my mother-in-law and her new husband, who drank, I used to say to Jim, "That's enough!" Later on, Jim no longer drank because of his position as a professor at Berkeley. But when he was young, he really did drink. I think it was a reaction to the war. He had some old friends, and.... All young Americans [back then] drank too much. But once he got married, and when he was studying and later teaching, he lost those bad habits. He was nice, though. When he drank too much, he fell asleep. I didn't like [his drinking]. But in every country there are people who drink too much and others who don't drink a lot.

Back then, we lived in an apartment, not a house, in the black district of San Francisco. I enjoyed that. People would ask me how I could live there. But I liked it. The Blacks laughed and were happy. For example, one night Jim had a cold and wanted some milk. It was midnight. I went down on Fillmore Street all by myself and started looking for milk. Some black people joked around with me, and I thought that was fun.

We were really Bohemians. We kept money in a drawer, and when we were hungry or wanted to travel, we'd just take out some money. One day, we opened the drawer, and there was practically nothing inside. Jim told me I had to go to work. I saw an ad for a job in an office. When I went there, the girl asked me, "Are you a French war bride?" I answered, "Yes. I love America, and my husband is very nice." "Well, you don't get the job," she said.

So, I answered a second ad. The guy who interviewed me looked at me and asked, "Are you from Paris, Madam?" I think he was very impressed. A lot of boys found me pretty back then.

So, I worked in offices. Jim went back to school, and I helped him get his degrees. Jim received a small war pension.[3] He studied to become an English teacher. Everybody knew my husband was a student, and they liked us because of that. Jim studied at Berkeley, and I worked in industry. He went up to the Master's level and then taught at a very good, a very well thought of, high school in San Francisco. He was offered a position at Berkeley, but he didn't have a Ph.D., so they suggested he get one. But he said, "No, I don't want to teach at the university level. I want to teach in a high school because that's where we mold young people." He loved the high school where he was. He loved teaching. He was much more of an intellectual than I was. Later on, he taught at Berkeley and was head of a small department, but he was always sorry to have left his high school students. Jim also loved San Francisco. But when he obtained his position as a professor at Berkeley, we left San Francisco and bought a house here in Orinda.

I worked in business for 20 years. Sometimes there were some old women in the office who didn't accept me. But too bad. I'd ask them, "How are you today?" and they wouldn't answer. There are people like that everywhere. One day, Jim said I should have the same profession as he did so that we could be together on vacations. It was true that when vacation time came round, I'd have to leave my job. People wouldn't give me two months' vacation. Jim said, "What you should do is go back to school. Get a degree in French and teach French. Then we'll both be in school and can study as well as teach." That's what I did, and we liked that a lot.

After he told me I should go back to school, I stopped working in business. I started studying at Berkeley, working towards an M.A. I taught in several schools in San Francisco. But then my professors wanted me to get a Ph.D., and I did, too. Jim said, "I don't know if you're going to like doing that, or if it's good for you. Working at a university is hard." He wasn't a proud man. I mean it didn't bother him if I had a Ph.D. and he didn't. He said everyone had to follow their own path. So I got a Ph.D. My dissertation was on Marie de France, a poetess. After that, I taught in a college that no longer exists: Lone Mountain. It belonged to the Sacred Heart nuns. I taught there for many years.

I had an experience at Lone Mountain. I had a student who, I'm sure, was a drug dealer. He was afraid of being arrested, so we hardly saw him in class. He'd come back and then go off again. I only saw him two or three weeks out of six. He was a very nice black student. But one day when I was correcting their exams, he came to see me with a friend of his who was just as big and just as handsome. He said, "Madame K.?" I answered, "Oh, there you are. And who's this? Is he your friend?" Then he said, "If you don't give me an A, I'll kill you." I replied, "Consider me dead then because you don't get an A!" Then I said, "Get out. Don't you see I'm busy?" I wasn't afraid. I liked him. After experiencing the war and the Germans [the German occupation], I wasn't afraid of a student. He got a B, but he deserved a C or a D.

In the beginning, when we were living in our small, modest apartment that wasn't expensive at all, we'd save everything Jim or I earned every month. Then we'd make a get away to France for June and July. I don't know how many times we went to France. I told myself that perhaps Jim would like it and want to stay, but he said, "Don't get it into your head that I want to live in France. I don't want to live in France. I still have an accent, and people make fun of me." I don't think anyone ever told him that. But he did feel a little inferior in France, and a man with an ego doesn't like experiencing that. You know, Americans are very proud of their country, and French people are often untactful; they say exactly what they think. It bothered him, and he didn't know French well enough to be able to have discussions. He liked going to France for awhile, but later on, starting at a certain point, he didn't like France as much, and he wanted to go there less. I never went to France without him, except after his death.

There were many French women in San Francisco. That's where I made the acquaintance of my very good friend, Colette. She'd also married an American. But our husbands didn't like each other very much. That's because Colette's husband was a worker, a workman.... I don't remember exactly what he did. And my husband was an intellectual. He loved the opera, the theater, the cinema. He was very *cultivé*.

Colette and I were both from Paris, so that was a link. We'd speak about France and the war. I think her father dealt a bit in the black market. He made jam, and if you had food, you could buy a lot of things. Money wasn't worth anything, but food was. We're still good friends. We don't see each other very often, because she's in South San Francisco and I'm in Orinda, but we call each other. All of a sudden one of us will feel like speaking to the other.

Colette had four children. I'm the godmother of the eldest one. I never regretted not having children because with all the arguments between children that occurred at my father and stepmother's house, I never really wanted to have children. Jim didn't want to have children, either. He wasn't sorry. He became a teacher almost at once, and he had children all day long. Well, too bad. We didn't have any children. Neither of us really minded. As it turned out, we were happy like that. Jim was intelligent. He wasn't selfish. On the contrary, he liked helping people.

In a way, I was his number one student. Each of us would write our own diary. That helped me a lot with my studies. When you write, you're obliged to formulate and to organize. Jim would give me advice. He'd say, "What you did is very good. It's well-organized."

It was Madame Hall, the president of the French War Brides, who introduced me to Colette. Madame Hall was a woman who came from the south of France—the *Midi*—like me. She was a war bride, *une mariée de guerre*, from the First World War. She never had children either. We had a lot in common, and we liked each other. We were like mother and daughter. She was from Bordeaux and had a Bordeaux accent. We actually weren't from very far apart. I lived in Paris, but I have a lot of Limousin blood, and I don't feel exactly like Parisian people.

Madame Hall worked for the American Red Cross in San Francisco. She also wrote for the French newspaper there, that is, *Le Courrier Français des Etats-Unis*. She was the one who brought me on board the paper. I stayed there from 1948 until 1963.

On December 1, 1948, I wrote an article about Madame Hall, who was, in fact, president of the National French War Brides Club. Here's an extract [from that article].

> The French War Brides Club, one of Madame Hall's main activities, could only have been created by an open-hearted, energetic, and active French woman, and one who is herself a French war bride.
>
> ...Madame Hall arrived for the first time in our great country in 1921 without even knowing the language. She overcame all her difficulties, doubts, and fears thanks to her desire to understand and to love and also to her confidence and her cheerfulness. Having "made a success of her life," she identified with other war brides and later wished to share her experience and offer her support to her young friends of the 1940s.

In June 1949, I wrote an article entitled "*Souvenirs de Guerre*" [war memories] in which I described Paris in June 1944: "Paris liberated, France liberated.... The years have gone by. My emotions and hopes from that time, like those of the people of France, have re-awoken on this anniversary...."[5]

The paper gave me a weekly column. Because I came from the center of France, I called these articles "Limousin Memories." The French people in San Francisco were all from the south of France, from the Auvergne, or from the Limousin, and they adored my articles. I wrote for more than 10 years. I was working at the same time. I wasn't paid. I did it out of love for my region.

Later, I wrote a column called "My Little Chronicle." And people loved it because I talked about them. I was a member of the French War Brides Club and belonged to the Alliance Française. I knew everyone in the French colony of San Francisco. The French newspaper attracted all the clubs. There were clubs like Peasants of the South, and others. I was mostly involved with the French War Brides. In January 1949, they organized a French gala, where I presented a little sketch that I'd written: "Mimi Learns English." It was about a love affair between a GI and a *Parisienne*.[6]

People liked my style of writing. They wanted to have me write articles for them. Writing all those articles made me feel like I wanted to write in French again, and I found my own style. When I was in school, I always liked to write. We had to do essays, *les compositions françaises*. I don't want to boast, but I was very good at them. There are a lot of things I can't do, but I do like to write. I adore it. For the first few years, I'd sign [my articles] "Antoinette K," but then, as of 1949, I became "Tony K." I still read those articles from time to time. There was a certain exaltation in the fact that I left France when it was in mourning and weakened—where things didn't work well and where we'd seen crimes. And I came here, to California and to the sun.

At one point, towards 1963, the paper was no longer going well. It was bought by *France-Amérique*. And the printer stole the lists of customers. In a way, I was a little like the soul of the paper, and they wanted me to continue writing, but I said *non*. Work for people who'd stolen those lists? *Non*. I was disgusted. Besides, we no longer lived in San Francisco. As long as I lived in San Francisco, it was okay. But when we left, it became more difficult. And by then, my courses required that I write.

There were about 50 of us in the war brides club. A lot of them arrived in San Francisco. Some of them stayed, but a lot left San Francisco because of their husband's work. And I knew some who didn't like America. There was one [war bride] who had a husband that Jim and I didn't like very much. His big fault was that he was tight with his money. His wife's name was Madeleine. He never wanted to spend his money; it was awful. My husband, on the contrary, was generous and open, and we spent our money. Later on, Madeleine's mother came to see her, and Madeleine went back to France with her mother. There were other French women who got divorced. The marriages worked better when the husband also spoke French. My husband spoke French at home. That's why I didn't lose my French. I know other war brides who today speak better English than French.

Jim died in 1976. We were supposed to go to France together, but he died several days before. One morning, a neighbor's daughter came to visit our garden, because we wanted her to water while we were away. And I remember that her mother came by car to pick her up and honked. And I said to her, "Adèle, don't honk. Don't do that. Jim is still asleep." They left, and I went in to see Jim. I thought it was a bit late—it was nine in the morning—for Jim to still be in bed. He was dead. It was horrible. It was his heart. He used to drink before, like a GI, but afterwards this wasn't good for him. He smoked a lot, and this gave me asthma. After he was buried, I wondered what I was going to do. I ended up by going to France on my own. I felt good—better—over there. I could speak French. I stayed with my grandniece.

Jim had been kind and clever. He had a strong personality that I really liked. He was intelligent, humorous, and also changeable from time to time. I never remarried. I had enough personality to get on without a husband. Except [for sex]. I didn't completely go without, but I didn't remarry. I regret this now. I would like *un petit mari* [a little husband] who's old like me.

I have to say that, before his death, Jim's and my love for each other was no longer what it was in the beginning. First off, because his position separated us. He preferred high school, and I preferred college. And that also implied deeper differences. He was very authoritarian, and I didn't like authority very much. As I was Catholic, getting a divorce never entered my mind. Let's just say, things weren't going as well as before. And then, there was *une petite femme* [a little woman].... One day, after he said something unpleasant to me, I answered: "*Mon vieux*, get a divorce if you want. But I'm keeping the house." He adored his house. All of a sudden, he didn't want to get divorced anymore. We still got on well, but it wasn't the same....

At the time of my husband's death, Lone Mountain College was having a lot of problems, and I decided to resign. It was impossible at my age to find another position near where we lived. I didn't want to go to Nebraska, or some other such place. So, what did I do? One day when I was reading the paper, I saw an ad: "Company selling wood is looking for..." I was a widow, and I needed money. I told myself I should apply. If they didn't want me, they didn't want me. Because I'd been told that when you're a professor and you want to work in business, you shouldn't say you're a professor. Well, I said, too bad. I'm not going to deny I'm a professor. And if they don't want me, I don't care.

So, I went [to the company] dressed in navy blue with a white blouse. The boss told me later that when he saw me, he thought, "If we don't take that woman, she'll go and enlist in the Navy." The assistant manager didn't want [to hire] me. He didn't want somebody who'd be showing off. But the owner of the company said, "Listen, it could be amusing. She'd bring in some new ideas." He hired me. And I succeeded in the business. I earned a lot of money [at that company]. I had a much better salary in business than I had in schools. Every three months, the boss would tally up the profits and share them with his workers.

All the while, I continued studying and writing. I am a specialist of French literature of the Middle Ages. I returned to Berkeley and the Department of Comparative Literature. I wrote a book about Marseilles that is really thick. My thesis was published. But the book I wrote on Saint Dominique was never published. I'm Catholic but not religious. Saint Dominique is [like] another god for some people. I said things the way they were, and the Dominicans didn't like this. And other people thought the things I said were too much in the vein of their [the Dominicans'] religion. In short, no one liked what I said. But I'm still pleased with my book.

I'd now like to write a book about Marie-Madeleine and entitle it *Marie-Madeleine Courtoise*. The word *courtoise* refers to the young girl—the young woman—who was courted by the troubadours of the twelfth century. And this was a period when Marie-Madeleine was very much in vogue in France.

People said things [to show] she was a saint, but all these things were invented. She was a woman who wrote *courtois* tales, and the vogue for Marie-Madeleine occurred when *courtois* literature—the literature that arose between the 1twelfth and thirteenth centuries—was flourishing. I want to explain why.

After receiving my doctorate, I studied Italian and Spanish. I never have an opportunity to speak these languages, but I can read them very well. I traveled everywhere. To Italy, France, in the east, in the south—everywhere—to give conferences. I received a grant from the AUW—American University Women—to go to Italy. I put them in my will to thank them. To my mind, I've had quite an extraordinary life. And [at first] I was just a shorthand typist.

During the war, I felt that I was called upon to do something important, something different. God helped me and guided me during all those times I crossed over into the Free Zone. I could have been captured on several occasions. This being said, they were especially looking for Jews.

I live all alone in this house today. I do a lot of things here. I spent $400 to have the trees in the back pruned. But the gardener didn't do the hill very well, so I was the one who finished it. My house is really clean. That's my peasant side. I have a swimming pool. I'm happy.

In the beginning, I liked everything French. But after 20 years, there were French people I didn't like. Instead of just liking French people, I now have a lot of American friends. I have some who speak French or have a little link with French people. But I like people because I like them and not because they like France. There are a lot [of people] I like at my church. There's a Jesuit, for example. People like the Jesuits a lot in France. The Jesuits were created in France.[7] When I was a little girl, I attended a Jesuit school.

I'm still a Catholic and I'm quite a practicing one. I went to mass this morning. I often go in the morning. But I don't belong to any special group. I'm just a member of the Church of Santa Maria.

I'm happy I came here. I feel very American, even though Americans still think I'm French, perhaps because of my accent. And the French think I'm really American.

I feel I'm both. I have American citizenship. Inside, there are things I approve of in the American environment, and there are French things I prefer. For example, the way cooking is done and French food. I wouldn't make porridge in the morning. In the morning, it's toast, eggs, fruit. But I make a French meal on Shrove Tuesday. I make crepes. I prefer a roast to stew. My mother-in-law never stopped making stews. I like roasted things, roast chicken.

I wouldn't dare drive here alone at night. But in France I would. And Frenchmen are really funny. "And what would *la petite dame* like?" "She's cute, *la petite*." An American would never say that. There's a certain openness in France. You don't know somebody in France, but you speak to them. Is that because here in Orinda, it's a bit *collet monté* [snobbish]? Perhaps. But when I'm a long time in Paris, I've had enough. I'm more independent in the United States. I've been alone in this house for 25 years. I lost my job, but I got other ones.

Twelve

"*MA PETITE FRANCE*"

When Jacqueline B-P. speaks about members of her family and close relations, she calls them "mon amour de père, mère, frère, amie..." meaning "my beloved father, mother, brother, friend..." And she calls her native France "mon joli petit pays" [my pretty little country] or "ma petite France" [my little France]. However, whenever her marriage to an ex-GI is spoken of, she is adamant in saying it was the worst bêtise *[stupidity] of her life.*

Jacqueline has been divorced for over 30 years and swore to herself she would never remarry. She raised her daughter, her only child, on her own. Her daughter went to college and is now a schoolteacher. As for Jacqueline, after a long career as an executive assistant, she is now retired and the grandmother of two little girls. She lives in Claremont, a small university town in the southern part of California.

During our conversation, Jacqueline was very frank, and she spoke to me as if I was a friend. We got on well and have remained in touch. Here is her story.

I was born in 1953 in Mirecourt, in the Vosges Mountains, but I spent most of my adolescence in Nancy. Papa was a judge. He was *un amour* of a father. I was very lucky insofar as my parents are concerned, and I had a happy childhood. Papa died very young, before I met my husband, but I also had *un amour* of a mother and *un amour* of a brother. I always say I had two wonderful men in my life: my father and my brother. And, after all, that isn't too bad. But having an adorable father is almost a handicap [afterwards], because no other man can ever measure up to him.

In Nancy, both during and after the war, we suffered greatly from hunger, as did most people who lived in cities. People in the country managed by exchanging and finding certain things. But people in the cities, even if they had money, couldn't find anything to eat. We were really not in a good way. And there wasn't anything for young people my age to do. There weren't any dances, and movies were only German propaganda, so we didn't go. There was a curfew, too. Sometimes it was at 7 p.m., sometimes at 5 p.m., after some Germans were killed by the Resistance. We had fun among ourselves because, you know, young people always find ways of having fun. But we were hungry, and we were dressed like beggars. It was a horrible time, and there was no entertainment. In five years, we lost the best years of our youth—I was, let's see, 17—well, the best years of our adolescence. Not only me, but my whole generation.

I studied in Nancy. I got my baccalaureate, and, at the same time, I studied at the Nancy Music Conservatory. I was a pianist. I took piano and organ classes, and also studied acting, but my real instrument was the piano. My cousin, who was also a graduate of the Conservatory, and I did some concerts. I gave piano lessons part-time in addition to my regular work as a cashier with the American army. This was first in Nancy and then later in Paris, where I worked in PX's [Post Exchanges]. We were still suffering from hunger, so I was really glad to work at a place where I could eat chocolate! I worked afterwards for the Joint Construction Agency. This was a group of American engineers working in conjunction with France's *Ponts et Chaussées* [corps of civil engineers]. They built railway systems, water towers, and all those American army bases.

I met my husband at an American club. At that time, after the war, we'd go dancing. There were clubs, American Red Cross dances. My husband was, in fact, my cousin's boyfriend. I swiped him, and I was really punished for it afterwards! But, I was young and innocent at the time. I thought he was sexy and had a lot of charm. And it's true that he really was charming, and he had a good sense of humor. He was very funny. But, of course, I realize now that I didn't always understand his [type of] humor. Anyway, he could be very funny. I thought I loved him! But, in fact, it was above all a question of sex. I got trapped in all that and didn't reflect on which qualities are really worthwhile.

When I first met him, he was working for the American Grave Registration Command, the AGRC. He was a prosthesist by trade, that is, he worked for dental laboratories making false teeth, bridges, things like that.

He'd fought in Italy. Once the war was over, he went back to the United States, to Washington D.C., to apply for a job, and he was sent back to

Europe as a civilian. He stayed in France for several years. I met him, I think, in 1945, or in 1946. We got married in 1948, and we stayed in France until 1950.

My whole family was against my marriage, but, of course, I thought I knew everything. When you're young, you think you know everything. I also think I was a bit angry with France at the time. Because *mon amour de Papa*—who'd lost a part of his foot during the First World War—had told me there'd never be another war. It was, people said, *la der des ders*—"the war to end all wars." But war was again declared, and that made *mon amour de Papa* a liar. On top of it all, we lost it [the "False War" of 1939–1940], and then there was the German occupation. That was why I was angry with France.

My husband wasn't mean, but he was a totally irresponsible man. He did whatever he wanted whenever he wanted to. He was, in fact, a bit of a victim of the war. And when he came to Europe, he fell in love with it and no longer wanted to go back to America. From that time on he detested America. And this didn't make it very easy for me when I arrived in the United States. Because instead of helping me adapt, he kept saying: "America's awful. We'd be better in France." And this didn't help the situation.

We started out in Buffalo. This was really just by chance, as my husband found a job there. He went there first, and I joined him there later. I had to wait in France because it was difficult getting my papers. Then I joined up with him in Buffalo, where we stayed for awhile. But my life with that man was really awful. He was so whimsical about keeping to a schedule that he often lost his job. He'd find another one, then lose it, too. He was the type who'd say, for example, "Hey. We don't have any more bread. I'll go and get some at the grocery store." And then he'd come back three weeks later—without any bread!

I often found myself alone. I hardly spoke English, and my husband left me without a penny for weeks. That was really very, very hard. I felt so desperate one day about being all alone in this country with such a husband that I took a walk along Niagara Falls intending to throw first my daughter, then myself [into the water]. But *un amour* of a Belgian lady, who lived in the same building and who was the same age as me, literally saved my life. She'd seen how my husband was treating me, and when she saw me leave the building, she followed me. I didn't know she was behind me. She really did save my life, and I'm very grateful to her. Unfortunately, she died several years ago.

The biggest problem was that my husband drank. He went to bars and only came back three weeks later. Sometimes he returned without the car because he'd lost it somewhere and he no longer remembered where. Nobody in my family drank. Of course, like a lot of French people, we lived like kings and queens when we ate or drank, but I never saw anyone in my family or among my acquaintances drink excessively. I didn't know alcoholics existed.

After awhile, my husband and I decided to separate amicably. I went back to France and lived with my mother and her maid. I found another job with the Americans and began a new life. Everything was going well. We lived at the time in a very pretty apartment, and I was happy to be with my mother and my little daughter. But, following an R.I.F. [Reduction in Force, or downsizing], I lost my job. And almost at the same time, *mon amour de Maman* died. I found myself completely at a loss, not knowing what to do.

Coincidentally, but also unfortunately, my husband arrived in Paris about that time. He told me, "I miss you. I miss the baby, etc." I was in such a sorry state that I thought that perhaps, after all, we could start again. I felt guilty because my daughter didn't have her father, and I'd adored my own Papa. So I came back, and that was my second big mistake.

This time we went to Los Angeles. My husband was originally from California. He was quite nice for a month, but then it all started again. Our situation was like a sinking ship. I wanted to save my daughter and myself from a shipwreck. So, I said I wanted a divorce. My husband didn't contend my decision. In fact, he completely disappeared. Even his mother—and I think he loved his mother, who was probably the only person in the world he loved—even she didn't know where he was. He completely disappeared. And, of course, he never gave me a penny for our daughter. He never helped me. I had a hard life, and that didn't help my liking the United States very much.

I also did something very stupid. My husband let me have custody of my little daughter, whom I adored. So I thought to myself, "This poor man. He doesn't have his daughter. He doesn't have anything." And I took out a loan to give him some money—this was in 1960—to help him start over a new life. It was 5,000 dollars, which was quite a lot of money in those days. The judge thought I was crazy, but I was a generous person. I borrowed money to help him start over, and he spent it in a month buying drinks for his friends. I took it to heart to pay back that loan because I didn't want people thinking French people don't pay back their debts.

So, because of my own stupidity, I found myself stuck in the United States. It took me years to pay back that money, and during that time my daughter grew up and became more American than French.

I was working then for an airbase in Ontario, here in California, of course—not in Canada. It wasn't very easy bringing up my daughter on my own. I couldn't ever save much money. I didn't have much income, but I wanted my daughter to continue her studies. I sent her to college and then for a Master's degree. We managed as best we could, but there was never much money left for little trips to Europe. But when I retired in 1992—no, it was in 1988—well, then I paid for three months' vacation in France. That made me really happy.

I didn't see my husband for at least 20 years and then—it's an absurd story—one day, out of the blue, when my daughter was 22 or 23, my husband's uncle came to tell us he was very ill. I answered that I was sorry, but that I couldn't do anything about that. Besides, I said, I no longer have anything to do with him.

But my daughter, who's *un amour* of a daughter, said, "But we should still take care of him." She asked what hospital he was in. He was at a veterans' hospital, something like a Veterans' Administration Hospital. But I told her she didn't owe the man anything, that he'd never done anything for her. However, she's *un amour* of a girl, and she went to see him in the hospital. She learned that he was about to be kicked out for one reason or another, and she thought it was terrible because he still needed care. Coincidentally, she had a doctor friend at that hospital. So she went to ask him if he could do something so that her father could stay at the hospital until he was better. That doctor was very nice. He arranged everything, and they took really good care of my husband. My daughter went every day to Long Beach to see him. And, you know, that's quite a trek. Her father ended up dying in that hospital at the age of 60. My daughter is happy to have done what she did, to have known her father, since she knew him so little when she was young.

I'll always regret making such a stupid mistake marrying that man. I got trapped by my own stupidity. I can't blame anyone else. I really regret ruining my life. And I'd been so lucky to have such good parents who'd provided me with as many opportunities as possible! I hadn't understood anything, and I ruined everything. But that's the way it is! And, after all, I'm not that unhappy, because I am lucky enough to have a nice daughter and nice grand-daughters. And I also have some nice friends.

I haven't had a boyfriend during all these years. I found that the men I met were always a little inferior to me, and I don't like living with inferior people! [Once] I said to my friend André, who's a Frenchman I know here, "You're almost at my level. Not entirely, but almost!" We laughed a lot about that. There aren't many good men, except for André. We women are fabulous!

I had to become an American citizen at the time when I was working for the Air Force because I had to have a Top Security Clearance—I don't know how you say that in French—and I had to become naturalized. I vote in the United States but without much conviction because I'm an idealist by temperament. I like to vote for someone I believe in, but in the end, I think they're all clowns. In fact, I only have two criteria when I vote. I look at the names, and then I vote for women and for Jews. First, I look for the women, but if there aren't enough with women's names, then I look for a Jewish name. Not because I'm Jewish myself, but because I'm a musician, and the Jews are the best musicians in the world. They have very pronounced sensitivity because they were persecuted for years. In fact, they're still being persecuted.

I find the English language rather easy. I studied German before, and I found German grammar very difficult. That's why when I arrived in the United States, I thought, grammatically speaking, English was a very easy language. It's also a very pretty language, and I like it a lot. But I think the pronunciation is still quite difficult for French people. I have an accent when I speak, but that doesn't bother me because Americans usually like a French accent. I can speak English very easily nowadays, and I don't even realize when I go from one language to the other. But when I'm in a crisis situation, or when I have a dream, it's always in French.

Many Americans are excessively nice, but the American way of life doesn't suit me. I don't like the fact that people don't eat meals together, that they grab a sandwich on the run. Not everyone, of course, but the majority of them. Someone meets you and takes the liberty of calling you "Jacqueline" right away. I don't like that. I don't like those types of manners. I call people "Mr." and "Mrs.," and I expect people to do the same.

I have some very good American friends whom I'm really fond of, but I must admit that I find most Americans very superficial in their affection. They seem to be your friend, and a week later, they don't remember who you are. That shocks me. I think we're much more cautious in France. It takes longer to make friends, but once you've made them, the relationship is very stable.

Even if I'm of French origin, I've never suffered from discrimination here. I think that's because Americans don't usually take French people very seriously. In a way, they think French women are *ooh la la* girls and that French men are "French lovers." It's a bit insulting, but it's not usually meant in a mean way. There's no animosity. I've never experienced any other kind of discrimination.

But I feel I'm constantly being suffocated by religion [here]. In France, I never think about it; no one pays any attention to it, and they don't talk about it all the time. I miss the secular environment of France. You hear

"God Bless America" all the time here. There are prayers and all that at each meeting you attend, and this gets on my nerves. There is supposedly separation of Church and State, but even on each dollar bill, there's "In God We Trust." It's completely incongruous. And there are so many different—so many useless—religious groups.

As for me, I'm an atheist. When Americans hear this, they say, "I'll pray for you." They say it nicely, but I find it insulting. So I usually reply, "Please don't!" I'd find it totally impossible to believe in anything. I believe in me; I believe in you. From time to time I go to an atheists' club in Los Angeles. They have a dinner at Christmastime, and it's marvelous to be among fellow atheists. The atmosphere is so healthy! There aren't all those superstitions and stupidities.

Yes, I really like going to that club, but it's quite far away for me to go there by myself. Los Angeles is so big, and you risk taking the wrong direction [when you go by car]. You really have to be careful. It's also very dangerous. Crimes exist everywhere, but I think in Los Angeles we take the cake! And I think since the Simpson trial racial differences are even more aggravated than before.

I'm constantly homesick. When I went back to France in 1988, after being there a week, I felt as if I'd never left. There'd been changes, of course. But there are things in *ma petite France* that have still remained the same.

I feel 200 percent French. The older I get, the more French I am. I'd like to get back my French citizenship. It's possible to do it, but I'd have to make the long trip to Los Angeles and go to the Consulate, where they're not always very nice. I don't really feel up to it. I have an old car, and I'm afraid to take it that far. And I tell myself that it's just a piece of paper, and in my heart I'm French. I'm very proud of French thought. I'm proud of our system . . . and of a whole lot of things.

In the United States I'm a Democrat, but in France I'm a Royalist. I like pretty things and castles. I'm so happy Louis XIV left us Versailles. I forgive him for everything he did because he gave us so much beauty! I think that's what I like most in the world—beauty, in all its forms. In music, in literature, in a rose. Among people, too, and not only physical beauty but beauty of the soul and beauty of emotion. I don't believe in God, but I do believe in beauty.

Thirteen

From New Caledonia to Los Angeles

After Georgette answered one of the ads I put in a French newspaper published in the United States, I interviewed her at her home in Los Angeles in 1995. We have seen each other several times since then in Paris when she comes over for the Paris Book Fair. Having lost her second husband since our original interview, she now devotes a great deal of time to writing and has produced two books. Georgette has always very much encouraged me in my own writing.

I was born in Noumea. Our family has been in New Caledonia since the end of the nineteenth century. It's a very beautiful island, and I am very attached to it, even though I have only been back there twice since when I left in 1945.

My great-grandfather was Irish. He left County Cork with his four brothers to make a fortune in the gold mines of Australia. Then, while they were in Australia, they heard that John Jacob Astor[1] was seeking sandalwood. At the time, Mr. Astor was transporting furs from Canada to China, and his ships returned empty from China. So my great-grandfather and three of his brothers bought a boat and started trading along the coasts of New Caledonia and other islands, swapping old nails and the rings around casks in exchange for sandalwood. Unfortunately, there was a huge storm during one of their voyages. My great-grandfather's boat ran aground on some reefs, and he was eaten by the indigenous people!

My grandfather, who was only 10 when his father died, was also Irish. He was the one who came to settle permanently in New Caledonia. He had

14 children. There are members of our family everywhere in New Caledonia nowadays. In the beginning, my grandfather only spoke English, but he had to learn French very quickly.

As for my father, despite his Irish name, he didn't speak a word of English. There's a family story about this. One day, some Australians came to see him. He kept saying to them, "You don't speak English. You don't speak English." The Australians were perplexed, but they went on talking. What Papa wanted to say, of course, was "*I* don't speak English" instead of "*You* don't speak English."

My parents had six children—three boys and three girls—and I was the eldest. I was brought up in a very strict, very Catholic, way by the sisters of Saint Joseph de Cluny. But I became disgusted by the church when I was about nine because I was told a girl couldn't be Pope! I studied until the baccalaureate. I had a very good teacher, Timothée Auriol, who was a former student of both Henri Bergson[2] and Pagnol.[3] I wanted to go to the Sorbonne to continue my studies because back then there wasn't a university in Noumea. In any case, it wouldn't have been possible. There was the war, and I also got married. But when I married my husband, I made him promise that one day I could continue my studies.

The Americans landed in Noumea in '42. I remember that day very well. It was March 12, 1942. I was riding my bicycle up the hill of the Colons Valley—it was a Saturday, and I was on my way to play tennis—when what do I see? Thousands and thousands of American soldiers coming down the hill! "March! March! Keep marching until nighttime!" Nobody knew they'd landed. We weren't told anything about the war.

I think something like a million American soldiers and sailors came through New Caledonia during the war. But we didn't know anything—or very little—about what was happening. From time to time, we'd see the wounded arrive, but that was all.

Thanks to the Americans, we were very, very lucky. The Japanese never bombed us or invaded [our island]. We also had a really good time with all those young Americans. Since there were very few women in relation to the number of men, we were [treated] absolutely like queens. When the Americans came back to New Caledonia from the war, there were lots of things for them. There were shows with Jack Benny and Larry Adler.[4] There were outdoor movie theaters and dances. It was a wonderful life!

The Americans also helped us financially. I remember one day I saw my sister sewing some little handkerchiefs. When I asked her what she was doing, she said, "I'm embroidering these little hankies to sell them to the Baland

Company. They buy them from me for a dollar each and then sell them to the Americans." I exclaimed, "But I can do that, too! I'm going to paint them." I'd taken some painting lessons and knew how to paint on material with some special paint.

So I got the whole family working on our kitchen table, which was very large. I bought material and cut it. Then Maman would spread out the material, one brother did this, another brother did that, a sister did something else, etc. After that, I painted on a little native girl with words like "Hi, Man!" or "Hello, Sweetheart!" We sold them to the Americans, and I made a small fortune. It worked so well that even if I was still young, I was able to open a souvenir shop.

I had a little apartment of my own and earned a rather good living. I was very independent. I used to shock my girlfriends. Even as a child, rather than playing dolls with the girls, I preferred playing football with the boys. I remember once I wanted to bike all over the island and asked two boys who were friends to accompany me. They said their parents wouldn't want them to. So I went to see their parents, and they agreed. They told their sons: "All right, but only because it's with Georgette."

One day, a young man, an American sailor, stops in front of my shop. He looks at me; I look at him. Then he asks me—in English, of course—if the shop belongs to me. I say "yes" and ask him who he is. He answers that he's Admiral Halsey's[5] photographer. His name is Glenn. He comes back several times to the shop. We begin to go out. And later we marry. This is in '45.

Glenn was from a small town in Texas. When he was young, say about 10, he met a man called "Willard the Wizard."[6] He was a [famous] magician who traveled from town to town. He made a great impression on my husband, and they became friends. Glenn introduced me to him later on. So when my husband was very young, he became a professional illusionist, and he joined the troop of the very famous Howard Thurston.[7]

Glenn had made J. Edgar Hoover's watch disappear, and he got a lot of publicity because of this. He went to England. Glenn was a marvelous man. He could be friends with the gardener or with kings and queens. He had a really good career in Europe. He learned how to use a Leica, and he became a good photographer. The army made him Admiral Halsey's aerial photographer. When [the battle of] Guadalcanal began, he flew over Guadalcanal and other islands taking photographs. He fought at Guadalcanal, but he really didn't like being a soldier.

We got married in the City Hall of Noumea at the end of 1945, and he was repatriated almost right afterwards. He left first in one ship, and

I followed him in another ship, the *General Polk*. There were about 10 women and hundreds of troops [on board]. We didn't mix at all. Glenn was already in San Francisco. We went under the Golden Gate, and there were all those ships, with firemen's boats spraying water everywhere to welcome us. The boats were all around us. There was music; they played "California Here We Come." We were among the first to come back after the war. It was really wonderful.

When I arrived, I was welcomed by a magician friend of Glenn's because Glenn hadn't been demobilized yet. His friend told me they'd reserved a room for me at the Hotel Mark Hopkins. Glen was demobilized that same day, and we celebrated at the Mark Hopkins. It was really fantastic—a real honeymoon. We were up there in the clouds with a marvelous view. But we could only stay for five days. No one could have a room for more than five days after the war.

We stayed for awhile in San Francisco. Glenn again started to get bookings. I replaced his sister, who'd been his assistant during the war. His show was called "Magic Flirtation." I'd hold a little parasol and wear a pretty long dress with a ribbon around the waist. We'd play the songs "A Pretty Girl is like a Melody" or "In a Small Hotel." Then Glenn would come towards me. To attract my attention, he'd catch the ribbon, pull it, and then cut it in two. I'd pretend to say: "Oh, no! He's cut my belt!" All of this was done in pantomime. And then, *voilà*! The ribbon was once again straight and uncut! I appeared astonished. After that, he'd ask to borrow my parasol. He'd take my little bag, open it, show the objects inside, put the parasol into a small, rolled-up, straw mat, do "hocus-pocus" over both the bag and the mat, and then take out the parasol again. All the various objects that were in my bag—my lipstick, comb, and mirror—would be hanging from the ends of the parasol. It was a very funny show.

I did that for five years. Glenn knew a lot of people, and I met many very interesting people. He loved to travel and to show me things. We went across America from coast to coast. We worked in Grand Canyon, Yellowstone, Yosemite, and Sequoia National Parks. When we were in New York, I said to him: "Do you remember you promised me one day I could go to college?" So, I took courses at Columbia University for a year.

Unfortunately, though, if your profession is being a magician, you can't stay in one place. You have to move. My husband went to work in New Orleans and Texas. He'd come back from time to time to see me in New York. He didn't like me staying in New York.

As for me, I was in seventh heaven. I lived in International House. Simone de Beauvoir[8] and Albert Camus[9] came to lecture at the French House, where

I belonged to a small group of students. I offered to show Albert Camus around New York and took him to the Empire State Building and other places. We became friends.

I really liked Columbia, but I realized I couldn't stay because you're either married or you're a student. In addition, my husband did something very clever. He found bookings in Paris. He knew very well that I wasn't going to stay in America with him in Paris.

We went to Europe towards the end of 1949. Our first booking was at the Enghien Casino [just outside Paris], then in La Baule, then in Paris at the Medrano Circus near Place Clichy.

My husband made a very good living. The only problem was that all the money disappeared in between bookings. I'd put money away in New Caledonia, and it was my money that paid the bills when we didn't have any bookings. This didn't bother me until the day when there wasn't any left.

Also, after five years together, I realized that this wasn't the kind of life I wanted. My husband liked to go from one city to the next meeting people. He was always invited out, and he drank too much. People kept buying him rounds of drinks. I tried, but I realized you can't change an alcoholic. He has to want to change.

What I wanted was to write. For example, I could've written like Colette[10] about the seamy side of music hall life, but I didn't really like that kind of life. I'd written a little bit for *France Illustration* and for *Paris Soir*, but that paid very little. In fact, I wanted to write what *I* wanted to write, not what somebody else told me to write. I wanted to be independent.

So when I saw that all my money was disappearing and that my husband was never going to change, I said to myself, "You're going to find yourself trapped with an alcoholic husband in a way of life you don't like. Get out quickly, my dear. It's over." I think I had $250 left in my pocket, and the trip to Los Angeles cost me about $180. When I got here, I only had $50 left in my pocket and a watch that my husband had given me when we first got here. I had to pawn it twice, but I still have it.

After arriving in Los Angeles, I worked in a souvenir shop, but this time it wasn't mine. I lived on hamburgers for many years. But little by little, I managed to get establishedp. I sold Avon and Fuller brush products, as well as vitamins, music classes, tulips, and chinchillas. I wrote for a newspaper and interviewed stars during the '50s and '60s. Finally, after buying and selling apartments, I carved out a good career for myself in real estate.

I love France and French culture. Everything I've written is in French. I also adore New Caledonia. I knew Melanesians[11] when I lived there, and

I know a lot of people from New Caledonia here in California. But I always wanted to travel, to see the world, to be near big cities.

I adore America. I feel more American than French in my way of thinking and being. I remarried in 1962. Robert, my second husband, was a diplomat and then worked in advertising. We share the same interests, and we've traveled a lot together. And now that we're both retired, I finally have time to write.

Fourteen

VIVE LA REINE!

Reine D. is the sister of a dear friend and colleague who passed away several years ago. The mother of eight children, nineteen grandchildren, and three great-grandchildren, she is the wife of a retired physician whom she met in Marseille during the war. The family live in Arkansas, and Reine speaks with a delightful Midwestern twang, whereas her sisters, both former English teachers in France, have very pronounced British accents. Reine provided very detailed written answers to my questionnaire, and we spoke at length on the phone

I was born in the summer of 1923 in the town of Mazamet in the *Montagne Noire* in the department of the Tarn. I was the third daughter and I was named "Reine" because people were sorry I was not a boy! They were sorry for my father and for me. [However,] when I was born, Paul M., a cousin in Paris who was a professor of mathematics at the Sorbonne sent a telegram with the words: *Vive la Reine!*

Mazamet was a small, Protestant, industrial town where they tanned skins and wove wool imported from Australia. My father was the principal of a technical school which was called Ecole de Commerce et d' Industrie at the time, and now called College Technique Marcel Pagnol.

Both my parents were school teachers and had been educated at the Ecole Normale [teacher training school] of Aix-en-Provence. They had high ideals and were the product of the Third Republic. They believed in free education for all. *Liberté, Egalité, Fraternité* was the motto. Public schools became secular but there very strict ethics.

When World War I broke out, my father was teaching applied mathematics and mechanics in a technical school in Marseille. He went through four years of war and became a lieutenant after being wounded. The last year of the war he taught airplane mechanics to American soldiers in Lyon. In 1934, he took my mother and me to see the battlefields in northern France.

My parents were married in 1918. Both families were from Marseille. Our ancestors were buried in the Jewish section of St. Pierre cemetery. The two families knew each other. Their backgrounds were *artisanat* [as artisans, craftsmen]. My father's ancestors worked on boats and on naval steam engines. They worked in shipyards and on the Suez Canal. My mother's father was a saddle and harness maker in the luxury category.

Living in the little town of Mazamet was a break from living in Marseille. Father had fought what he believed would be the last war. The school was a boarding school, and my parents had an apartment in the school. My mother was the purser and dietitian. She had a cook, a cleaning woman, and a laundry woman. I was born in the upstairs master bedroom.

After two years in Mazamet, my parents moved to a larger school in Agen, in the Lot et Garonne. The school was a boys' school and had just moved to a building that had been a seminary. At the entrance door of the school were the words we read every day: *Liberté, Egalité, Fraternité* engraved in stone. The school had dormitories and a big park in the back with linden and horse chestnut trees, and on one side, old canons and a canteen from the war of 1870. During summer vacations, my sisters and I had lots of fun running around there. I can say we had a happy childhood.

My father was active. He would awake early and go and hand ring the bell to get the students started for the day. We were a happy family raised with moral values. My father would talk to us about philosophy and religion. He was a freemason, and one of his grandparents was Jewish. But he always told us that he wouldn't impose religious beliefs on us. We could make our own decisions when we were mature.

We lived in Agen from 1924 to 1934. During that period we had English girls living *au pair* [as live-in babysitters] in our home. They would learn French and speak English with us. I became bilingual at three years of age. My sisters and I went to school at the *lycée de jeunes filles* [girls' high school]. We rode bicycles, played tennis, had vacations in the Pyrenees and the Basque country.

Agen was a town that had no Jews. One day in 1933, someone called me a "dirty Jew." I was 10 years old. Hitler had a "fifth column" somewhere around town.

In the summer of 1934 my parents moved back to Marseille. My father became principal of the Technical School there. It had been his dream to occupy that position since World War I had interrupted his teaching career. He was a very good principal. He had many friends in industry and was trusted by many other principals, the mayor of the town, and the rector of the *Académie* [regional education authority] wherever we lived. Shortly before World War II, he was decorated with the *Légion d'honneur* for his work in technical education, and he had the highest level of the *Palmes Académiques* [honorary award to teachers and professors]. We had a large apartment with a view on the Mediterranean Sea.

I attended classes at the Lycée Montgrand. We spent weekends and holidays with our cousins. We would go to Les Lecques, La Ciotat, Bandol, or on picnics at Gemenos. In winter, we'd go and have tea on the Cours Mirabeau in Aix-en-Provence.

One sunny afternoon in October, Father told us he noticed from our apartment window a flotilla of navy vessels escorting the boat carrying King Alexander of Yugoslavia. But, a few minutes after being greeted by the members of the French government, the car of the King and Minister Barthou was gunned down by an *Oustachi*.[1] They were both killed,[2] and the *oustachi* got away. We were in school when this happened, but afterwards, schools were all closed.

I realized that living in a big town was quite different from living in Agen. Life continued normally after this serious incident. But the people of Marseille did not forget it. In 1944,[3] when Yugoslavia joined the allies, even though we were under German occupation, we deposited flowers at the place where the King died.

After our arrival in Marseille, my parents' goal was for us to complete our education. My sisters studied for the baccalaureate. Alice was so young she had to ask for special permission to take the exam. I was a good student, even though I didn't like to read very much and never really learned how to study. Most of the knowledge I acquired was from Father's conversations and from my sisters' *répétitions*. I could reason, and I was good in science and geography; I loved maps. Mathematics came to me naturally. I took the A *bac* [Latin, English, and math] exam and passed in 1940. For the second part, I chose science and mathematics, but it took me two years to get it because the curriculum was hard and I was distracted by the war.

In September 1939 I'd seen big tears come down Father's cheeks. The myth of World War I being the last war was shattered. But life went on anyway. From 1939 to the Armistice of 1940, during what was called the *drôle de guerre*, Father had the school shops participate in war manufacture. We still lived inside the school. The basement was made into a shelter during the day for Father's students, and at night for the neighborhood. We learned how to have our gas masks ready. At the sound of the siren, we would get dressed, close the shutters, leave the window slightly open, turn off the gas and electricity, and rush downstairs. One day, the doorkeeper told my mother: "Madame, even if the bomb fell close by, your hat would still be on at the right angle!" We had to keep our dignity. My Mother loved perfection.

Then came the first day of school, October 1941. With one telephone call, Father was dismissed, with no salary, from his position as principal. What was the reason? The Vichy government's *statut des juifs et des franc-maçons.*[4] Father only had one Jewish grandparent on his father's side. According to Vichy law, you were only Jewish if you had three Jewish grandparents. He had married a Jewish lady, but at the City Hall of Marseille, not at church. Apparently, this was a sign that he wanted to be Jewish. On top of everything, he had arrived at a high degree in masonry. All of this was the reason for his dismissal.

Papa's family was an old family from Provence and the Comtat. My father's mother was born near Gap in the Alps at Serres. My grandfather had had relatives in La Ciotat and Nice. Before the Third Republic there was no separation of church and state. Marriages and births were only recognized if they were registered by the Catholic church. Apparently, my grandparents did not want to have a Catholic wedding. After 1870, when it was the City Hall that registered vital statistics, my grandparents registered four children and their nuptial vows. They had many more children after that and the whole situation became legal. They lived close to the synagogue. The older children went to school there. That school became a public school and my father, who was number seven in the family, went to grade school there.

After 1940, I remember my mother repeating many times that Napoléon had emancipated French Jews. They were equal to any French citizens. Those of Provence had had citizenship much longer than any others in France. They had had an important role in French history. The government of Vichy would not touch them. It was tragic for her when these laws were applied and extended and French Jews were taken to the Holocaust.

We had to get out of the school apartment. My father didn't have any income, just a very small pension for being a veteran of World War I that the Vichy government didn't dare take away. He rented a bungalow on a small farm at Camp Major near Aubagne. It could be reached by a tramway line from Marseille. He had to sell the family car, a *Citroën familiale*. My sisters finished the year at Aix-en-Provence, where they lived at the university residence. The dining room there was divided between the occupying Germans and the students. The menu was different on both sides: lots of butter and meat for the Germans, and ration tickets on the other side.

By the end of the year, both of my sisters were qualified to teach but they couldn't because they were considered Jewish. So they studied in a private secretarial school and got jobs in Marseille. By then, we were living in another apartment, but we would visit the bungalow in Camp Major on the weekend and buy vegetables, fruit, and sometimes a chicken from people who had land. We didn't smoke, but my sister Elise, who had practical ideas, subscribed for tobacco rations and used them to barter for potatoes. That was our *Système D*.[5]

The Occupation was a progressive system. Everyday something worse was announced. First came the ration coupons for bread, meat, oil, butter fats, beans, potatoes, soap, and toothpaste. To obtain the coupons, identification cards were needed. Should we declare ourselves as Jews? My mother had four Jewish grandparents, my sisters and I had three, and all the ancestors were buried at the Jewish cemetery. So like many, we were honest and had our identification card stamped *juif*. In the southern zone we didn't have to wear the yellow Star of David.[6] I studied at the science faculty. Three percent of the students were allowed to be Jews.[7] To apply, I had to present a family history and take an entrance exam.

One morning in November 1943, I remember leaving the university and taking the street car home. It always made a stop at a place where I could see the family leather shop, which had a beautiful leather goods display in the window. Inside the shop was a full-size horse, set up by a taxidermist, with fine leather saddles. After my grandmother died in 1940, my Uncle Albert, who was 40, became owner of the shop. He lived with my Aunt Laure, who was my mother's and my uncle's sister, above the store. She was 43 years old and had recently been widowed, so she'd decided to come to Marseille from Romans in the Drôme to attend the same secretarial school where my sisters had gone.

When I looked at the shop that day around 10 a.m., the wooden shutters were halfway closed and flapping in the wind. There had been a *grande rafle* [roundup] the night before. Marseille had to fulfill a quota of deportees for the Germans, so the French police had gathered up lots of people. Neighbors told us the police came to the apartment above the store and called my uncle by nickname. He opened the door, and they grabbed him. The neighbors said he fought, but Albert and Laure were both taken away. For a long time we never heard anything about them. Much later in 2000, when I was in Israel, I visited a memorial to the French who'd been deported and saw the names of Albert and Laure and other people we knew, as well as the number of their convoy. They perished in Auschwitz,

After that, we decided to stay in Camp Major, and I stopped going to the university until the end of the war. The dean said he could not guarantee my safety. We decided to erase the stamp *juif* on our identification cards by using 40 percent peroxide and coal dust to make it look old. We avoided crowds. I tutored some students in math and physics in Marseille one day a week, and took the streetcar into town. I'd get the mail, buy a few rations, and check if our numbers showed up at the butcher shop.

Marseille felt like it was under siege. The circle of the Gestapo got tighter and tighter. There were lots of curfews—sometimes the time of the curfew was different on each side of the street. Elsie was lucky because she was in Camp Major when a bomb fell on the office she'd been working at in the rue de Rome on June 3, 1944. We stayed in Camp Major until the middle of September 1944, when Marseille and Aubagne were liberated. Then we returned to Marseille. The Dean of the Faculty helped me get a scholarship to finish my degree in chemistry. Little by little the situation got better for Father. He was reinstated, retired, and given four years of back pay. My sister Elise got a job with the U.S. Civil Affairs and my sister Alice started teaching in Digne.

We lived near where the Medical School was located. The U.S. Army First Medical and Fourth Medical Laboratories had established a general medical laboratory and blood bank at that location. An extension of the blood bank opened up in the remains of a department store on the Canebière, the main street of Marseille. I had to walk in front of it every day before reaching the University. I lived on avenue Pasteur, a street that went to the Pharo, and I used to watch some of the American soldiers doing phlebotomies from our living room balcony ride by in an open truck on their way to the Pharo. They looked like students my age who were with me at the Chemistry Faculty. They looked like a happy group.

One day I was walking on the Canebière, and I stopped by to give some blood. The blood was to go to the soldiers at the Battle of the Bulge.[8] I did not have type "O," which they were collecting at the time, but I met a fellow named David who was about my age. He said he had a "friend" and that one day when they were free, they would like to see more of Marseille. I don't remember how we decided on the time and date, but I do remember that we walked to Notre Dame de la Garde and the Corniche.

After that, we went to my house for refreshments. The "friend" was a very quiet man, whose name was, I learned later, Arthur. He had blue eyes and a blond moustache; and he quietly observed everything around him. At the time, he was 23 years old and I was 21. He was a medical lab technician, a phlebotomist, and a typist for the organization.

Arthur was from a Kansas farm near Ruleton, a farm town of about 65 people. The French have very good maps, but Ruleton was not on any of them! His father was a wheat farmer and a rural mail carrier; his mother taught grade school. He had five brothers and three sisters. They were Protestants and Republicans.

Arthur was recruited after Pearl Harbor. He had wanted to go to medical school but it had to be postponed. He was selected to be trained as a medical laboratory technician and was assigned to the First Medical Mobile Field Laboratory. The staff was composed of doctors of medicine, doctors of veterinary medicine, and sanitary engineers. The group included pharmacists, school teachers, and college students—all about the same age.

After training in Springfield, Missouri, and San Antonio, Texas, the Laboratory was sent to Algeria, Tunisia, Sicily, Naples, and eventually to southern France for the landing. The First and Fourth Medical Laboratories stopped off in Marseille and then divided up. One part followed the troops to the Battle of the Bulge, while the other stayed south and eventually set up in Istres, which was where Arthur was assigned. Arthur would come from Istres every Sunday and visit with us between 3 and 5 p.m.

After his furlough in London he wanted to get married. A group of officers of the Laboratory staff came to our house with an interpreter for an official interview. Our family passed the "test." But my father decided that Arthur might have only wanted to get married because he was homesick. Therefore, he told Arthur he should return to Kansas and, if he really liked me, he could then come back and get me. In October of 1945 he returned to Kansas and was discharged from the Army. He saved up his money for our plane tickets, and then he came back to my house in June of 1947.

While he was away, I became a part-time secretary at the France-Amérique Committee in Marseille. Our office was at the French Information Service. I met lots of people, including Edmonde Charles Roux and her aunt, Madame Bourde, the widow of the surgeon who died in the Resistance. Gaston Deferre was mayor of Marseille and director of the *Provençal*.

Arthur and I corresponded for two years. My sisters thought it was funny when he sent a Bible and a cookbook. He also gave me a chemistry book about fats which gave references I needed for my Master's thesis. During our brief courtship, we had developed an intellectual friendship. Sometimes we held hands, and once he kissed me on the cheek when he gave me my engagement ring.

1947 came. The Pastor who married us gave us a talk beforehand. He said that it takes at least three years to get adjusted to married life. We would be giving a promise to God and we were obliged to keep it. After Arthur's arrival in Marseille, the dressmaker started my wedding dress. There were visits to our relatives and friends—the announcements were printed and published. The wedding date was set.

The civil ceremony was the first of July at the *Mairie* [city hall] of Marseille. My aunt, who was an alderman, presided over the vows. The third of July was the church wedding at the Temple Protestant, rue Grignon in Marseille. None of Arthur's relatives were there, so my sister Alice was his "best man." My sister Elise and a friend were bridesmaids, and my uncle provided the transportation.

Our honeymoon was at Bormes les Mimosas, so we took a bus to go there. From then on we were starting something new! We went back home to Marseille on the *Micheline* train after 10 days of honeymoon. Then came the packing before our departure to America. My parents were quite emotional about my leaving.

We were going to fly on a TWA transcontinental "Constellation" from Le Bourget airport in Paris. My sisters were in Paris attending a seminar at Lycée Louis le Grand. Since our flight was delayed five days because the plane was coming from Egypt, where there was the plague, we had more time to visit Paris and Versailles. I remember there was a heat wave at the time, and the fish were dying in the Seine. I spent almost all my French money in Paris because I was only allowed to convert the equivalent of $50 to take to the States. We also finished all our bread ration tickets. The last day I went to a *boulangerie* [bakery shop] close to the hotel and they sold me some leftover bread without asking for ration tickets. I also bought some beautiful peaches, and that was the end of my French money. We just had enough to pay for the hotel and to take a taxi to Le Bourget the next day.

I remember at Le Bourget I presented my passport, and the man at the counter read "Profession: chemist," so he asked me if "Vinyl" was made out of wine. I said "No." I mumbled the word *polymerization,* and he seemed satisfied. We flew to Gander Airport in Newfoundland. My husband sent a telegram from there back to my parents to say that we were on our way to Chicago.

The air in Newfoundland was cool and smelled of pine trees. We were served turkey and cranberry sauce and some huge peas with green coloring, but I was not very hungry! Next, we stopped in Detroit, where they cleaned the airplane, weighed us, and took our body temperature. Then we flew on to Chicago. That's where I had my first contact with the Immigration Service. I was asked whether I was a communist. To enter the United States, I had to pay an $8 head tax, then be fingerprinted. When I asked to wash my hands, a huge agent with a gun on his belt followed me to the lady's room to make sure that I only washed my hands and didn't run away!

Arthur took a room at La Salle Hotel. I remember that everything around was black from a recent fire in the area. Arthur had a pharmacist friend from the Med Lab & Blood Bank who took us around the shore of Lake Michigan and then to a restaurant. I ate very little. But the next day I went to the beauty shop. Then we boarded the Rock Island Rocket, a fast train, for Goodland, Kansas. It was air conditioned with big blocks of ice and I saw iced tea prepared in front of a customer for the first time. Although the train was fast I caught up on my sleep. But suddenly the train slowed down nearly to a stop, and we were in the middle of a flood of the Ohio River.

I was in a different world. Mennonite women with bonnets and cotton dresses! Catholic priests going to Des Moines, Iowa, dressed as if in the Middle Ages! We finally arrived in Goodland, Kansas at 5 a.m. The sun was already bright. My husband had a great big smile. The Goodland railway station was a regular stop for the Rocket on its way to Denver. Close by there was a hotel with outdoor tables, so I sat there.

In front of me there was a great plain, and to visualize it, just think of the pictures of Alice Springs in Australia. Goodland is on a plateau at 3,800 feet. Arthur called his family at the farm, and shortly afterwards his dad arrived in a nice Ford with his two younger children, Rachel and Norman. Everyone was smiling.

The farm was 10 miles west, and there was a big, long breakfast table waiting for us with his mother and most of his brothers and sisters. I think they were as shy as I was, but I certainly received a good looking over and a very polite reception. A few days later some neighbors gave us a *charivari*,[9] pronounced *sheeveree*. Then I met a Swiss family, the Meinens. Later, I was taken over to the local newspaper office, where they told me that I spoke better English than many people in the county.

After 55 years, I am an American. I did not leave France because I did not like it. For 10 years, I lived in a building where there was an engraving of *Liberté, Egalité, Fraternité*, and I still believe in that. I was not prejudiced against the Americans. I lived in farming communities in the Middle West where people had a lot of common sense. They spoke what they thought.

The women were industrious and could do many things: jump on a tractor, a combine, take a pattern and sew dresses out of feed sacks, wear them with fine stockings and patent shoes, and curl their hair. They baked their own bread and rolls. Many played piano and organ and wind instruments, they took notes as secretaries of their clubs, and so on.

We have lived in Fayetteville, Arkansas, since August of 1959. We moved here because Fayetteville has a university and good, integrated schools and is quite international. It was the home of Senator Fulbright. His mother, Roberta, was the owner of the town newspaper. The Library was named after her. His father owned the Coca-Cola plant. I used to go and hear the senator speak when he came out here from Washington.

Before moving to Fayetteville, we lived in Concordia, Kansas. We also lived in Lawrence and Sunflower, Kansas, while my husband was in medical school. We moved to Denver, Colorado, when he started his residency in internal medicine at the Presbyterian Hospital. From there we went to Clifton, Kansas, where he tried the experience of being a "Country Doctor." He decided to finish his residency, and he was given a position at the Veterans Administration Hospital in Houston, Texas. He also taught at Baylor University's School of Medicine.

In 1947, I taught French conversation at the University of Kansas when we were living in Laurence. I had fun and the colleagues were kind and helpful. I was puzzled by the girl students who were members of sororities. Some of them belonged to farm societies. They were a bit jealous of me because I was a war bride. It was hard for them to make the transition from farm girl to the "prissy" attitude they had on the campus.

Then, I started having a family. I was close to my children. I went to clubs. First to the medical [students'] wives' clubs, then to the doctors' wives' clubs. I met English war brides and some French war brides, too. For many years I stayed at home. After my eighth child was born, I started taking correspondence courses in secondary education. Two principals, one a veteran of World War I and another a veteran of the landing in Normandy, invited me to come and substitute teach in many subjects. I made friends with school teachers. This was a circle I liked. I could step into any class and with a few instructions from the absentee teacher I could handle the situation. I did that from 1965 to 1985.

My husband and I never had any problems with alcohol or tobacco. He never drank or smoked all through his three years of military service. While in medical school, he saw how harmful these intoxicants could be. He became a pioneer in forbidding smoking in hospital wards and also in prescribing the use of a small amounts of aspirin for heart disease patients. He's now retired. We celebrated the 50th anniversary of his graduation from Kansas University's School of Medicine in September 2002.

In 2001, Arthur was given a diploma for having participated in the liberation of France from 1944 to 1945. The diploma was given to him by the French Consul in Houston, Texas, during a ceremony at the Capital building in Little Rock, Arkansas. Some of our children and grandchildren attended.

I became a naturalized American in September 1950 and have always voted in elections. My children all had university educations and went up to the Master's degree level. They all got hired in their respective professions. I don't know if they could have accomplished all this in France. I have kept contact with France and French by writing letters about every 10 days to my family and friends, and I subscribe to French magazines. I speak French and English, and I think in both languages. I have always spoken English with my husband.

Each of the children went to France in their senior year of high school and stayed with their grandmother and their Aunt Elise in Marseille and their Aunt Alice in Paris. Some went more than once. I returned to France to visit in 1958, 1976, 1979, 1983, 1984, 1994, and 1998. I was sad to leave my family, but I was glad to come back to my home in Fayetteville.

I've been very fortunate because I have a wonderful French family, as well as a good husband, in-laws, and many relations in Arkansas, Colorado, and Kansas. When Arthur and I got married, we had great hopes for our children. I've always had a positive outlook on life, and I easily forgot the mishaps.

Fifteen

"I KNITTED SOCKS"

I very much enjoyed speaking with Pierrette S. As both of us have had careers in teaching, we understood each other when speaking about differences between the American and French educational systems. Dynamic and entrepreneurial, she feels comfortable in the United States and is not afraid to say so.

I was born in 1924 in Marseille. My mother was from Paris, and that's why I don't have a Marseille accent. She detested that accent, so at home we had to speak with a Parisian accent. Papa was a commercial artist and worked in advertising.

I went to a regular French elementary school in Marseille and then to Anatole-France, an "upper school" there. I took the exam to get into the *Ecole Normale* [teacher training college], and placed thirteenth out of 600 candidates. Only the first 30 were admitted. The *Ecole Normale* was supposed to be in Aix-en-Provence, but because of the war and the Occupation, they put us in Marseille. I later decided I preferred to teach in a high school rather than in an elementary school, so [after the *Ecole Normale*] I continued my studies at the university. I did a *licence* [a B.A.]—a "classical" *licence*—in English. Since I'd never done any Latin before, I had to cram all the Latin [on the program] in three years. Latin mattered a lot in France back then.

As I said, there were 30 of us women admitted that year to the *Ecole Normale*. We were all boarders, and we were very well-protected, as if we were studying at a nuns' school. This was during the Occupation. We couldn't go dancing during our free time because the Germans forbade it. But we danced clandestinely. We did everything they outlawed us to do. Officially, though, I didn't go dancing.

When the Americans came, the first thing they did was to hold dances and to invite the local girls from Marseille. It was all chaperoned and very respectable. The American Red Cross organized everything. So then we were able to go dancing. And when I went out on my own with a young man, we'd go to the movies. The Americans had movie theaters with American films. So those of us who were students of English could once again see American movies. During the war, we'd been cut off from them. There were only very mediocre French films and horrible German ones. Then, all of a sudden, we got to see "Gone with the Wind."

In fact, my life totally changed when the Americans arrived. It was from one day to the next. The Germans left one day with their means of camouflage, and then, the next day, the Americans arrived. It was a really extraordinary moment when they came. Of course, *I* wanted to speak English, so I went up to a group in a Jeep and asked, "Where did you land?" They didn't understand me, but they gave me some cigarettes, which I didn't want. Later, though, they answered: "Saint-Tropez." I remember that day very, very well. But the French were jealous. I had a French boyfriend who was with the FFI at the Liberation. He was furious because he was sure I'd gone out with American soldiers. But my girlfriends and I were very sensible. We never went in cars with men. We went by train or on foot. So absolutely nothing happened, and that was fine with us.

On the other hand, one of my classmates at the *Ecole Normale* was really unlucky. She was hitchhiking between Aix-en-Provence and Marseille, or someplace like that. Nowadays, it isn't wise to hitchhike, but, back then, we young French people used to do it all the time. So, she was hitchhiking after the Americans arrived, and she was picked up by two black Americans, who raped and killed her. She was only 19 or 20. It was horrible! We'd been studying together for four years and were like sisters. That was really hard. No, the Americans weren't all gentlemen.

As for me, I had nothing to complain about when I went out with an American soldier. He respected me. First of all, because I worked for the American Red Cross and usually wore my uniform when I went out with them. And also because I behaved correctly. I can't complain. You know, we might have been a little silly back then, but at least we knew what to expect, and we were careful.

Paul, my future husband, came from a place near Fresno, California. He'd been a [college] student before the war. We met at the If Castle near

Marseille. I was working as an interpreter for the Red Cross, and twice a week I gave tours [to the castle] for American soldiers.... I'd talk to them about the Count of Monte-Cristo, and at one point during the tour I'd show them a hole between two cells. That particular day, I was telling them that the week before, an American had wanted to go though the hole, when I realized that my flashlight didn't work, probably because the battery was too old. So a soldier lent me his. Afterwards, when I wanted to return it to him, he gave it to me as a present. And that soldier was Paul. We ran into each other again in the street two or three days later. That's how it all started. We went out for awhile, but then Paul left for the United States. He then re-enlisted for two years in the army and came back to Europe, this time to Germany.

I was in love with America, but I think I was also really in love with Paul. My parents were very nice with me. They realized how strong my feelings were. They asked me to think about it. I thought about it; I didn't rush. It wasn't like those people who met one day and got married the next. We got married in 1947. Despite the restrictions, my father succeeded in providing a wonderful wedding meal with ingredients [bought] on the black market. We even had *vol-au-vent* [Chicken a la King] as a starter. It must have cost a fortune. My parents really went out of their way. Everything was delicious.

There was just one thing that shocked my parents a bit. It was that in France at the time, people would [first] get information about the young man their daughter was going to marry. As a matter of fact, it wasn't really such a bad idea. Agencies handled it, and they'd tell you if the boy had a police record or not—things like that. But it was much more difficult to do this type of research when it was for an American. So I told Papa: "*Non, non*. Don't waste your money. *I* know he's a good person." And he *was* a good person in the beginning. It was afterwards that things didn't go well. Anyway, it really bothered Papa that he hadn't gotten information about my husband before our wedding.

After we got married, we lived together in Germany for about a year. We had a house, and I gave lessons. Then, in 1948, we sailed to America.

As a matter of fact, one day—I don't remember exactly when—I wrote a little piece about our trip. Here's what I wrote:

I arrived in America in 1948 on an army ship called the *Zebulon Vance*. The crossing from Bremerhaven, Germany, to New York lasted two weeks. The boat was grey and dismal—full of U.S. army men and their war brides. We'd all been carefully examined—our lungs, blood tests, etc.—to see if there was any risk of illness, and we were impatient to begin a new life in the United States, which seemed to be a happy land compared to our European countries, where we'd undergone six years of terror, rationing, and bombings.

Those of us who weren't prepared for it were very disappointed once they got on board. We weren't going to travel with our husbands in comfortable cabins, but rather in dormitories of about 40 people [women] each. The berth assignment for each bride was done according to very simple selection criteria. Age—we were all young—nationality, or race weren't taken into account at all, according to *her* system. *She* asked us: "Are you pregnant?" And if we weren't, *she* simply gave us an upper berth. *She* was the witch in charge.

What a difference in lifestyle compared to the one we had in Germany, where [all of us brides] were very spoiled and had servants and gardeners. But those two weeks weren't really unpleasant, either.

My fear of scurvy—it was my first Atlantic crossing—quickly disappeared when I saw we could eat as many apples as we wanted. The food wasn't good, but it was abundant. I wonder if anything served on those metal, compartmentalized trays could taste good. After several days, all the flowers [people had] given to wish us *bon voyage* had withered. Our dormitories were gloomy.

It was about that time that my husband Paul, after washing one of his shirts, asked me if I could iron it. I'd already seen people iron shirts, but I'd never done it myself before. I thought anyone could do that kind of work, so I put my name on the waiting list for the ironing board. But when my turn finally came, it was during the middle of a storm and the laundry room was completely empty.

I found myself all alone with the ironing board, the iron, and the shirt. The boat and I were rolling from one side to the other in a very comical way, and I hardly ever got to reach the shirt. It took me a really long time. When the shirt finally looked presentable enough, I took it to my dormitory. It was really hard to hold on to both the shirt and the ramp, but I was lucky and I succeeded.

It was the middle of the afternoon, but I climbed up into my bunk. That was when I realized the dormitory was full of people, and that most of them were seasick. I heard moans and groans. A box of candy had fallen and split open, and pieces of candy were rolling back and forth on the floor, following the movement of the boat. The noise prevented everyone from sleeping. I lay there, daydreaming, under the ceiling. I wondered what would happen to all my companions once they were scattered all over America. How many of these marriages would last? We were all young, in love, and full of hope.

When the tug boat towed us into the port of New York, the fog was so thick we couldn't see anything. This didn't matter to me. They'd misplaced my

medical record, so I had to stay two or three more days onboard. I finally got
to see *them*—I mean Manhattan, the Statue of Liberty, the gold buttons on
the immigration officer's large chest. He began by asking me if I intended to
overthrow the government of the United States. I couldn't prevent myself from
thinking that if I were, he'd be the last person I'd tell! As I walked down a street
in New York, I heard Jean Sablon singing *"La Mer"* ["Beyond the Sea"], and I
felt a little bit less of an exile...

What were my impressions when I arrived in the United States? On the
whole, I was enchanted. Several years ago, I tried to remember how I felt back
then, and I wrote another little piece:

> The America I discovered was young, kind, clean, optimistic, and hard work-
> ing. She hadn't gone to Vietnam yet, she'd had very little experience with
> drugs, and none at all with AIDS. She was still racist and sexist but was making
> great progress in these two areas.
>
> I was ready to love *my* America. But I was going from surprise to surprise.
> At the American officers' mess in Frankfurt, Germany, I'd already seen very
> distinguished-looking men throw themselves on their corn-on-the-cob like
> dogs on a bone. And in the United States, I soon discovered that dinner guests
> who kept their left hands under the table weren't stealing my silverware!
>
> My surprises were usually good ones. In restaurants, they served the salad at
> the beginning of meals, meaning right away. I liked the rapid and courteous ser-
> vice. I quickly discovered lemon pies, corn flakes, and hamburgers. Above all,
> I came to realize that American kindness wasn't a myth, and I still believe this.

My husband had requested to be sent as close as possible to California,
and, of course, they sent him to New Jersey! I was used to good, Mediterranean temperatures, and I suffered a lot in New Jersey. It was also a horrible
year because we didn't have any money. Life was hard. Paul was in the army,
and the apartment we finally found cost as much as his salary as a sergeant.
So, I knitted socks and sold them for a dollar a pair so we could eat.

At that time, the schools of Trenton, New Jersey, weren't hiring married
women or foreigners. Therefore, I couldn't work in public schools. So
I became a substitute in private schools. I also worked as a sales lady in a shop.
I did a bit of everything. But what really worked well was that everyday
I made a pair of socks. I took them to a very elegant shop, and it sold them
for me. In a way, I think [knitting and selling those socks] was a good thing
because I never needed [to ask for any financial] assistance.

Afterwards, we went to California, where I met my parents-in-law.
My father-in-law was of Prussian origin. He criticized France a lot. But I very

much liked my mother-in-law. She was wonderful. She'd had 13 children, and she taught me how to do natural childbirth.

In California, I began to study to get a teaching credential. I did correspondence courses through the University of California. At the same time, I worked—when I had the right to—and I knitted socks.

My husband went to college on the GI Bill, and he worked at the same time so that we'd have more money to live more comfortably. In a word, we never died of hunger. When he got his first job as an engineer, we were able to buy our first house here. Our son was born in 1955. But it was already not going very well between my husband and me. I realized that, deep down, he'd never accept my French culture. He didn't want me to speak French. He didn't want me to make French girlfriends in the United States. He didn't want us to go back to France, even for a visit. He wanted me to forget my country. And, because of him, I stayed away from France for 11 years! He didn't take much care of his son, either.

I remained a number of years with my husband because of my son, but around 1962 I asked for a divorce. I remember what the lawyer said to me: "You'll be lucky if the judge gives you custody of your child. French women, you know, have a bad reputation here. As a matter of fact, your husband accuses you of being unfaithful."

That beat everything! Me, unfaithful? I was never unfaithful. I wouldn't have had time. I worked very hard. I gave lessons during the day, and at night I had our child and the correspondence courses.

My husband didn't want me to leave him. He emptied our bank account. It was very complicated, but I got the divorce and custody of our son. The court took away his visiting rights because he didn't pay alimony for our child. He disappeared completely out of my life after the divorce.

I remarried, and my second husband adopted my son, who has his name. On a California birth certificate, a child has the name of the father who adopted him, not of the natural father. My second husband and I were very happy together, but he died in 1974. My third marriage—with my present husband—took place in 1981.

I was in a terrible state—completely broken up—after the death of my second husband. We were both on sabbatical just before he died. He was an "eternal student," just like me. When he died, I was in the middle of a research project. I'd written a long essay on women in Mexican literature, and I'd started taking Spanish. So, rather than shoot myself in the head, I decided to do a doctorate in France. I left to do research in Paris and Montpellier and then in Mexico. I defended my dissertation in 1976 and obtained a doctorate in comparative literature from Paul-Valéry University in Montpellier. I was 50. But several members of the jury over there weren't very nice. I could see that they were wondering what "that American" wanted. No, they didn't treat me very well. I really earned that doctorate!

I think I obtained American citizenship about two years after coming here. It was automatic. And I think that is how it should be when you teach. Because, at school in the morning, the pupils get up and recite the Pledge of Allegiance, and if you're not an American, you can't salute the flag. On top of it all, I wanted to vote. I really like politics. I like it a bit less nowadays, but I always vote and I keep well-informed.

I think it's very important to take an interest in what's happening. For example, my neighbor here is mayor of our town. From time to time, we go to receptions together. My husband and I give to charities. I believe that when you have a fairly good salary, you should give back a little to the community.

I'm retired now. I was a French teacher at a high school for 36 years and had the same classroom [all that time]! I still teach, but only to adults. I have a rather good retirement and enough money, so if I'm offered a class that I don't like, I can say no. That's what's wonderful. Last spring, I did a course on Provence, and that was wonderful. Provence is my stomping ground!

When you teach in a high school here, the parents make life very difficult for you. They want their children to have good grades, no matter what their level is. You have students who don't study at all, but the parents accuse the teacher if the students don't have good grades. They need A's in order to get into college. The parents don't care if their child doesn't know how to conjugate the verb "to be." That's why I don't miss that high school. But I do greatly miss the students, and, by the way, this feeling is reciprocal. Some of them still write and telephone me. But the big problem is the parents! They're probably the big tumor in education at the moment.

Also, here in the United States we have a term that is very much in use. . . . It's *self-esteem*—esteem for oneself. You have to lie, to create a fake personality. When a child does a drawing that is totally mediocre, we say: "Well, this is fantastic! What a young artist!" Why would he make an effort after that if he's already received compliments? I've been told it's the other extreme in France. Students there aren't encouraged. There should be a happy medium. Don't tell a kid "it's very good" if it isn't good, but don't treat him like an imbecile, either. I remember when I was a student in France, if we made a mathematical mistake, for example, we were called, "You imbecile!" If I said that here, I'd be fired right away.

There is so much diversity in California. For example, there's a school here where students speak 53 different languages! And if you look at a class list, there are very few names like "Smith" or "Jones." There are an enormous number of Asian, Polish, Russian, and Spanish [names]. But the students don't mix, and, unfortunately, there are some who never learn English. We're told: "You have to let them keep their own culture." That's fine, but are they going to become lawyers and doctors like that? After all, their families decided to come here. It's a little like me. No one translated for me when I arrived in the United States. I had a lot of trouble understanding people in the street, even though I had a *licence* [B.A.] in English. It wasn't Shakespearean English I was hearing.

I've always liked the people here. Americans are very nice. But it's probably a little unfair of me to say that, because I've never lived in France during normal times and as an adult. Wartime wasn't a normal time. People were suffering from hunger and were ready to fight over a piece of bread. I think the French are calmer these days. Still, sometimes I feel like a foreigner there because France has made incredible progress. And if you don't know the system—how to weigh vegetables in a supermarket or how to punch your ticket at a train station—well, then....

I know other French war brides here. Most of them didn't stay married to the same man, but they still stayed in America. I sometimes wonder if the marriages failed because they were bad marriages or whether it was because the man or the woman didn't know the family and the past of the other well enough. In my case, for example, I was raised in a family that appreciated the arts and museums. There are other families where the arts aren't so important. It doesn't matter whether you're French or American. Deep down, what's important is how you look at life.

Like the other war brides I know here, I stayed in America. I undoubtedly made a bad marriage the first time. But I think we do what we can in life, and we shouldn't try to redo what has already been done.

CONCLUSION

Eighty-nine years after the Armistice of 1918 and 62 years after the end of World War II, the *mademoiselles* are now deceased or have, in many cases, become white-haired, French-American grandmothers. But their memories live on, as shown in the stories included here and in others I have collected. We can but admire their resilience in living out *la grande aventure* that began for them back in the 1940s, when they met their Doughboy or GI husbands, married, and then moved to America.

It's been quite a journey—for them and for us. From their childhoods in different parts of France or in French colonies, we traveled through the war years, the Occupation, and then the Liberation. We listened while two of the women explained how they participated in the Resistance. We heard about some of the women's contact with German soldiers in occupied France and how others (particularly those in New Caledonia or Algeria) only saw Allied combatants. Some told of witnessing unbearable or striking scenes; others had few or flawed memories of the war period.

But all of the women met, at some point, an American soldier in uniform, and we learned how, in their late teen years or early twenties, their lives changed dramatically. Leaving France behind, they usually voyaged to America on converted Liberty ships. After being welcomed at the dock, they were transferred to a train or were fetched by car, and then taken to their final destination—be it Chicago, rural Iowa, segregated Alabama, or sunny Los Angeles. These places would then be their homes for decades to come, or just an interim location until they moved elsewhere.

Once they were settled, another adventure began—that of housewife and mother, sometimes coupled with a career—in conventional, Eisenhower-era America of the 1950s, with its cult of domestic life. Many had to combat an unflattering stereotype of French women. They had to learn a new language and adapt to a new culture. Over the years, some had happy marriages and remained married to the husband they had met during the war. Others divorced and later remarried. A few stayed single. Some lived in areas where there were other French people or French clubs; others did not. If they worked outside the home, they became, more often than not, high school French teachers, university lecturers of French, or bilingual secretaries. Depending on their financial situation, some would return to France every few years to visit family and friends. However, with age, especially following a husband's retirement or death, their own retirement, or the passing away of family members and friends, their trips back to their native land have now dwindled. And very few (only two of our sample group) returned permanently to France to live.

Although these women's stories now appear here in print, I first heard them in person. Journeying down "memory lane" with these women, I made tape recordings of their tales. Then, after listening to the tapes, reading the transcripts, and rewriting the stories, I realized that certain common themes emerged.

Foremost among these themes, of course, is "the American dream," or some variation of it. Although anti-American sentiment existed in France after the war, most French women looked favorably upon America as a place of "milk and honey," and "our" war brides were no exception. After years of penury and deprivation, they discovered a place where food was plentiful, houses well-heated, and daily existence materially comfortable. Although, in a few cases, some of the women discovered a way of life in the United States that was somewhat more "primitive" than what they had known before, on the whole, their living conditions were better.

French women adapted well to American domesticity of the time. Coming mostly from traditional French families, where "a woman's place was in the home," they were usually excellent cooks, good homemakers, and attentive mothers. And even if some of them later worked outside the home, like many modern-day French "super-women," they managed to combine holding a job, cooking delicious *petits plats* [dishes], and maintaining a well-run household. Over the years, they became used to the spacious houses and the material comforts. Indeed, in most of the personal accounts, this aspect of American life is almost always mentioned.

In addition, for young women who had spent their formative years in dreary and restricted circumstances, America represented a land of opportunity and a chance for adventure. Looking back over the years, many of the women in my sample said they had really appreciated the opportunities for study and professional achievement that America had offered them. Several implied that their marriage and subsequent move to the United States were a way for them to escape over-protective parents or difficult situations.

Indeed, the question might be asked whether marrying a Doughboy or a GI after a world war represented a free trip to the New World, all expenses paid by the U.S. government. In other words, did they *use* their GI husbands as a means of getting to America? Was their marriage a springboard, so to speak, to a better life? Some people might think so and, to a certain degree, this was sometimes the case. But the reality was undoubtedly more complex, for, as we have seen, most of the women I interviewed really believed they were in love when they married.

We must not forget how *young* these women were when they married. And also how young their GI husbands were. Just examining the dates on the marriage records in French town halls or on the tombstones at the American cemetery in Colleville confirms this. Many of the "boys" had been drafted straight out of secondary school, and some of them had never even been away from home before. Some of them had probably had some sort of romantic adventure in England before D-Day, but many probably hadn't. Perhaps they were still pining for a childhood sweetheart back home, unsure whether she would still be waiting for them when they returned. As for the French girls, most of whom came from strict Catholic families, many of them had never "dated" before or had a steady boyfriend. Or if they did, they often feared their loved one would never return. Other factors could also come into play. Sometimes the opposition of the girls' family spurred them on to a romantic entanglement; and in a few cases, it was actually the *parents* who encouraged the girls to go out with a GI.

Furthermore, the times were exhilarating, and there was a sense of urgency in the air. When would Harry or Dick have to leave again for the front? Would he be killed or wounded? Would Jeanette or Marie remain faithful? When would they see each other again? Then, after the war in Europe was over, the question was: "When would he have to go back to the United States?" This sense of urgency, together with the heightened sense of sexual awareness that goes along with youth and war, helped these people "fall in love" quickly. Sometimes they waited till after marriage to have sexual relations, sometimes they didn't. But if they didn't, and the girl became pregnant, the GI would propose marriage. Or at least that is what happened to the women in this book. It was the gentlemanly, virtuous, "American" way to do things for many young men of the time.

Another theme that appears in the stories is a certain amount of naiveté and unconsciousness on the part of the young war brides. They made the hasty decision to marry a man they hardly knew, to leave their native land and to immigrate to America, often without considering the consequences should it not work out. Indeed, for most war brides, the sea voyage to America was a one-way trip; neither they nor their parents could afford to pay for a return ticket. Nor would most of them even dare to return, since they would have had to face the recriminations of their families, especially if they "had" to get married in the first place.

Marrying a man they barely knew, the women had romantic notions that everything would be fine once they were together, that love would "conquer all." Or if it didn't, as one woman said: "I wasn't *really* in love, but when you're 19, you're always a little in love...so I said to myself 'it doesn't really matter. I'll divorce if it doesn't work out.'"

But, as this woman would discover, divorce proceedings in America were not always so easy to initiate, especially if you were a foreigner. And, as often happened, it could turn out to be the husband who left or asked for a divorce, sometimes leaving the abandoned French-born wife in difficult financial circumstances with no child support.[1]

Another problem the women had not reckoned on was suffering from "culture shock." Although America and the American way of life had often been an ideal for them, the reality of adapting to a new culture on their own without the support of family and friends was fraught with difficulties. As intercultural researchers tell us, first you adapt on the superficial level: you learn the language, you adopt the dress and habits, you cook the food. Then you discover that there are so many hidden differences—the underside of the "iceberg," so to speak—the ways of thinking, the norms and values, the core beliefs. These are much more difficult to adapt to, and for a young French woman back in the 1940s, it was no easy task. Moreover, most of the time, they had to fend for themselves. Their husbands did not realize or did not acknowledge the changes the women were confronting or the efforts they were making. And, although "back then" there were, in certain places, Red Cross orientation programs and French War Brides clubs, there were no cross-cultural seminars, no books on culture shock, no "survival kits for overseas living."[2]

No wonder many of the marriages ended in divorce! Marriage is hard enough, but when it is a "mixed" or exogamous[3] marriage, it is even harder.

What *is* admirable, however, is that the women who divorced were courageous enough to stay on and to make lives for themselves in their adopted country. This is not to say that the women whose marriages lasted were not courageous. It is just that a divorced woman faces additional difficulties, especially when living in a country whose language is not their own and where the legal system is different. The French brides discovered that American states each had separate divorce laws, and the legal rights of foreign residents were not always clear. In some states, it seems, a husband was not even required to notify his wife that she was being, or had been, divorced!⁴

In all truth, though, it must be said that it would also have been very difficult for the women to get a divorce in France or to even return after obtaining one in America. Most of the women's families were Catholic, and divorce in France in the 1950s still carried with it a stigma that was even worse than the one it had in conventional 1950s America.

For the women whose marriages ended in divorce, incompatibility— whether owing to cultural differences, lack of common interest, or other factors—was a big issue. But incompatibility could exist even when the marriage lasted. As often happened back in those days, and as still happens today in certain circles, despite the problems, women stayed on in unhappy marriages because of children, material security, or various other reasons.

According to the French women I interviewed, one of the problems that could lead to incompatibility in the couple was the "education gap" between them and their GI husbands. Although only several from my sample actually had a college degree before marrying, the women I spoke to were, on the whole, fairly well-educated before marrying. A few of them had started taking university courses at the outbreak of the war, and almost all of them had a *brevet supérieur*, or the equivalent, at the time, of a French baccalaureate or an American high school diploma. Several were musicians; one was a ballerina with the Paris opera. Very few had stopped school at an early age.

As we have already mentioned, their husbands had often gone off to the war straight out of high school or after some sort of vocational training. Even if the French girls had only gone to a French secondary school, their educational level and cultural awareness were usually greater than that of the average American of the same age. There were good schools in America, of course, but in the 1940s, and still today, it all depended on where you lived. Farm boys and boys who lived in city ghettos obviously did not get much "book learning," as the saying goes. Whereas in France, with its universal, nationalized system of education, *lycées* [high schools] throughout the country had good standards, and if you succeeded academically in actually reaching high school, you had a rather good educational level.

In addition, since French schools have always tended to teach "Culture" (with a capital C)—history, literature, philosophy, art, music, and so on—the women were obviously more *cultivée* [cultured] than their American husbands. Of course, there were exceptions. For example, the husband, if he were an officer, might have attended college or come from a well-educated family. Or the wife, if she were an orphan or a farm girl or came from a poor family, might have had to leave school early and go off to work at the age of 15. On the whole, however, the women I interviewed were a fairly educated group, and some of them complained about the cultural and educational disparity between them and their husbands and his family.

With regard to the husband's family, another problem that could cause difficulties was the French wives' American in-laws, with whom the newlyweds often had to live for the first few months or even years of their marriage. In several cases, the in-laws were themselves first or second generation immigrants, and, as often happens, newly arrived immigrants are often "more American" (or more "French," "Italian," "British," and so forth) than the native-born. Consequently, the in-laws would be disappointed that their GI son had brought back a foreign, non-English-speaking wife or fiancée, a floozy *French* girl at that! A mother-in-law could be particularly critical. The properly behaved young bride, who was often extremely homesick for her own mother, would thus have to contend not only with the unbecoming stereotype of French girls, but also with a disapproving mother-in-law. Fortunately, not all of the women in my sample had such experiences. In certain cases, the mother-in-law was kind and supportive and helped the French bride adapt to American life.

A husband's alcoholism could also be the cause of incompatibility. Many of the men started drinking as soldiers, be it beer in boot camp in the United States, whiskey in British pubs, Calvados in Normandy, wine in Parisian cafés and nightspots, and the list goes on. After the war was over, they continued drinking with their "pals" while waiting to go back home, and then carried on with the habit once they were back in America. An evocative scene in the 1947 film *The Best Years of Our Lives* shows the three returning soldiers leaving their families and meeting up in a bar their first night home.

Heavy drinking was not always considered alcoholism or an "addiction" in 1950s America. It was a "man's thing," and many a wife at the time tolerated it at home and did not speak about the problem openly. But, for some of the women I talked to, such heavy drinking came as a real shock. They said they had been brought up in families where people drank a good deal of wine, but they had never seen the dark side of drunkenness, which some of their husbands displayed. Like many of their American counterparts of the time, however, they rarely dared confide to others about the problem.

The real issue, of course, was *why* these men drank. In the case of Sergeant Al Simpson, an upper class, happily married man and father in the film *The Best Years of Our Lives*, it was because, following his return from the war, he could not readapt to his former "normal" way of life: the job at the bank and the business lunches. It all seemed so superficial and worthless to him after seeing the horrors of the battlefield and his men dying. Indeed, many of the returning GI's of World War II suffered from this same type of what would be called after the war in Vietnam "posttraumatic stress disorder." Unfortunately, however, in the 1940s and 1950s the men's condition was not recognized as such, and they did not, or were not encouraged to, seek medical help. The consequence was that the men drank or became depressed or suicidal, and their condition could last for years afterwards, destroying marriages and families along the way.

Some of the women I spoke to found themselves in these sorts of situations, where a husband drank or acted strangely. Often they divorced, and many of them had difficult lives as a result. But rather than remarrying, a certain number of the wives sought solace in their faith, their work, their children, or in volunteer work or the arts. Very few turned bitter or complained about their fate.[5]

What is somewhat surprising, however, is that during their interviews, few of the women actually analyzed the reasons for their divorce or marriage difficulties. Moreover, the theme of the husband's war experiences is often missing from their stories. Many of the women did not know, or could not remember, where their husbands had been or what they had done during the war. Nor did they reflect on how the men they loved had been traumatized by what was undoubtedly the most influential experience of their lives.

This is possibly due to the fact that the women I interviewed are not only French-born, but also of another generation and thus little prone to psychological analysis, as we are nowadays. When these women were growing up in France, a war was going on, and no one had time for "analyzing" things. There were a few exceptions, of course, but on the whole, just as young brides they did not reflect on their true sentiments when marrying, so as elderly women they have never really dwelt on the underlying causes of their marriage difficulties or on their own shortcomings.

Consequently, just as many of the husbands did not empathize with their French wives with regard to the difficulty they were having adapting to America and American culture, few of the women seemed to empathize with their husbands (or ex-husbands) about their war experiences. Indeed, examining the situation from a "modern" vantage point, we might say that neither the husbands nor the wives recognized the underlying issues or had a sense of how to go about "working on" their relationship.

But there again, these women and the men they married were all so young "back then," and at the time, even among Americans, such therapeutic undertakings were the exception rather than the rule. Back in the 1940s and 1950s, people did not consult therapists or air their problems so openly as they do now. And bad memories of war (or the Holocaust) were kept secret or only shared with others "who had been there" and "who would understand." These memories were parts of your lives you put behind you and tried to forget.

My own father, for example, never shared his war experiences in the Pacific with us, and I doubt that my mother, herself a war bride, ever asked him much about them at the beginning of their marriage. Whereas nowadays, particularly since the 50th Anniversary of D-Day and with the publication of various books on "the Greatest Generation," we talk about war and the Holocaust, and veterans and survivors are encouraged to share their personal reminiscences and feelings.

In the women's stories, other themes, such as religious differences, views on child-rearing, and everyday living also emerged, but these could be expected. Less obvious, however, was such a theme as the lack of political consciousness among my interviewees. Although many of the women have always felt strongly about retaining their French identity, they also feel American; most acquired American citizenship (and subsequently lost their French citizenship) as far back as the late 1940s or early 1950s. But very few of them actually *vote* in national or local elections or favor one party or the other. Indeed, many seem apolitical. Surprising as this may seem, it could possibly be explained by the fact that they were born and brought up in a country where women only received the vote from General DeGaulle in 1945!

Similarly, and this too was probably due to their French upbringing and also to their generation, most of the women I interviewed were very reserved when it came to speaking about anything "intimate," such as being sexually attracted to their husband, having had sexual relations before marriage, or getting pregnant. One war bride did admit she was expecting a child before she married. Another spoke freely about her sexual life, both before, during, and after marriage. But these two women were the exception. All of the others avoided the subject and were very discreet. In some cases, I suspected that a woman had been "with child" before marriage, but I felt it inappropriate to question her about this. Women of this generation obviously have a certain sense of propriety. Indeed, I remember in one case, just after reading a rather "feminist" oral history manual, I tried to prod and "delve" into sexual mores among French women of the time. Several days after our conversation, the woman I had taped told me she had been shocked and had almost stopped the interview!

Needless to say, and as alluded to in the Introduction, not all French women of the time were so demure and modest about their sexuality, but in many ways the attitudes and behaviors of the vast majority of the women I interviewed certainly belies the American stereotype of sensual "ooh-la-la girl."

This "sexy" image of French women has been longstanding. in the United States. As we have seen, the myth was perpetrated after World War I by American Doughboys, to such an extent that GIs came to France in 1944 thinking that all French girls would be ready to jump into bed with them. But going even further back, it is linked to the French women who went out West after the discovery of gold. Employed as *dames de comptoir* [barmaids] in gambling houses, restaurants, and saloons, they were much appreciated. A French scholar writes:

> The French woman was . . . a new object of attention. Her way of walking, her lithe, graceful casualness and charming behavior that can only be found chez nous was an irresistible attraction. Men followed the French woman whenever she strolled down the street. For them, she was a rare curiosity which they never tired of watching and admiring. [6]

Many of these women had been dancers, actresses, and dancers in Paris before the Revolution of 1848. They came to California with the hope of starting anew—and also making a good deal of money—often in "the oldest profession in the world." But not all of them were prostitutes, and according to Annick Foucrier in *Le Rêve Californien*, herein lies a certain cultural gap between French and Americans:

> There is often a very fine line between liberated woman, libertine, courtesan, kept woman, woman of easy virtue and prostitute. And from one culture to the next, the distinctions get confused, depending on the woman's position in society, her possibilities for economic and emotional autonomy, the degree

of social mobility in relation to marriage, and the relationship between money and sexuality.[7]

Prostitute, libertine, ooh-la-la girl—this was the image of French women the war brides I interviewed often had to contend with when they arrived in the United States in the late 1940s and 1950s.[8] Whereas the truth was that most French war brides came from strict, very protective backgrounds and were somewhat naïve when they married. And although some of them were quite beautiful when they were young, others were not. Indeed, writer Alice Kaplan remembers her first French teacher, a war bride supplementing a husband's slender income and putting her daughter through private school, as "a tired, dowdy woman with very black hair, beige clothes, and an almost sickly pale skin punctuated by a mole."[9]

Hence, for the war brides, forging a French-American identity over the years has not always been easy. As their stories reveal, the women had to adapt their French experiences, values, and upbringing to cross-national marriage and the American culture of the time, becoming "hyphenated Americans" along the way. Because they emigrated as individuals and intermarried, they have tended to live among non-French people. And like other first-generation French immigrants to America, they integrated rather quickly into American society. They had to, as they usually found themselves isolated from other French people. This is because, according to anthropologist Jacqueline Lindenfeld,

> the current French population in the United States is numerically insignificant and has no territorial identity, given its scattered geographical distribution and the absence of spatially defined communities populated by direct immigrants from France. It has a low degree of institutional identity grounded in a weak religious, educational, and political infrastructure.[10]

Most of the French war brides took on American citizenship quite quickly, have spoken English in the home, and raised children who are much more American than French and may not even speak their mother's language.[11]

Nevertheless, all of the women I interviewed remain deeply attached to France, the distant homeland, the place they were born. Whenever possible, they return on visits or open their homes to French family and friends. Although sometimes a bit "rusty," they still speak French, and many of the women continue to teach it, even at an advanced age. Even though French people tend not to be "joiners," some of the women are members of the Alliance Française or a local French woman's group. Others live in places where these associations do not exist or are difficult to reach. In several cases, the women confided to me that they did not like the *ringard* [old-fashioned] atmosphere of certain French organizations in the United States.

* * *

The World War II French war brides married and crossed the Atlantic in the late 1940s. Some 20 years later, in the late 1960s, I married a Frenchman and moved to France. Indeed, my own marriage and emigration experience is, in many ways, the mirror image of theirs. Like most of the war brides, I raised bicultural children, whose "mother tongue" is, in fact, not the language of their "foreign" mother but rather that of their father and the surrounding environment. Like these women, I speak my "adopted language" fluently, but with *une petite trace d'accent* [a slight accent], described so aptly by Nancy Huston. Like her, when I let out "an a-typical melody or phrasing, a mistake in gender, an imperceptibly clumsy verb form...that's all that's needed to... denounce me!"[12]

Some of us have divorced, but after so many years away from our native land, our lives are now based in our adopted country. This is where we have spent our adulthood; this is where our children and grandchildren are. We "can't go home again," as James Jones once said. And besides, where is "home" anyway?

When I married my French husband, I flew to Paris, and yet I also share with the French war brides a transatlantic seafaring experience. In 1968, I traveled from Le Havre to New York on an overcrowded Italian ship, the *S.S. Aurelia*, whose passengers were mostly European students, many of them Fulbright scholars, en route to the United States for the first time. Just as back in the 1940s the YWCA and the Red Cross gave orientation sessions to the war brides, so did the Council on International Educational Exchange offer ship-board activities in the 1960s that introduced America and the American way of life to newcomers. Conditions on board the *Aurelia*, as on the converted troop ships, were hardly luxurious—four to six berths to a cabin, rough seas and seasickness stand out in my memory—but the nine-day crossing provided plenty of time for entertainment and romance. Thanks to the *Aurelia*, many a cross-cultural marriage ensued—including my own!

My return to France a year later with my French fiancé would not be the first time I had lived there. In the early 1960s, my father worked in Paris on a two-year assignment and brought the family with him. But our lives revolved around the American community of Paris: my brother and I attended the American School, we went to Sunday services at the American Cathedral, and we shopped at the PX in Camp des Loges.[13]

How different it was being with a Frenchman and his family! Just like many of the war brides, I found myself living with my in-laws for the first few months, while my fiancé went off to do his military service in the French navy. And like them, all I dreamt about during those months was having our own place and starting our married life together—alone.

In the years following our marriage, like the French brides, I discovered those "cultural misunderstandings" between American and French people so aptly described by French anthropologist Raymonde Carroll,[14] and, more recently, by such authors as Pascal Baudry,[15] Harriet Welty Rochefort,[16] and Gilles Asselin and Ruth Mastron.[17] These misunderstandings were, and are, everywhere: different assumptions with regard to food, privacy, family, love, marriage, sex, raising children, money, the sharing of information, and the list goes on. Trying to comprehend and adapt—with more or less success—to the many differences in attitudes, values, beliefs, and behaviors, I somehow managed to forge my own French-American identity in France, just as the French war brides did in America.

The parallels exist, but not just between the women and me. Mixed marriage, voluntary or forced migration, problems of language and identity—these are all part of the human experience, accentuated even more today because of increased emigration and immigration, globalization, travel, and international exchanges. As Amin Maalouf, the French author of Lebanese descent has written: "We are all compelled to live in a universe that barely resembles our original *terroir*;[18] we must all learn other languages, other ways of speaking, other codes."[19]

Some of the bi-cultural marriages of these women lasted; others ended in divorce. But in either case, the women carried on and made a "personal construction"[20] of their lives. There is thus a poignant, universal quality about their experience which goes far beyond the Franco-American dimension of their encounters and marriages with GI's.

NOTES

PROLOGUE

1. The term "war bride" is used in this book to distinguish women who married American soldiers after World War I and World War II and who, in many cases, were transported to America by the U.S. Army.

INTRODUCTION

1. Various legends exist as to the origin of the term. One plausible theory states that, in the nineteenth century, the word "Doughboy" meant a small, round doughnut. During the American Civil War, the term was applied to the large buttons on the infantry uniforms and then to the infantrymen themselves. This same term was later used as the popular name for the American infantry soldiers in World War I.

2. Mary Blum, "The Gentleman Volunteers of WWI," *International Herald Tribune*, August 31-September 1, 1996, back page.

3. Ernest P. Bicknell, *With the Red Cross in Europe 1917-1922* (Washington, D.C.: American National Red Cross, 1938).

4. "*Trois années de guerre dans des conditions très pénibles, l'échec d'offensives, souvent sanglantes, voulues par des chefs dans lesquels on a perdu confiance...expliquent, plus encore que la diffusion d'idées révolutionnaires et pacifistes, cette grave crise de discipline qui menace la cohesion de l'armée française. A l'intérieur du pays apparaissent également des indices de fléchissement moral. A Paris, puis en province, les milieux ouvriers s'agitent.*" Yves-Henri Nouailhat, *Les Américains à Nantes et Saint-Nazaire, 1917-1919* (Paris: Les Belles Lettres, 1972), 190.

5. Susan Zeiger, *In Uncle Sam's Service: Women Workers with the American Expedition Force 1917-1919* (Ithaca and London: Cornell University Press, 1999), 56.

6. Jean-Yves Le Naour, "Le Sexe et la Guerre: Divergences Franco-Américaines pendant la Grande Guerre (1917-1918)," *Guerres mondiales et conflits contemporains* 197, March 2000, pp.115-129.

7. Quoted in Edward M. Coffman, *The War to End All Wars: The American Military Experience in WWI* (Madison: University of Wisconsin Press, 1986), 133.

8. Mark Meigs, *Optimism at Armageddon: Voices of American Participants in the First World War* (New York: New York University Press, 1997), 114.

9. Ibid., 125-127.

10. Nina Mjagkij, "Forgotten Women: War Brides of WWI," *Amerikastudien/ American Studies* 32 (2) (1987): 192-193.

11 *Stars and Stripes*, December 6, 1918, 1.

12. Susan Zeiger, *In Uncle Sam's Service: Women Workers with the American Expedition Force 1917-1919* (Ithaca and London: Cornell University Press, 1999), 52. Zeiger breaks this number down as follows: 3,198 with the YMCA, 2,503 with the ARC, 260 with the YWCA, 104 with the Salvation Army, and 76 with the Jewish Welfare Board.

13. Ibid., 73.

14. Undated report by Dean Beekman, archives of the American Cathedral of Paris.

15. Joseph Wilson Cochran, *Friendly Adventures: a History of the American Church from 1857 to 1931* (Paris: Brentanos, 1931), 163.

16. Ibid., 160-161.

17. *Stars and Stripes*.

18. *Coming Back*, National War Work Council of the YMCA of the U.S., June 27, 1919, 1.

19. Ibid., April 11, 1919, 1.

20. Mjagkij, 191.

21. Meigs, 112.

22. *Stars and Stripes*, May 24, 1918, 8.

23. *Stars and Stripes*, May 9, 1919, 8

24. Tyler Stovall, *African Americans in the City of Light* (New York: Houghton Mifflin, 1996), 15.

25. Ibid., 17.

26. *Stars and Stripes*, June 6, 1919, p. 7.

27. Mjagkij, 193.

28. Ibid., 196.

29. Ibid., 194.

30. Ibid., 193.

31. *Stars and Stripes*, January 31, 1919, 1.

32. Mjagkij, 196.

33. Archives of the French Ministry of Foreign Affairs. *Série B, Amérique*, 1944-1952: *Corps diplomatique, Représentation française*, vol. 5 (December 1945-October 1951).

34. *Le Courrier français des Etats-Unis*, December 1, 1948, 5.

35. *New York Times*, September 2, 1919, 16, col. 5.

36. *New York Times*, Section VII, December 14, 1919, 7, col. 1.

37. *New York Times*, Section II, December 4, 1921, 1:6.

38. "GI" is said to refer to the words "government issue" printed on the soldiers' clothes and gear. Or it might originally have referred to the "galvanized iron" of the trash cans used by the American army.

39. French historian André Kaspi has written that New Caledonia was indispensable for carrying out American operations in the area. André Kaspi, *La Deuxième Guerre mondiale: Chronologie Commentée* (Paris: Perrin, 1990), 295.

40. Later to be adapted to the screen as the popular musical comedy "South Pacific."

41. James Michener, *Tales of the South Pacific* (New York: Macmillan, 1947), 2.

42. Jenel Virden, *Good-by, Piccadilly: British War Brides in America* (Urbana: University of Illinois Press, 1996), 17.

43. Philippe Masson, *Précis d'histoire de la Second Guerre Mondiale* (Paris: Perrin, 1992), 235.

44. J. Robert Lilly, *La Face Cachée des GI's: Les viols commis par des soldats américains en France, en Angleterre et en Allemagne pendant la Seconde Guerre mondiale* (Paris: Editions Payot & Rivages, 2003), 43.

45. According to Section 303 of the act, Indian and southeast Asian women were considered "racially ineligible" for immigration into the United States.

46. When the Oriental Exclusion Act was rescinded.

47. Roland W. Charles, *Troopships of WWII* (Washington, D.C.: The Army Transport Association, 1947), Appendix G, "Ships Adapted to Carry War Brides and Military Dependents," 361.

48. Virden, 2.

49. Memorandum to Colonel Barnes, with attn. to Miss Mabel Coleman, Director of the Army Service of the ARC, August 5, 1946.

50. B-21-1, No 56 am, Vol. 295, *Affaires Etrangères*, 1-2.

51. Martin Blumenson, *La Deuxième Guerre Mondiale-la Libération* (Paris: Time Life Books, 1981), 126.

52. Elizabeth Brugnon, *AAWE News* (Paris) (February-March, 2003), 13.

53. Charles Lemeland quoted in Hilary Kaiser, *Veteran Recall: Americans in France Remember the War* (Bayeux: Editions Heimdal, 2004), 90.

54. Ibid., 89.

55. Aubert Lemeland quoted in Hilary Kaiser, *Veteran Recall*, 93.

56. Sim Copans quoted in Hilary Kaiser, *Veteran Recall*, 83.

57. Ernie Pyle, *Brave Men* (New York: Henry Holt & Co., 1944), 456.

58. John O'Reilly, "Liberation—and a Year Later," *New York Herald Tribune* (Paris), August 26, 1945, 2.

59. Pyle, 463.

60. Edouard Bonnefous, *La Vie de 1940 à 1970* (Paris: Editions Fernand Nathan, 1987), 330.

61. Percy Knauth, "A War Is a War," *Life*, April 16, 1945, p. 14.

62. O'Reilly.

63. Ibid.

64. Foreword, *112 Gripes about the French* (Paris, Information & Education Division of the U.S. Occupation Forces, 1945). This booklet was recently translated into French and is being sold to the general public by a French publisher. *Nos Amis les Français: Guide Pratique à l'usage des GI's en France 1944-1945* (Paris: Le Cherche Midi, 2003).

65. A 13-page restricted report on Franco-American relations in the mid-1940s was discovered by the author at the library of the French Ministry of Foreign Affairs. Written by an unnamed American officer three months after V-E Day, it analyzes the factors responsible for the deterioration of relations between the two countries. Surprisingly, much of what he attributed to the state of affairs back then is still valid with regard to the difficult diplomatic and cross-cultural situation that exists today.

66. Antony Beevor and Artemis Cooper, *Paris after the Liberation, 1944-1949* (New York: Doubleday, 1994), 128.

67. The answer to "Gripe No. 10" lists a number of these. Cf. *112 Gripes about the French*.

68. *Time* 46 (21), November 19, 1945, 19.

69. Alfred Fabre-Luce, as quoted in Beevor and Cooper, 133.

70. André Kaspi, *La Libération de la France* (Paris: Perrin, 1995), 471.

71. Ibid.; and Doris Weatherford, *American Women and WWII* (New York and Oxford: Facts on File, 1990), 259.

72. Hervé le Boterf, *La Vie Parisienne sous l'Occupation*, Vol. 2 (Paris: Edition France Empire, 1975), 162.

73. Weatherford, 259.

74. Beevor and Cooper, 129.

75. *112 Gripes about the French*.

76. Roger Lantagne, quoted in Kaiser, *Veteran Recall*, 50-51.

77. Interview with Reine D.

78. Lilly, 180. Lilly says that this was why the victims of rape in these areas were particularly "vulnerable."

79. Quoted in Beevor and Cooper, 129.

80. Benoîte Groult, *Les Trois Quarts du Temps* (Paris: Editions Grasset & Fasquelle, 1983), 177.

81. Beevor and Cooper, 129.

82. *Time*, November 19, 1945.

83. *New York Herald Tribune* (Paris), February 27, 1946.

84. Ibid.

85. The first train left St. Lazare for Le Havre on February 28, 1946. According to a *New York Herald Tribune* article, an Army band was there to serenade the departing brides, and the Red Cross was on hand to distribute coffee and doughnuts.

86. "War Brides and Their Shipment to the U.S.," in *Occupation Forces in Europe Series 1945-1946*, Office of the Chief Historian European Command, 74.

87. This program was for British war brides on the *SS Santa Paula*, but interviews with French war brides and reports by ARC workers on Le Havre New York-bound ships indicate that similar programs existed on most of the other war bride ships.

88. Juliet Gardiner, *Oversexed, Overpaid and Over Here: The American GI in World War II Britain* (New York: Canopy Books, 1992.) 210.

89. *Stars and Stripes, Warweek*, June 15, 1944, 3.

90. *Stars and Stripes, Warweek*, June 1, 1944, 3.

91. *Stars and Stripes*, June 19, 1944.

92. Ibid.

93. *Warweek*, September 28, 1944, 1.

94. *The Best from Yank*, 102.

95. *Stars and Stripes*, August 28, 1944, 6.

96. Ibid., 5.

97. A children's game in which kisses are exchanged for pretended letters.

98. *Stars and Stripes*, September 25, 1944.

99. *Stars and Stripes*, December 14, 1944, 2.

100. Private First Class.

101. *Stars and Stripes*, December 29, 1944, 2.

102. *Life*, November 26, 1945, 29.

103. Ibid., 33.

104. Ibid.

105. Ibid.

106. Ibid., 32

107. Stovall, 139.

108. Stovall, 138.

109. *Life*, April 26, 1946, 83.

110. *Life*, September 10, 1945, 91.

111. Ibid.

112. *The Stars and Stripes*, August 5, 1945.

113. R.G. 165, 463, June 1946-December 1947.

114. *The Stars and Stripes*, September 16, 1945.

115. The GI Bill of Rights, officially known as the Servicemen's Readjustment Act of 1944, was signed by President Roosevelt on June 22, 1944. Among other benefits,

the act provided federal aid for veterans to continue their education in school or college.

116. *Stars and Stripes*, September 28, 1945, 4.

117. Stovall, 140.

118. Ibid.

119. *Life*, December 3, 1945, 31.

120. *Life*, November 12, 1945, 49.

121. *Life*, November 26, 1945, 95.

122. *Life*, December 3, 1945, 31.

123. These two photographers' photos were lent to the author by Raymonde Cole.

124. *The Stars and Stripes*, September 8, 1945.

125. *Marie-France*, No. 44, September 20, 1945, 5.

126. *Marie-France*, No. 110, December 25, 1946.

127. *Elle*, March 26, 1946 (no19), 4-5.

128. B. Amérique 1944-1952, Etats-Unis; Français aux Etats-Unis, October 1944-December 1946, No 294 and January 1947-1951, No 295.

129. Letter from Henri Bonnet to Leon Blum, 8 January 1947, 3.

130. Ibid., 2.

131. *Elle*, September 3, 1946, 20.

132. *Marie Claire*, December 1954, 106-109.

133. *Marie-Claire*, December 1954.

134. In the 2002 film *Catch Me If You Can*, which is based on the true story of master fake Frank Abagnale, Jr., the portrayal of Abagnale's mother, a French war bride whom Agagnale's father met in a village in France just after the end of World War II, is a case in point.

CHAPTER 1

1. Bishops and cardinals of the Catholic church usually wear rings set with a large amethyst.

CHAPTER 2

1. Taken from the *Fremont Messenger*, April 10, 1918. Notice the play on words: *vrille*/free and grave/brave.

2. Rutherford B. Hayes, a Republican, was president of the United States from 1877 to 1881.

3. May 1 is the *Fête de Travail*, Labor Day, in France. Traditionally, people buy and give *muguet* to friends and family to as a sign of happiness and good luck.

4. Lily Pons was a well-known American soprano of French origin.

5. These are honorary awards for devotion and accomplishment in the areas of teaching, scholarship, and research. They were originally initiated by Napoleon.

6. Edouard Daladier was Prime Minister of France for a third time from April 10, 1938 until March 21, 1940.

7. Hitler and Chamberlain signed a resolution determining to resolve all future disputes between Germany and the United Kingdom through peaceful means.

8. Letter taken from the personal archives of Myriam H.

9. *Oberlin Review*, Oberlin College student newspaper.

CHAPTER 3

1. The name her father officially registered at the town hall when she was born was "Lillian," but she goes by the unofficial, Frenchified, "Liliane."

2. Liliane Schroeder, *Journal de l'Occupation: Paris 1940-1944* (Paris: François-Xavier de Guibert, 2000), 8.

3. The S.S. *Lusitania* was a British steamship that was torpedoed by a German submarine on May 7, 1915, off the coast of Ireland. Of the 1,200 victims, 120 were American.

4. Private diary of Robert J, as quoted to Kaiser.

5. The *Escadrille Lafayette* was a squadron of volunteer American pilots established in April 1916. It was incorporated into the American army in January 1918 and became its first fighting squadron.

6. *L'Officiel de la Couture et de la Mode de Paris*, March-April 1945.

7. Liliane Schroeder, *Journal de l'Occupation*, 262.

CHAPTER 4

1. This was a certificate pupils received at age 14 at the end of primary school.

2. Monoprix, at the time, was like a five-and-dime.

3. These were the Sherman tanks of the French *2eDB* (second armored division), so they were not driven by Americans but by French soldiers, who entered Paris on August 25, 1944. Several of their units were deployed on the rue de Rivoli. However, the American 4th division entered the city the same day by the Porte d'Italie. So it probably was an American to whom Marcelle is referring.

4. Strictly speaking, the militia were a paramilitary force rather than police, even though the head of the French militia, Joseph Darnand, was the Secretary General of the Vichy government's *Maintien de l'Ordre* (the police department).

5. The camps of the Civilian Conservation Corps, founded in 1933 under the tutelage of the American army, were created to employ young, single men between the ages of 18 and 25.

6. The *Pieds-Noirs*, literally "black feet," were the people of European or Jewish descent living in North Africa, particularly Algeria. Many of those in Algeria fled to France in 1962 following the declaration of independence of this former French colony.

CHAPTER 5

1. The OSS was created by President Franklin D. Roosevelt in July 1942 and was the precursor of the CIA.

2. Jacqueline undoubtedly meant the MI-6 (and not the M6), which is the British Secret Intelligence Service.

3. A while after our interview took place, Jacqueline remembered the name of the book: *Un Petit Bateau tout blanc* [A Little, All-White Boat]. The title evokes the coded groups used on Radio London by the Free French. See Ernest-Fred Floege, alias Paul-Frédéric Fontaine, *Un Petit Bateau tout blanc: la Résistance française vue par un officier américain* [A Little, All-White Boat: The French Resistance as Seen by an American Officer] (Le Mans, France: Le Mans, 1962).

4. Flossenbürg was a concentration camp in Germany. It was liberated by the Americans on April 23, 1945. However, in the face of the Allied advance, the SS forced 14,000 prisoners to evacuate the camp. Four thousand died in this "death march."

5. The trio—comprising Patty, LaVerne, and Maxene Andrews—was formed in 1932 and was very popular during the 1940s and 1950s. Maxene died in 1995, about a year before our first interview.

6. The Hmongs and the Miens were originally of Chinese origin. They live today in the mountainous areas of China, Vietnam, Laos, and Thailand and are divided into different ethnic groups distinguished by their language and dress.

CHAPTER 6

1. Young men between 20 and 22 years of age had to do obligatory work service, *service du travail obligatoire* (STO).

2. Following the close of World War II, the U.S. Army founded American universities in Biarritz (France), Florence (Italy), and Shrivenham (England), where American soldiers in the ETO could take courses for college credit.

3. This cake is probably a *pièce montée*, which is a traditional French wedding cake made of cream puffs and caramel and assembled in a conical shape.

4. Nicole once worked as a counselor at a huge summer camp for children of employees of Renault, the French car company.

5. In the original letter, Nicole uses the word *librairie*, which is a "false friend" in English and means a "bookstore," but afterwards Nicole told me she meant a "library," which is the word *bibliothèque* in French.

6. A Neopolitan ice cream.

7. This is, of course, an exaggeration.

CHAPTER 7

1. The landing in North Africa (Algeria and Morocco) by the British and Americans occurred on November 8, 1942.

2. Marcelle S., another war bride from Algeria who was on the same ship and whom the author interviewed for this book, said that it was a merchant marine ship.

3. This would mean the crossing lasted three weeks. Marcelle S. said it took nine days.

4. Federal law imposed prohibition of the consumption of alcohol from 1919 to 1933, but certain states remained "dry" even after the federal law was rescinded.

5. The French word *brassière* usually means a baby's undershirt or a life-jacket.

6. Jeanne-Marie is probably confusing the *agrégation*, which is a national competitive examination to become a teacher as a French civil servant, with a French university degree such as the *licence* [equivalent of the B.A.].

7. Whittier is the birthplace of Richard Nixon.

8. Notre Dame de Paris (or "Our Lady of Paris") is a Gothic cathedral found on the Ile de la Cité. It is still used for Catholic church services but is also a popular tourist attraction.

CHAPTER 8

1. This was a pure coincidence. See the story "New York Sandals."

2. Albert Camus (1913-1960), the French philosopher and writer, was born in Algeria of a Spanish mother and a French father. He received the Nobel Prize for literature in 1957. His best-known novels are *The Stranger* (1942) and *The Plague* (1947).

CHAPTER 9

1. There were younger ones. A report written in the 1940s by an employee of the American Red Cross speaks of a war bride who was only 15.

2. See Introduction. The film *The Best Years of Our Lives* refers to this.

CHAPTER 10

1. Raymonde made a mistake here. The Korean War actually took place later on, between 1950 and 1953. Perhaps the woman's son was one of the American troops who disarmed the Japanese in Korea at the 38th parallel at the end of World War II and then stayed on afterwards.

2. The firm was named after Earl "Madman" Muntz, one of the pioneers in large-scale production of television sets at the end of the 1940s.

3. Antoine de Laumet de Lamothe Cadillac (1658-1730) founded the city of Detroit in 1701.

4. It was Laumont, in the municipality of Saint-Nicolas-de-la-Grave.

CHAPTER 11

1. In 1944 and 1945, a great many French women who'd gone out with Germans during the war had their hair shaven in public.

2. Tony probably means the GI Bill.

3. Again, Tony is probably referring to the GI Bill.

4. *Le Courrier Français des Etats-Unis*, December 1, 1948, p. 5.

5. *Le Courrier Français des Etats-Unis,* June 1949.

6. Tony promised to send me a copy of this short play, but then she left for the retirement home, and afterwards nobody seemed to know what happened to her documents.

7. The order was created in Paris on August 15, 1534, when Saint Ignace de Loyola and his six companions took an oath.

CHAPTER 13

1. John Jacob Astor (1763-1848) was of German origin. The success of his American Fur Company, created in 1810, made him the richest man in the United States at the time.

2. Henri Bergson (1859-1941) was a French philosopher who won the Nobel Prize for literature in 1927.

3. Marcel Pagnol (1895-1974), the French film director and playwright from Provence, is famous for his trilogy: *Marius, Fanny,* and *César.*

4. Jack Benny and Larry Adler were comedians whose USO shows were very popular among troops in Europe and the Pacific.

5. William Frederick Halsey (1882-1939) was commander of the South Pacific Area from 1942-1945 and then of the Third Fleet (1944-1945) in the Pacific Theater.

6. Harry Francis Willard (1895-1970).

7. Howard Thurston (1869-1936) was the most famous illusionist in the United States at the beginning of the twentieth century.

8. Simone de Beauvoir (1908-1986) was a French philosopher, political activist, novelist, and essayist. She is particularly well-known in the United States for her two-volume feminist work *The Second Sex* (1949). She was also the lifelong companion of French philosopher and writer Jean-Paul Sartre.

9. See the note on Camus in the chapter "Morry and I."

10. Sidonie-Gabrielle Colette (1873-1954), known as "Colette," was a prolific French novelist and short-story writer whose works dealt mostly with passionate love and female sexuality. Her *Music-Hall Sidelights* (1913) was adapted to the screen in 1935.

11. Melanesians are the native inhabitants of the part of Oceania called Melanesia.

CHAPTER 14

1. The Oustachis were Croatian separatists who supported Hitler during World War II.

2. This was on October 9, 1934.

3. It was actually in March 1941.

4. Reine is referring to two separate laws: the anti-Semitic *statuts des juifs* of October 3, 1940, and June 14, 1945, and the August 14, 1940, law against "secret associations" like the masons.

5. French term meaning "way of getting around things."

6. Jews in the Occupied Zone had to wear the star of David as of May 29, 1942. In December of the same year a law was passed to include the southern zone, but the law was never applied.

7. According to a law of June 23, 1941, there was a 3 percent quota on entrance of Jews into French universities.

8. The Battle of the Bulge was the German counter-offensive against the Allies in the Ardennes in December 1944 and January 1945.

9. A charivari is a serenade with kettles, pans, and horns for a newly married couple.

CONCLUSION

1. One woman whom I interviewed but who did not want to have her story published told me that her husband had left her alone with two children and all of $15 in her pocket.

2. A reference to the well-known 1984 handbook by cross-cultural specialist, L. Robert Kohls.

3. Marriage outside a tribe or similar social unit.

4. Virden, 92.

5. Two instances come to mind: one, of a French war bride in the Midwest who associated her ex-husband with all Americans, who only drink beer, watch TV, and lack "culture." The other, of a war bride in southern California who answered my advertisement. I remember her accusing me of having become "more fucking French than the French." Before meeting with me, she and a lawyer had drawn up a two-page list of questions for me to answer, including what her percentage of royalties would be. The bitterness of these two women was definitely the exception, however, and I decided not to include their interviews in this book.

6. Albert Benard de Russailh, *Journal de voyage en Californie à l'époque de la ruée vers l'or 1850-1852* (Paris: Aubier, 1980), 205; quoted in Annick Foucrier, *Le Rêve californien : migrants français sur la côte Pacifique (XVIIIe-XXe siècles)* (Paris: Belin, 1999), 161.

7. Foucrier, 164.

8. There are still sequels to this today. A French friend of mine recently recounted how her daughter, who now lives and works in San Francisco, was dubbed a "French bitch" and a "man-stealer" by some of her American colleagues.

9. Alice Kaplan, *French Lessons: A Memoir* (Chicago: University of Chicago Press, 1993), 126.

10. Jacqueline Lindenfeld, *The French in the United States: An Ethnographic Study* (Westport, CT: Bergin & Garvey, 2000), 140.

11. An interesting study could be made of the degree of "Frenchness" and bilingualism of the warbrides' children and grandchildren.

12. Nancy Huston, *Nord Perdu* (Paris: Actes Sud, 1999), 33.

13. Camp des Loges was an American army camp near St. Germain-en-Laye, on the outskirts of Paris. The U.S. army remained in France until 1966, when President DeGaulle withdrew French forces from NATO.

14. Raymonde Carroll, *Cultural Misunderstandings: The French-American Experience* (Chicago: University of Chicago Press, 1988). Originally published as *Evidences Invisibles* (Paris: Editions du Seuil, 1987).

15. Pascal Baudry, *Français & Américains* (Paris: Pearson Education France, 2003).

16. Harrriet Welty Rochefort, *French Toast* (New York : Saint Martin's Press, 1997).

17. Gilles Asselin & Ruth Mastron, *Au Contraire! Figuring Out the French* (Yarmouth, ME: Intercultural Press, 2001).

18. *Terroir* is a word which is very difficult to translate into English. It is related to the soil, to the native land.

19. Amin Maalouf, *Les Identités meurtrières* (Paris: Editions Grasset & Fasquelle, 1998), 47.

20. Lindenfeld, 144.

SELECT BIBLIOGRAPHY

The Best from Yank, the Army Weekly, Selected by the Editors of Yank. New York: E.P. Dutton & Co., Inc., 1945.

Carroll, Raymonde. *Cultural Misunderstandings: The French-American Experience.* Chicago: University of Chicago Press, 1988. This book first appeared in French under the title *Evidences invisibles: Américains et Français au quotidien.* Paris: Editions du Seuil, 1987.

Coquart, Elizabeth. *La France des GI's: Histoire d'un amour déçu.* Paris: Albin Michel, 2003.

Hillel, Marc. *Vie et Mœurs des GI's en Europe: 1942–1947.* Paris, Balland; 1981.

Kaiser, Hilary. *Veteran Recall: Americans in France Remember the War.* Bayeux: Editions Heimdal, 2004. This book also exists in French under the title *Souvenirs de Vétérans.* Bayeux: Editions Heimdal, 2004.

Kaspi, André, et al. *La Libération de la France: Juin 1944-janvier 1946.* Paris: Perrin, 1995.

Katz, Balbino, ed. *Nos amis les Français: guide pratique à l'usage des GI's en France, 1944–1945.* Paris: Le Cherche Midi, 2003. This is a French translation of *112 Gripes about the French.* Paris: Information and Education Division of the U.S. Occupation Forces, 1945.

Lilly, J. Robert, *La Face Cachée des GI's: Les viols commis par des soldats américains en France, en Angleterre et en Allemagne pendant la Seconde Guerre mondiale* Paris: Editions Payot & Rivages, 2003. Translated from English by Benjamin and Julien Guerif, with a preface by Fabrice Virgili. This book was originally written in English under the title *Taken by Force: Rape and American Soldiers in the European Theater of Operations during World War II. England, France,*

Germany, 1942–1945. It was published for the first time in the United States by Palgrave-Macmillan in August 2007 under the title *Taken by Force: Rape and American GIs in Europe during WWII.*

Meigs, Mark. *Optimism at Armageddon: Voices of American Participants in the First World War.* New York: New York University Press, 1997.

Schroeder, Liliane. *Journal d'Occupation: Paris, 1940–1944. Chronique au jour le jour d'une époque oubliée.* Paris: François-Xavier de Guibert, 2000.

Stovall, Tyler Edward. *Paris noir: African-Americans in the City of Light.* Boston: Houghton Mifflin, 1996.

Virden, Jenel. *Good-bye, Piccadilly: British War Brides in America.* Urbana: University of Illinois Press, 1996.

INDEX

ABOUT THE AUTHOR

HILARY KAISER is American by birth and the daughter of a GI who fought in Japan during World War II. She is an Associate Professor at the University of Paris-Sud and has done many oral histories of Americans living in France. The second edition of her book *Veteran Recall: Americans in France Remember the War* was published in June 2004.

DATE DUE

GAYLORD

PRINTED IN U.S.A.